Leaving New York

Leaving New York

Writers Look Back

EDITED BY

Kathleen Norris

Hungry Mind Press

First U.S. Edition
Published by Hungry Mind Press
57 Macalester Street
Saint Paul, MN 55105

9 8 7 6 5 4
First Hungry Mind Press printing, 1995

Library of Congress Catalog Card Number: 95-079536

ISBN: 1-886913-00-5

Printed in the United States of America

Jacket design: Adrian Morgan/Red Letter Design
Front cover photograph: courtesy Photonica
Book design: Will H. Powers
Typesetting: Stanton Publication Services, Inc.

Special thanks to
Eva Hooker
Christopher Hubbuch
and
Phil Patrick

Leaving New York

Leaving New York

Kathleen Norris

Introduction

NEW YORK, NEW YORK, full of surprises. William H. Bonney, better known as Billy the Kid, was born there in 1859, and Bat Masterson died there in 1921 at his desk at the *New York Morning Telegraph* where he was working on a review of a prize-fight. He'd had a column at the paper since moving from Denver in 1903. Gunfighters, gamblers, icons of the West—the city takes them in its stride. Poets and novelists, prophets and hacks. The city sees them come and go.

Willa Cather had her best writing years in Greenwich Village, where she lived from 1912 to 1927, when the most celebrated of her Nebraska novels were published. To do fictional justice to Nebraska, apparently, she found it necessary to remain in New York. Her contemporaries, F. Scott and Zelda Fitzgerald also came to the city from the provinces, and although F. Scott perfectly captures an aspect of New York society in *The Great Gatsby,* the Fitzgeralds didn't remain long, but moved on to Europe. On their return, Zelda descended into madness and F. Scott moved on to Hollywood, which disappointed him.

Many other twentieth-century writers whose work is strongly associated with other places—Djuna Barnes, Sinclair Lewis, Carson McCullers, Flannery O'Connor, Eugene O'Neill, Tennessee Williams, Thomas Wolfe, James Wright—either lived in the city for a time, or had strong ties there, in some cases, relationships with editors and publishers that ultimately helped them survive as writers elsewhere. New York City still attracts young American writers to its literary hothouse, and while

1

that can narrow down to blatant careerism, it doesn't have to.

The New York experience often broadens a young writer's perspective; think of Mark Van Doren, who taught for years at Columbia, influencing poets as diverse as John Berryman, Allen Ginsberg, Delmore Schwartz and Louis Simpson. And the city has long been a temporary home for writers from other countries who come to give readings or to teach. Federico Garcia Lorca comes to mind, so taken with the city that he wrote a luminous memoir entitled *Poet in New York*. There is Dietrich Bonhoeffer, who studied at Union Theological Seminary in the late 1920s and returned in 1939, seeking refuge from Nazi Germany. He left New York to die at Buchenwald. Helped by W. H. Auden, poet Joseph Brodsky came to the city in the early 1970s; nervous about being exiled from immersion in his native tongue, he nevertheless found life in New York preferable to being imprisoned as a "social parasite" in what was then the Soviet Union.

It's easy to see why New York draws professionals in the performing arts—it's where much of the work is, for one thing, as well as the necessary group dynamics. One is more likely to be able to put together a top-notch modern dance company, for instance, or the cast of an opera, in Manhattan, New York, than in Manhattan, Kansas. Maybe that rankles those of us in the hinterlands—I have credentials in that regard, as I live in the hick part of South Dakota, west of the Missouri River—maybe we feel that it *shouldn't* be this way, but it is the case. I should add that one of my favorite modern dance companies is happily situated in Ames, Iowa.

But writing is a solitary activity, and I've often wondered why it is that so many writers drift, in their formative years, to a city that specializes in demolishing the internal and external quiet that most writers need. Young writers usually can't afford the quieter neighborhoods; they are plunged headlong into the city's noise and heady variety—"millions of stories," Bill McKibben exclaims—all very different from the homogenous, constricting small town or suburban atmospheres from which they've so often come. In his memoir, *A Second Flowering,* Malcolm Cowley tells us that the young E. E. Cummings, rebelling against a clergyman father "famous for his rectitude," rented an apartment in Greenwich Village that Cowley describes as "a model of squalor." Cummings liked to roam through the Lower East Side and the Syrian quarter near the southern tip of Manhattan. He kept a New York apartment all his life, although in his later years he lived mostly in New Hampshire.

American literature would look very different were it not for New York City—Poe wrote "The Raven" in the Bronx—and this anthology, the inaugural book of the Hungry Mind Press, is an intriguing compilation of some contemporary reflections on the city. Le Corbusier once called New York a magnificent disaster, and that tension surfaces in the following essays. Bill McKibben sees a "great collection of human talent and energy and angst"; Frank Conroy speaks of being both "addicted and ambivalent"; he has a grim tale to tell.

Native New Yorker Leslie Brody, in her stunning "Jewish Geography," speaks of living most of her life in "self-imposed exile" from the city, and confesses that the farther away from New York she is, the more devoted to it she becomes. Wisconsin native Mona Simpson, who comes for graduate school and settles in for twelve years, admits in her essay "The Things We Do for Love" that "for a long time I resisted New York the way one might resist a person, whom you suspect has the power to overwhelm you." Yet leaving did not come easily: "After talking about leaving New York for more than a decade," she says, "I finally did so only in a rush and when I didn't want to."

One of the ironies of putting a book such as this together is that the more literature you discover, the more you sense that the subject is inexhaustible. I recently found that the British travel writer Jonathan Raban, in *Hunting Mister Heartbreak,* had done a savage take on Manhattan in the 1980s, where the rich got richer and the poor got homeless. Even the "dirty porcelain of the Holland Tunnel" cheers him as he heads for the South, "sick of the city, its tense days and sleepless nights."

I also noticed that James Merrill had opened his 1993 memoir, *A Different Person,* with a comment that summarizes the reason many young writers leave New York. They've simply outgrown the need to travel in a pack to readings, receptions, taverns. "Meaning to stay as long as possible," Merrill wrote, "I sailed for Europe. It was March, 1950. New York and most of the people I knew had begun to close in."

Merrill had become weary of what he terms "the allusive chatter" of his acquaintants in the literary world—one of those provincial "city microcosms" that A. J. Liebling speaks of, small, ingrown worlds in which people come to dwell, calling it New York. Like Joan Didion, Merrill was tired of seeing the same faces. Didion's "Goodbye to All That," an essay I devoured when I was in my early twenties and had somehow mustered the nerve to move to Manhattan, explained to me what I had been experiencing. Days of terror, when I was unable even to walk out of the apartment; days when all things seemed possible, and I had Manhattan in the palm of my hand.

Like Bill McKibben, another writer who came to New York fresh out of college, I was sure that I had "the best job in the world," and for a time it was. And then it wasn't. Frank Conroy's "Change" is a brilliant evocation of how the city can suddenly get to a person. Becoming aware of the sensory and emotional filters he carried with him through the streets—"hearing, but not hearing, the screams from the streets. Seeing, but not seeing, the ragged figure sleeping in a doorway. Reflexively averting the head to avoid the smells of piss and funk," he suddenly realized, "*this is no way to live*." The story of how this idea evolved into his conviction that "*this is no place to live*" (emphasis mine) is one of the most gripping in the book.

I still love to visit New York, and now will be unable to ride the subway without thanking Derek Walcott for telling me where I am. *Of course*, this dank, foul place is the River Styx, and a uniformed, officious "Charon in his grilled cell / grows vague about our crime, our destination." Li-Young Lee has made it possible for me to see one of my favorite cities in terms of one of my favorite books of the Bible, the Song of Songs. I'll never pass the Morton Street Pier without thinking of Edward Hoagland and a doomed diamondback turtle.

It is good to be reminded that the city is, in Tom Wolfe's phrase, "New York high and low," still full of Liebling's "worlds of the weight-lifters, yodelers, tugboat captains and sideshow barkers, of the book-dutchers, sparring partners, song pluggers, sporting girls and religious painters, of the dealers in rhesus monkeys and the bishops of churches . . ." all working like "a complicated Renaissance clock."

It is also good to picture a black-crowned night heron fishing at dusk in the marshes of Pelham Bay Park, within view of the gigantic Coop City apartment houses, good to read Terry Tempest Williams' account of an intrepid ornithologist from the American Museum of Natural History, who braves the city's polluted, watery edges in order to better teach city schoolchildren about a natural environment that's been all but obliterated by development. It is "the water songs of the red-winged blackbirds," Williams says, that "keep her attentive in a city that has little memory of wildness."

There are many ways to leave New York. The heron and the blackbirds can simply fly away. People fly too, but only after contending with principalities and powers to get to one of the city's three major airports. It's remarkably easy to leave New York, come to think of it—by train or bus or limo, by tube train to New Jersey. One might even board a luxury liner at a West Side pier. Few people hitchhike, but New York being New York, I'm sure someone's doing it at this very moment.

When I first heard Bob Dylan's ironic "Talking New York," I was a high school student in Honolulu. For my fifteenth birthday, I'd asked my parents for a subscription to *The New Yorker,* but never imagined that I'd live in the city. The last lines of the Dylan song "So Long, New York. / Howdy, East Orange" were utterly mysterious to me. I assumed that they were an exercise in surrealism. It wasn't until years later, when I better understood the geography of the New York City region, that I realized that Dylan had actually been getting down to the nitty gritty, which is what a person has to do in order to leave New York.

My thanks to the brave souls at the Hungry Mind Press, who imagined this book and then patiently and lovingly brought it into being. Thanks also to researchers Philip Patrick and Christopher Hubbuch. I owe a very great debt to Eva Hooker, my co-editor, who did so much of the work of compiling, ordering and editing manuscripts.

APRIL 1995

The City that Danced with Them

Toni Morrison

excerpt from Jazz

I'm crazy about this City.

Daylight slants like a razor cutting the buildings in half. In the top half I see looking faces and it's not easy to tell which are people, which the work of stone-masons. Below is shadow where any blasé thing takes place: clarinets and lovemaking, fists and the voices of sorrowful women. A city like this one makes me dream tall and feel in on things. Hep. It's the bright steel rocking above the shade below that does it. When I look over strips of green grass lining the river, at church steeples and into the cream-and-copper halls of apartment buildings, I'm strong. Alone, yes, but top-notch and indestructible—like the City in 1926 when all the wars are over and there will never be another one. The people down there in the shadow are happy about that. At last, at last, everything's ahead. The smart ones say so and people listening to them and reading what they write down agree: Here comes the new. Look out. There goes the sad stuff. The bad stuff. The things-nobody-could-help stuff. The way everybody was then and there. Forget that. History is over, you all, and everything's ahead at last. In halls and offices people are sitting around thinking future thoughts about projects and bridges and fast-clicking trains underneath. The A&P hires a colored clerk. Big-legged women with pink kitty tongues roll money into green tubes for later on; then they laugh and put their arms around each other. Regular people corner thieves in alleys for quick retribution and, if he is stupid and has robbed wrong, thieves corner him too. Hoodlums hand out goodies, do their best to stay interesting, and since they are being watched for excitement, they pay attention to their clothes and the carving out of insults. Nobody wants to be an emergency at Harlem Hospital but if the Negro surgeon is visiting, pride cuts down the pain. And although the hair of the first class of colored nurses was declared unseemly for the official Bellevue nurse's cap, there are thirty-five of them now—all dedicated and superb in their profession.

Nobody says it's pretty here; nobody says it's easy either. What it is is decisive, and if you pay attention to the street plans, all laid out, the City can't hurt you.

I haven't got any muscles, so I can't really be expected to defend myself. But I do know how to take precaution. Mostly it's making sure no one knows all there is to know about me. Second, I watch everything and everyone and try to figure out their plans, their reasonings, long before they do. You have to understand what it's like, taking on a big city: I'm exposed to all sorts of ignorance and criminality. Still, this is the only life for me. I like the way the City makes people think they can do what they want and get away with it. I see them all over the place: wealthy whites, and plain ones too, pile into mansions decorated and redecorated by black women richer than they are, and both are pleased with the spectacle of the other. I've seen the eyes of black Jews, brimful of pity for everyone not themselves, graze the food stalls and the ankles of loose women, while a breeze stirs the white plumes on the helmets of the UNIA men. A colored man floats down out of the sky blowing a saxophone, and below him, in the space between two buildings, a girl talks earnestly to a man in a straw hat. He touches her lip to remove a bit of something there. Suddenly she is quiet. He tilts her chin up. They stand there. Her grip on her purse slackens and her neck makes a nice curve. The man puts his hand on the stone wall above her head. By the way his jaw moves and the turn of his head I know he has a golden tongue. The sun sneaks into the alley behind them. It makes a pretty picture on its way down.

Do what you please in the City, it is there to back and frame you no matter what you do. And what goes on on its blocks and lots and side streets is anything the strong can think of and the weak will admire. All you have to do is heed the design—the way it's laid out for you, considerate, mindful of where you want to go and what you might need tomorrow.

I lived a long time, maybe too much, in my own mind. People say I should come out more. Mix. I agree that I close off in places, but if you have been left standing, as I have, while your partner overstays at another appointment, or promises to give you exclusive attention after supper, but is falling asleep just as you have begun to speak—well, it can make you inhospitable if you aren't careful, the last thing I want to be.

Hospitality is gold in this City; you have to be clever to figure out how to be welcoming and defensive at the same time. When to love something and when to quit. If you don't know how, you can end up out of control or controlled by some outside thing like that hard case last winter. Word was that underneath the good times and the easy money something evil ran the streets and nothing was safe—not even the dead. Proof of this being Violet's outright attack on the very subject of a funeral ceremony. Barely three days into 1926. A host of thoughtful people looked at the signs (the weather, the number, their own dreams) and believed it was the commencement of all sorts of destruction. That the scandal was a message sent to warn the good and rip up the faithless. I don't know who was more ambitious— the doomsayers or Violet—but it's hard to match the superstitious for great expectations. . . .

. . . When the train trembled approaching the water surrounding the City, they thought it was like them: nervous at having gotten there at last, but terrified of what was on the other side. Eager, a little scared, they did not even nap during the fourteen hours of a ride smoother than a rocking cradle. The quick darkness in the carriage cars when they shot through a tunnel made them wonder if maybe there was a wall ahead to crash into or a cliff hanging over nothing. The train shivered with them at the thought but went on and sure enough there was ground up ahead and the trembling became the dancing under their feet. Joe stood up, his fingers clutching the baggage rack above his head. He felt the dancing better that way, and told Violet to do the same.

They were hanging there, a young country couple, laughing and tapping back at the tracks, when the attendant came through, pleasant but unsmiling now that he didn't have to smile in this car full of colored people.

"Breakfast in the dining car. Breakfast in the dining car. Good morning. Full breakfast in the dining car." He held a carriage blanket over his arm and from underneath it drew a pint bottle of milk, which he placed in the hands of a young woman with a baby asleep across her knees. "Full breakfast."

He never got his way, this attendant. He wanted the whole coach to file into the dining car, now that they could. Immediately, now that they were out of Delaware and a long way from Maryland there would be no green-as-poison curtain separating the colored people eating from the rest of the diners. The cooks would not feel obliged to pile extra helpings on the plates headed for the curtain; three lemon slices in the iced tea, two pieces of coconut cake arranged to look like one—to take the sting out of the curtain; homey it up with a little extra on the plate. Now, skirting the City, there were no green curtains; the whole car could be full of colored people and everybody on a first-come first-serve basis. If only they would. If only they would tuck those little boxes and baskets underneath the seat; close those paper bags, for once, put the bacon-stuffed biscuits back into the cloth they were wrapped in, and troop single file through the five cars ahead on into the dining car, where the table linen was at least as white as the sheets they dried on juniper bushes; where the napkins were folded with a crease as stiff as the ones they ironed for Sunday dinner; where the gravy was as smooth as their own, and the biscuits did not take second place to the bacon-stuffed ones they wrapped in cloth. Once in a while it happened. Some well-shod woman with two young girls, a preacherly kind of man with a watch chain and a rolled-brim hat might stand up, adjust their clothes and weave through the coaches toward the tables, foamy white with heavy silvery knives and forks. Presided over and waited upon by a black man who did not have to lace his dignity with a smile.

Joe and Violet wouldn't think of it—paying money for a meal they had not missed and that required them to sit still at, or worse, separated by, a table. Not now. Not entering the lip of the City dancing all the way. Her hip bones rubbed his thigh as they stood in the aisle unable to stop smiling. They weren't even there yet and already the City was speaking to them. They were dancing. And like a million others, chests pounding, tracks controlling their feet, they stared out the windows for first sight of the City that danced with them, proving already how much it loved them. Like a million more they could hardly wait to get there and love it back.

Some were slow about it and traveled from Georgia to Illinois, to the City, back to Georgia, out to San Diego and finally, shaking their heads, surrendered themselves to the City. Others knew right away that it was for them, this City and no other. They came on a whim because there it was and why not? They came after much planning, many letters written to and from, to make sure and know how and how much and where. They came for a visit and forgot to go back to tall cotton or short. Discharged with or without notice, they hung around for a while and then could not imagine themselves anywhere else. Others came because a relative or hometown buddy said, Man, you best see this place before you die; or, We got room now, so pack your suitcase and don't bring no high-top shoes.

However they came, when or why, the minute the leather of their soles hit the pavement—there was no turning around. Even if the room they rented was smaller than the heifer's stall and darker than a morning privy, they stayed to look at their number, hear themselves in an audience, feel themselves moving down the street among hundreds of others who moved the way they did, and who, when they spoke, regardless of the accent, treated language like the same intricate, malleable toy designed for their play. Part of why they loved it was the specter they left behind. The slumped spines of the veterans of the 27th Battalion betrayed by the commander for whom they had fought like lunatics. The eyes of thousands, stupefied with disgust at having been imported by Mr. Armour, Mr. Swift, Mr. Montgomery Ward to break strikes then dismissed for having done so. The broken shoes of two thousand Galveston longshoremen that Mr. Mallory would never pay fifty cents an hour like the white ones. The praying palms, the raspy breathing, the quiet children of the ones who had escaped from Springfield Ohio, Springfield Indiana, Greensburg Indiana, Wilmington Delaware, New Orleans Louisiana, after raving whites had foamed all over the lanes and yards of home.

The wave of black people running from want and violence crested in the 1870s; the '80s; the '90s but was a steady stream in 1906 when Joe and Violet joined it. Like the others, they were country people, but how soon country people forget. When they fall in love with a city, it is for forever, and it is like forever. As though there never was a time when they didn't love it. The minute they arrive at the train station or get off the ferry and glimpse the wide streets and the wasteful lamps lighting them, they know they are born for it. There, in a city, they are not so much new as themselves: their stronger, riskier selves. And in the beginning when they first arrive, and twenty years later when they and the City have grown up, they love that part of themselves so much they forget what loving other people was like—if they ever knew, that is. I don't mean they hate them, no, just that what they start to love is the way a person is in the City; the way a schoolgirl never pauses at a stoplight but looks up and down the street before stepping off the curb; how men accommodate themselves to tall buildings and wee porches, what a woman looks like moving in a crowd, or how shocking her profile is against the backdrop of the East River. The restfulness in kitchen chores when she knows the lamp oil or the staple is just around the corner and not seven miles away; the amazement of throwing open the window and being hypnotized for hours by people on the street below.

Little of that makes for love, but it does pump desire. The woman who churned a man's blood as she leaned all alone on a fence by a country road might not expect even to catch his eye in the City. But if she is clipping quickly down the big-city street in heels, swinging her purse, or sitting on a stoop with a cool beer in her hand, dangling her shoe from the toes of her foot, the man, reacting to her posture, to soft skin on stone, the weight of the building stressing the delicate, dangling shoe, is captured. And he'd think it was the woman he wanted, and not some combination of curved stone, and a swinging, high-heeled shoe moving in and out of sunlight. He would know right away the deception, the trick of shapes and light and movement, but it wouldn't matter at all because the deception was part of it too. Anyway, he could feel his lungs going in and out. There is no air in the City but there is breath, and every morning it races through him like laughing gas brightening his eyes, his talk, and his expectations. In no time at all he forgets little pebbly creeks and apple trees so old they lay their branches along the ground and you have to reach down or stoop to pick the fruit. He forgets a sun that used to slide up like the yolk of a good country egg, thick and red-orange at the bottom of the sky, and he doesn't miss it, doesn't look up to see what happened to it or to stars made irrelevant by the light of thrilling, wasteful street lamps.

That kind of fascination, permanent and out of control, seizes children, young girls, men of every description, mothers, brides, and barfly women, and if they have their way and get to the City, they feel more like themselves, more like the people they always believed they were. Nothing can pry them away from that; the City is what they want it to be: thriftless, warm, scary and full of amiable strangers. No wonder they forget pebbly creeks and when they do not forget the sky completely think of it as a tiny piece of information about the time of day or night.

But I have seen the City do an unbelievable sky. Redcaps and dining-car attendants who wouldn't think of moving out of the City sometimes go on at great length about country skies they have seen from the windows of trains. But there is nothing to beat what the City can make of a nightsky. It can empty itself of surface, and more like the ocean than the ocean itself, go deep, starless. Close up on the tops of buildings, near, nearer than the cap you are wearing, such a citysky presses and retreats, presses and retreats, making me think of the free but illegal love of sweethearts before they are discovered. Looking at it, this nightsky booming over a glittering city, it's possible for me to avoid dreaming of what I know is in the ocean, and the bays and tributaries it feeds: the two-seat aeroplanes, nose down in the muck, pilot and passenger staring at schools of passing bluefish; money, soaked and salty in canvas bags, or waving their edges gently from metal bands made to hold them forever. They are down there, along with yellow flowers that eat water beetles and eggs floating away from thrashing fins; along with the children who made a mistake in the parents they chose; along with slabs of Carrara pried from unfashionable buildings. There are bottles too, made of glass beautiful enough to rival stars I cannot see above me because the citysky has hidden them. Otherwise, if it wanted to, it could show me stars cut from the lamé gowns of chorus girls, or mirrored in the eyes of sweethearts furtive and happy under the pressure of a deep, touchable sky.

But that's not all a citysky can do. It can go purple and keep an orange heart so the clothes of the people on the streets glow like dance-hall costumes. I have seen women stir shirts into boiled starch or put the tiniest stitches into their hose while a girl straightens the hair of her sister at the stove, and all the while heaven, unnoticed and as beautiful as an Iroquois, drifts past their windows. As well as the windows where sweethearts, free and illegal, tell each other things.

Twenty years after Joe and Violet train-danced on into the City, they were still a couple but barely speaking to each other, let alone laughing together or acting like the ground was a dance-hall floor. Convinced that he alone remembers those days, and wants them back, aware of what it looked like but not at all of what it felt like, he coupled himself elsewhere. He rented a room from a neighbor who knows the exact cost of her discretion. Six hours a week he has purchased. Time for the citysky to move from a thin ice blue to purple with a heart of gold. And time enough, when the sun sinks, to tell his new love things he never told his wife.

———————

Born in Lorain, Ohio in 1931, TONI MORRISON *completed two degrees, had two children, and became a senior editor at Random House before her first novel,* The Bluest Eye, *was published in 1970. Morrison published three more novels, including* Song of Solomon *for which she was awarded the National Book Critics' Circle Award, and taught at Yale University and Bard College before leaving Random House in 1984. In 1988 she was awarded the Pulitzer Prize for her fifth novel,* Beloved. *In 1994 she received the Nobel Prize for Literature. The preceding excerpts are taken from her 1992 novel,* Jazz.

2

The City Dweller Leaves

Frank Conroy

Change

The only constant in life is change.
HERACLITUS

I suppose the thought—unbidden and unwanted—first popped into my head sometime in the early sixties, as I came home from a night of playing jazz in the Village. My wife and I lived in Park West Village. Two and a half rooms on the fourteenth floor of 788 Columbus Avenue: a flat, slab building, replicas of which I was to see many times on the outskirts of Moscow twenty-five years later. It was two or three in the morning as I walked up Amsterdam Avenue, cut across the side street, and approached the building from the back. It was hot, and unusually quiet—no sirens, none of the anonymous, mysterious screams from the street to which we had become accustomed.

Fifty yards from home something made me stop and look up. What was it? I'd walked from the 96th Street subway dozens of times at roughly the same hour and never had I stopped. I looked at the towering wall of the building. Then, as if some cosmic sound engineer had turned a dial, I began to hear. The air-conditioners. A hundred of them jutting out from seventeen stories of red brick. A continuous sigh, a humming, a quiet but deep windy sound, somehow ominous. I felt a mild shock at the realization that the sound had always been there, and yet it was only now that I heard it, as if it had to break through some filter in order to reach my brain in order to be processed.

Something like a revelation followed. All at once I became aware of other filters, other forces bearing on perception itself built so deeply into me as to escape notice. Hearing, but not hearing, the screams from the streets. Seeing, but not seeing, the ragged figure sleeping in a doorway. Reflexively averting the head to avoid the smells of piss and funk. Closing my ears against the roar of the subway. Automatically minimizing tactile contact with any public surface. And by extension backing off from processing the sudden ugliness—the fight outside the Irish bar, the psychotic spitting curses at someone not there, the beggars, the potential muggers, the depression on the grass patch to the left of the main entrance to 788 Columbus Avenue where a suicide from the sixteenth floor had landed, garbage spilling, rats dancing, traffic arguments—these uglinesses and others, a daily ambush of various uglinesses backed away from, not processed, effectively denied. I'd been born in New York City, and spent most of my life there, and all at once I realized what it had done to me. Tunnel vision is the metaphor of the whole sensorium, and eventually of the soul. It took no more than a minute, and the frightening thought emerged with unusual clarity: *this is no way to live*.

So, move to Brooklyn. Brooklyn Heights, to be precise, which at that time had not yet been "discovered." Another part of the city, and yet from the stunned disbelief of our friends in Manhattan, you might have thought it was another world. "Brooklyn! Why on earth would you want to do that?" For space, for a residential neighborhood, for non-thru streets, for trees, for quiet nights, for clean sidewalks—for a lot of reasons, the most important being our desire to have a child, and then another child, which would not have been possible for two responsible people living in an apartment on Columbus Avenue. (Although people had been doing it all around us, their children playing in the chain-linked fenced-in cement and steel playgrounds sprinkled here and there in odd corners of the complex.) For many years Brooklyn worked well for us. We congratulated ourselves on getting there early, while it was cheap, as more and more people came over from Manhattan, driving up real estate and thus taxes.

And if, after three thefts, it was no longer possible for our boys to have bikes, nor to go to the nearby park without a large group of pals alongside them, that was simply a price of city life. When parking spaces became harder and harder to find it was an inconvenience. But when the City of New York became addicted to higher and higher parking fines, tow-away cash transactions, etc., when the numbers of legal spaces were actually *reduced* in order to increase civic revenues, the situation turned ugly. (Of course, only certain neighborhoods were targeted for these schemes, the middle-class neighborhoods where the residents were thought to be "good citizens" who would pay their fines by mail, without the expensive business of chasing them down.) It became impossible to own a car, and I had no illusions about who forced me to sell our beat-up station wagon. The City of New York forced me, and many others, in the start of what was to be a protracted war, an economic war against its own citizens which eventually drove out the middle classes. It is a truism that no community can work without the presence and participation of the middle classes. The catastrophe that is New York City today occurred by policy and by increments, and the work-ethic, family-oriented, planning-for-the-future folks who cooperated with their government were actually helping to braid the cat-o'-nine-tails with which they would be whipped. It was betrayal on a grand scale, and meanwhile, in actual fact, the rich got richer, the poor got poorer, and all the poisonous effects of that schism grew increasingly corrosive to everyone.

My boys went to private school in the neighborhood. (The public school—even for a parent like me who had attended public schools right up to college— P.S. 6, Stuyvesant High School were unthinkable.) The boys would walk, usually with a few pals from the block who also attended St. Ann's. One of their classmates was late one morning and had to walk by himself. He was set upon by three kids from the neighborhood across the park, robbed, and then kidnapped and taken to a deserted brownstone where he was sodomized, hung out a fourth floor window by his heels, beaten, and then released with instructions to go home, get money, and return with it. He returned with the police.

Okay, one might say, things like this happen when you have such an enormous density of population. It's a statistical matter, so many criminal, sexually precocious juvenile sociopaths per hundred thousand. Perhaps, although none of the St. Ann's parents put forward that view. But what I found even more ominous than the event was the fatalistic calmness with which subsequent developments were received. The three young criminals were apprehended, released to the custody of their families, and told to show up in court. They did, and because of their youth and the disinclination (in my view irresponsible) of the victim's parents to have the boy testify to the details of the sodomy, all three were forthwith released. Again, I heard a voice. *This is no place to live*.

But I hung on. The city was not without its delights. Music, movies, my favorite bar, and the excitement of meeting new people after my first book came out. There was a kind of forward momentum I never questioned, but simply rode, night after night, a continuous social stimulation to which I became addicted. And the more my marriage weakened, the more desperately I tore around town. Much deeply foolish behavior, and I blame no one but myself for that. Years of hysteria.

After the divorce I subleased a one-room apartment in Manhattan. I had no job, unpredictable income as a pianist and freelance magazine writer, no savings, and at the age of thirty-five, no plan. "Don't sink," my divorce lawyer told me. I didn't want to sink. I could not allow myself to sink, and yet I didn't know what to do. When the sublease expired and I looked around for some place to stay I realized I could not possibly afford the rents that were being asked, no matter how my luck ran.

The big apple! It had been my city, but now I saw it as a vast machine which would only grind me down bit by bit, forcing me into escalating debt, the charity of friends, or various other humiliating scenarios. God knows I had judged some of my fellow New York artists harshly enough—those who lived off women, or hus-

tled the rich, or sold drugs, or anything at all to keep
from driving a cab—and I was not about to join their
ranks. I had, after all, not only to look at my face in the
mirror, I had to look into the faces of my children.

My story is so common as to be banal, but there it is.
I'd been ambivalent about New York City, but also
addicted to it. Personal catastrophe finally drove me
out, cold turkey. My friends, vaguely threatened by
such radical action, did everything they could to dis-
suade me. If Brooklyn had been another world, then
leaving altogether was disappearing into another universe. It was, all agreed, unthinkable. An insane, self-
destructive proposition.

In fact, as it turned out, it was how I saved myself. I
did not sink, as I doubtless would have had I stayed.
I built a new life a good deal less provincial than the old
one.

––––––

FRANK CONROY *was born in New York City in 1936. A
graduate of Haverford College, he has worked as a jazz
pianist, a scallop fisherman, a federal bureaucrat, and a
teacher. He now teaches at the University of Iowa, where he
is director of the Iowa Writers' Workshop.*

Frank Conroy's work has been published in The
New Yorker, Esquire, Partisan Review, Gentlemen's
Quarterly, *and* Harper's *magazine. His autobiography,*
Stop-Time, *was released in 1967. A collection of his stories,*
Midair, *was published in 1985.*

About the New York of his 1993 novel, Body and Soul,
*Conroy writes: ". . . the New York described in its pages is
long gone, replaced by another city of the same name."*

*Conroy divides his time between Iowa City and
Nantucket. "Change" was written for* Leaving New York.

Kathleen Norris

Leaving New York and Staying: How Much of a New Yorker Am I?

In the supermarket—how much of a New Yorker am I? I press against the supermarket's dairy bin and the refrigerated air wells up over me and out of the past, the dark, cold air of the apple shed in Tonasket. My feet are ice cold and my sinuses begin to ache. The checkout cashier, a Puerto Rican girl with a scarred mouth and a pleasant face, packs my grocery bag and winces when she lifts a heavy bag of onions. What hurts? The pain bites into my right shoulder. It's from lifting over and over with the same arm. I'm feeling old. *Yes,* I say, *at nineteen, I felt this pain. I'm getting old, I thought, and I haven't even gone to college.*

These few words, scrawled by a friend, Betty Kray, on a paper plate that I found among her papers after she died, epitomize a truth about New York; many of its most loyal citizens—those we think of as consummate New Yorkers—have actually come from somewhere else. They are denizens in the ecological sense of the word, "naturalized in a region." Having fully acclimated to New York City over the years, having taken root in its institutions—in Betty's case, as Executive Director of the YMHA Poetry Center and later the Academy of American Poets, and as co-founder, with Stanley Kunitz, of Poet's House—they come to seem native. They thrive in the overcharged air.

But Tonasket looms—Tonasket, Washington, an isolated village in the remote Okanogan Valley, northeast of Seattle via 250 miles of two-lane blacktop. Tonasket, a sour memory jostled to the surface in a crowded supermarket near Columbia University, on the edge of Harlem, the pained face of a young checkout clerk. An unnerving question penetrates the public facade—*how much of a New Yorker am I?* Over the years, one invents a New York self, but when Tonasket returns, it jolts us and pulls us back to its provincialism, its dark, musty places, the fear of being buried alive in the root cellar. Nineteen years old, and no way out.

Tonasket reminds the New York émigré that place is inescapable, that lying just below our veneer of sophistication is the weary, scared kid who's afraid of being stuck forever in the provinces. A ghost all too easily summoned, she becomes a question and a reproach—what if you had left me here, to be worn down before I had a chance to receive an education? What if you'd never had the nerve to make your way in the world outside Tonasket? Where would I be? Where—who—am I now?

New York City has long attracted people who leave places like Tonasket, Washington in order to make their way in the professions and the arts. From the vantage point of New York and Europe, many writers have immortalized their Tonaskets: the Red Cloud, Nebraska of Willa Cather, the Sauk Center, Minnesota of Sinclair Lewis, or F. Scott Fitzgerald's Saint Paul. The Montgomery, Alabama of Zelda Fitzgerald. Other contemporary writers—Carol Bly, Robert Bly, and Larry Woiwode among them—were drawn in their youth to the literary world of New York, but in discovering their authority as writers, they eventually left it behind.

I moved to New York City in 1969, long before I knew I was a writer. I'd recently graduated from Bennington College and was adrift. My family was and is close-knit, but my rootless childhood as a Navy brat had left me feeling placeless. New York seemed as good a place as any to take my plunge into adulthood and my first real job, as an assistant to Betty Kray at the Academy of American Poets.

It was a dream job for a budding poet, mainly because I was able to hear so much poetry read aloud, not only at the Academy series, but at the YMHA, St. Mark's in the Bowery, and at other series that were springing up all over town. Good poetry read badly, bad poetry read well, and vice versa. My roommate, a friend from college, was a Juilliard student, so I attended many concerts as well. I was surprised to discover that among my new friends and acquaintances, born-and-bred New Yorkers were a rarity. Most of us had come from other places, small towns or cities in the Carolinas, Arkansas, Tennessee, Oklahoma, Ohio, Missouri, Kansas. So many of these people seemed marvelously sophisticated to me. They'd been around long enough to establish themselves as New Yorkers, at least by my naive definition. They held on stubbornly, working as studio musicians, editors, actors, museum curators, opera singers and voice teachers when they could, and as waiters, strippers, taxi drivers, messengers and office temps when the good jobs evaporated. I wondered if I had their nerve.

Some of them may still be New Yorkers; I left after six years, having discovered that I had the nerve to move to South Dakota. Now, when I write about leaving New York, I find that I must also write about my good friend and mentor Betty Kray, who came to New York City in the early 1950s and never left. After her death, in the process of working for her executors, I discovered a cache of private writings in which Betty had written, in middle-age, about the young woman she'd been when she arrived in Manhattan. She could have been describing me, twenty years later, when full of bravado and insecurity, I tested the city to see if I might become a real New Yorker: what I thought I was coming to, what I thought I'd left far behind, and the dire importance, in Manhattan, of appearances. Betty wrote:

When I first came to New York that immunity the city grants a newcomer covered me like a corn husk. I felt untouched, invulnerable, at a virginal distance. The city seemed a game I could enter or leave at will. . . .I had that gray suit. I wore it because it was my best. I could be a careless young woman in a suit that cost $125.00. And Susan [a distant relative] walked next to me, buoying me up. How dead she is—twenty years now. Mother had just died, and Susan bought me the suit as a consolation.

All of my dead (some of them then living) were helping me enter New York; I see that now that I no longer have them. But then I thought they were hindrances, to be shoved aside, repressed, diminished. The incredible professionalism of New Yorkers hit me more than anything else, and it seemed to me then as now that I'd always be an amateur. I could never escape my background.

I must have looked attractive. Sometimes the mirror said yes, but I needed more than that. I'd look for approval in people's faces. I was never sure. I wore the gray suit in Manhattan's terrible heat and looked for a job.

Place was always an important theme in my friendship with Betty, and in her mentoring of me as a poet. She was one of the very few New Yorkers of my acquaintance who understood that my move out of Manhattan to my grandparents' home in Lemmon, South Dakota might be necessary for me as a writer. But it's only recently that I've come to understand Betty's fears for me as I showed signs of settling in— "you're isolating yourself too much from other writers," she would say, reprovingly. "You need to get out more." It's only after her death that I discovered that Betty's gentle reproaches came not only from a distaste for Tonasket's provincialism, but from a hidden grief and shame that made it impossible for her ever to visit me on the western Plains.

At Bennington I had encountered for the first time the provincialism of urban Easterners, who had a working knowledge of the Northeast and Southern California, but only a dim idea of the vastness of America, what they would refer to as "flyover country." So I was surprised to find, on interviewing with Betty Kray for a job at the Academy, that one wall of her cluttered office was dominated by a large map of the country. As I recall, she never did get around to asking me how well I typed, because in our initial small talk I happened to reveal that I was flying to South Dakota the next morning, to visit my grandparents over Christmas. Betty insisted that I show her on the map exactly where I was going, even though this involved moving some reference books and papers aside to get within pointing range of western South Dakota.

"Well," I said, "I'll fly to Bismarck." (It was, and is, the nearest commercial airport). "But I'll still be over a hundred miles away. Then I'll fly in a small plane, probably a four-seater, down to Lemmon, right across the border of South Dakota." Betty was full of questions about my grandparents, about how often I saw them, about my ties to South Dakota (which in my early twenties I considered tenuous at best). Then Betty said, proudly, "I'm a Westerner, too. I came here years ago from Seattle." She told me that one of her ancestors had been a surveyor and engineer who had helped map the Continental Divide. She also told me that I had the job.

Language as Salvation

In my relatively sheltered, lower-middle class life—my parents (musicians and teachers) had more books and music on hand than money—it had never occurred to me that one might have to leave home in order to find people who knew that one might live by music, or by words. I didn't know that exile from one's roots might be the cost of finding a language that would save you. But now I suspect that this is the reason so many young writers try the New York life, at least for a while. I suspect that for writers and passionate lovers of poetry like Betty Kray, language is at the heart of the process of deciding, "how much of a New Yorker am I?"

For some writers, myself included, the story goes much as it did for Larry Woiwode, who in an essay entitled "The Spirit of Place" has said that in the mid-1960s, when he began writing seriously "that is, willing to give up my life for it, I was in a room in New York that I rented for nine dollars a week." Influenced by writers such as Beckett, Joyce, Babel, Kafka and Nabokov, his style was what he now terms as "modishly experimental, on the cusp of Postmodernism." But one day, he says, "my maternal grandmother entered my mind with such force it occurred to me that she had influenced me more than any of these writers." Eventually his assent to tell her story led to what may be the ultimate North Dakota novel, *Beyond the Bedroom Wall*. He now lives and farms about forty miles to the north of me.

I left New York, and left off writing fashionably cerebral poetry, under much the same auspices. One day when I was alone in my apartment in New York I heard the unmistakable, tinkly laughter of my South

Dakota grandmother. Pressed to define the experience, I'd say that it was my conscience speaking, but in my grandmother's light, high voice, asking me pointed questions that left my newfound literary pretensions in a shambles. Her language—plain English, gloriously inflected with the King James idiom of a late-19th century girlhood in Virginia—reminded me who I was, and eventually called me back to South Dakota.

Betty Kray remained in New York City until she died in 1987. And language caused her to remain, and drove her to make her life's work one that benefited poets and poetry. (She succeeded so well at this that at her funeral Stanley Kunitz said, "American poets just lost one of the best friends they ever had.") In a 1966 letter to her friend Denise Levertov, who had written for permission to dedicate a book of poems to her, Betty wrote:

If you put me on your dedication page, I should want to be Betty Kray. As such I couldn't be called an ardent and steadfast friend of poetry, which maybe Elizabeth Ussachevsky could smilingly and publicly accept, but Betty Kray, my childhood name, is closest to my real self, and as BK I scarcely befriended poetry but rather used it ruthlessly ever after discovering it. I think poetry is to be used. It's like an otter's toboggan slide, it's for fun, merry-making, a quick plunge, of infinite use. I'm trying to figure out how to explain to you who grew up in an atmosphere charged with language how it was to have grown up in a relatively mute world, as I did. Or at least where language was regarded as a practical instrument for everyday dealings or as a didactic instrument, and as such blunt and heavy, a killer.

The best language I heard spoken I now realize was that of my mother, whose speech came from a small southerly town where the style was simple and vividly related to the physical landscape. A refinement of college and gentility overlay this speech, but as she grew older the refinement dissolved into the understratum. My grandfather wrote didactic articles and as a consequence spoke pompously, but would lapse into a biblical idiom—he was a Bible reader—and this saved him. My father tried to sound like a cross between an engineer's and a lawyer's brief, a composite of the two. They (and the community) were essentially non-fluent . . .

Discovering poetry gave Betty a glimpse of another way of using words, a way past the utilitarian language that had threatened to strand her in Tonasket. "If one is not used to hearing original ideas, and feelings, articulated by ordinary people" she explained to Levertov, "then language becomes a nagging puzzle." The fluency of poetry had seemed to her a secret spring, "hidden, forceful, compared to its flood. Poetry takes one to the fountain. It's a main stream," she said finally, "a river Jordan sluicing the barren west."

Betty was well aware that there were "barren wests" in all corners of the world, even in the sophisticated environs of New York City. Her years in Tonasket had made her extraordinarily sensitive to provincialism. She knew it when she saw it; the provincialism of the New York City Board of Education, for example, which treated Betty with great suspicion when she approached them in the early 1960s with a radical proposal that would allow the Academy of American Poets to send poets to read their poetry in city schools, and to conduct in-service courses on the teaching of poetry for public school teachers. Only after a heroic effort on Betty's part was the Academy able to establish this pilot program, funded in part by the Rockefeller Foundation. It eventually became a model for the nationwide artists-in-the-schools program that the National Endowment for the Arts established in the 1970s.

But in May of 1965 Betty wrote to Gerald Freund of the Rockefeller Foundation that "it has taken a year to convince the [Board of Education] In-Service people of the merits of any program offering discussions of poetry . . . We found ourselves explaining that 'poets are articulate.'" The Board's provincialism, so typical of an entrenched bureaucracy, might best be exposed with a glance at the roster for the proposed in-service course, which was finally held in 1966. The moderator was Stanley Kunitz, and guest lecturers included W. H. Auden, Anthony Hecht, Robert Lowell, Denise Levertov, Howard Nemerov, Louis Simpson, W. D. Snodgrass and Allen Tate. Younger poets hired by the Academy to read in the schools throughout the city in that first year of the program included David Antin,

Paul Blackburn, Ed Field, Kathleen Fraser, Louise Glück, David Ignatow, Emmett Jarrett, June Jordan, Galway Kinnell, Harvey Shapiro, Diane Wakoski and Jay Wright.

During my tenure at the Academy in the early 1970s, I recall Betty's dismay over a situation that developed when we sent a young Puerto Rican-American poet to work in a junior high school on the Upper West Side of Manhattan. The student body had changed in the previous decade from mostly white (predominantly Jewish) to Hispanic and Caribbean black. One older teacher complained to us because the poet had read several poems, his own and those of others, that included obscenities. They turned out to be everyday Spanish words and phrases, not obscene at all; images of vegetables in a grocery store bin, and of mothers carrying infants. As Betty and I talked with the man, we sensed that our program had become the focus of his resentment over all the changes in his neighborhood and school. He had come to equate Spanish words with obscenity.

Betty was more stunned than angry. But as she continued to engage the man in conversation, and he revealed that he had always wanted to be a rabbi, but had more or less settled for teaching in a public school, her face clouded. I had never heard Betty speak of Tonasket, Washington, but I now know that in this sad, frightened man she had encountered its ghosts. He'd never dared to enlarge his world, and the failing had come to haunt him. He was, he told us, beginning to take some classes at Yeshiva—clearly they were the light of his life. But his life at school was hell. Provincialism had not only cut him off from his students, it had blinded him to the glories of Spanish and Spanish-American literature, a literature that might have helped him to better connect with those around him.

For over thirty years Betty Kray was a force behind the scenes in American poetry. She helped to generate the first nationwide poetry reading circuits, as well as several poetry contests and translation projects—many things that American poets now take for granted. But in a letter to Denise Levertov, Betty spoke of her work

on behalf of poetry as merely a form of "self-charity."
Tonasket had taught her what would save her, and I
believe that its pull—that strange, haunted question—
"how much of a New Yorker am I?"—not only explains
the energy with which Betty applied herself to promot-
ing poetry, but also reveals why she felt that she needed
to remain in New York City and bring the world to her.

And the world came. Betty used Russian contacts to
offer Andrei Voznesensky his first invitation to read in
the United States; the Academy of American Poets
sponsored a New York City reading and a national tour
in 1966. As far as I know, Betty was the first to invite the
Blackfeet writer James Welch to New York; he read on
the Academy series and also visited several Manhattan
elementary schools. During my time at the Academy I
worked on a project in which American poets translated 20th century Brazilian poetry; the book that
resulted, edited by Elizabeth Bishop and Emanual
Brasil, and published by Wesleyan, is a classic. We also
sponsored a New York reading and nationwide tour by
several eminent Japanese poets. Around the time I was
leaving, in early 1974, the Academy was developing a
series of panel discussions and readings to be held
throughout the country, in which several Chinese poets
would join American writers such as Robert Bly, David
Lattimore, Kenneth Rexroth, Gary Snyder and James
Wright in discussing the influence of Chinese verse on
American poets and poetry.

Language as Homeland

For many years most of my income was derived from
working as a visiting poet in North and South Dakota
schools. It pleased Betty that a program she had helped
to initiate in the mid-1960s was helping me in the '70s
and '80s to earn a living on the Great Plains. I often
wrote to her from the little towns, sharing stories of the
children and their teachers. But Betty died before I
could relate one episode that would have resonated
deeply with her. One snowy afternoon a teacher's aide
approached me in the school library, asking apologeti-
cally if I could help one of her charges. Pointing to a
glum-looking teenaged girl seated at a table across the

room, she told me, "She has to come up with three metaphors for English class, and she can't think of any."

I felt as if the shiny linoleum floor had opened suddenly, and become a treacherous sea. A darkness so vast had intruded on the false cheer of the fluorescent-lit room that the light changed utterly, and I felt as if I had to gasp for air. All I could do at first was to sputter with phrases that made no sense to the girl. " . . . But you make up metaphors all the time, and you have since you were a little kid. It's how you learned to talk . . . it's how the English language works, how your mind works."

The girl gazed at me, blankly, miserably. I realized that if, as Czeslaw Milosz has said, language is the only homeland, this young girl's education had made her an exile in her own country. I thought of Betty, and Tonasket, and wondered what she would say in this situation. I thought she might simply whisper in the girl's ear, *get out—get as far away from this place as you can—while you're still young—get out of the barren stream before it dries you to a husk.* I recalled Betty's response to Marilynne Robinson's novel *Housekeeping,* which my husband and I had given her. It's a classic tale of small-town provincialism, of children's pitiful attempts to make sense of the grown-ups around them, who seem (and are) so gratuitously cruel. Betty confessed to us that not long after starting the novel, she had turned to the last few pages. "I had to make sure," she said, "that someone got out of there alive."

Betty got out of Tonasket, and stayed out. I got out of New York and settled, improbably, in the town my mother had left after graduating from high school in the 1930s. Both she and Betty Kray—I think of them as my two mothers—were afraid that if I stayed too long in western South Dakota my college education and city smarts might go to waste. When I took up knitting and bread-making their suspicions were confirmed. When a casserole that I entered one year in the county fair made it to the finals, I wouldn't be surprised to learn that they consulted with one another about how best to get me out.

But my mother also enjoyed having me here,

because it's given her an unexpected opportunity to stay in touch with her childhood home. And over the years Betty slowly resigned herself to the fact that I enjoyed living in isolated circumstances. She sympathized when several of my best friends, ministers in local churches, were being run out of town. "I am accustomed to these situations," Betty wrote to me late in 1983, "I grew up among people like this in Washington state, which accounts for much of my suspicion and hostility toward small town people. My favorite English teacher was practically drummed out of town because she had us read Huxley's *Brave New World*. (My mother and father fought for her)."

The Mute World

It wasn't until several years after Betty's death that I learned of her deep connection to the western Plains. In discussing their family history, her brother told me a story that I know well, a story of misguided, overzealous homesteading and bitter failure, of farms abandoned, and a diaspora that has scattered the children of Great Plains homesteaders all across America. Their paternal grandfather had been a tailor in a town near Prague. Certain that war was coming, and desiring to avoid being drafted in the Austro-Hungarian army, he brought his family to America. They settled in the Sandhills of western Nebraska. The Czech tailor soon discovered that he was no farmer, and eventually he left, abandoning his wife and ten children.

The woman managed, not only to survive, but to see that all of the children received a high school education, something that was not common on the western Plains even in my mother's generation. But, as Betty's brother put it, "our father used to speak of gruesomely hard times." As the oldest child, their father bore much of the responsibility for the family, but eventually he graduated from the University of Nebraska and became a civil engineer.

I knew Betty Kray for fifteen years; worked closely with her for six, and she had known from the beginning of our friendship that we both had roots on the western prairie. Yet she never mentioned it. Her brother feels that she was deeply ashamed of this episode in the family history. Knowing this helps me to understand the fears Betty had for me when I left New York City for the Plains. I recall that Betty spoke to me not long before I left New York about how in a small town I'd need to be "self-protective" in a different way than on city streets. It confused me at the time, but I understand it now.

New York City is a place where you can protect yourself by keeping the past hidden, where you can essentially reinvent yourself as a New Yorker. Betty did invent a magnificent and thoroughly cultured life for herself in New York, and she did it in the best possible way. Her life was one of service to language, to poets and poetry. Still, "the mute world" of Tonasket and western Nebraska, its language tuned to survival, rather than to beauty, never quite let Betty go. She was a brave woman, and the delicious ambiguity of poetry became her fortress. But the Plains haunted her, and silenced her.

I have a map of the New York City subway system on a wall in my house in Lemmon, South Dakota. It tells me where I've been. It also reminds me of one marvelous irony of my friendship with Betty—the Plains that made her mute have given me my voice. It was here that I became a poet. All of my dead—Betty Kray among them now—helped me to enter this place called South Dakota. Betty's rich, religious idiom says it best. "Poetry," she said, "is a main stream, a river Jordan sluicing the barren West. . . ."

———

A New Yorker for nearly six years, KATHLEEN NORRIS *moved twenty years ago, with her husband, poet David Dwyer, to the house built by her grandparents in Lemmon, South Dakota. There in the "humbling . . . largeness of earth and sky," she confronts her heritage, religion, language, and landscape. Her book* Dakota: A Spiritual Geography *was a* New York Times *Notable Book in 1993.*

Born in 1947 in Washington, D.C., and a graduate of

Bennington College in Vermont, Norris is also the author of three books of poetry, Falling Off *(1971),* The Middle of the World *(1981), and* Little Girls in Church *(1995).*

Along with the introduction, Kathleen Norris wrote the preceding essay especially for Leaving New York.

Leslie Brody

Jewish Geography

1– A Dream New York

Walking uptown recently on a beautiful October evening, (after dinner in a piano bar overlooking the bridge homes of hobos and the condominiums of millionaires), I saw a young couple emerge from the gate to the United Nations. He was tall, blonde, square jawed in his London Fog raincoat and holding an umbrella that skimmed the hair of his equally tall companion. She, coatless in a short chic frock, her high heels clicking on the pavement, wiped a stray lock out of her eyes. That hair-do, upswept, bee-hived made her look as if she'd walked out of a James Bond movie. Together they looked like a 1960s cigarette commercial. Interpreters, I thought, linguists or negotiators. And I wondered what it would be like to be young, accomplished and Norwegian in New York. They were, I thought, quintessential out-of-towners who lived there. I, on the other hand, am a dyed-in-the wool New Yorker who has never spent more than two consecutive weeks in town.

Except in my infancy, I have never lived in New York City. I was born in the Bronx (which qualifies as the city, but not the "town"). My youth was spent on Long Island, in Riverhead, a farming community then (ducks and potatoes). For another child this might have been bliss. (My father had a wrecking yard five acres large, where my brothers played bumper cars with scrap autos.) But I was the sort of child who'd rather be lost at the Met than in the hills. My father left New York so he could be his own boss. My mother left reluctantly. Long

after we'd moved to where there was none, she pined for
pavement. Every Saturday, she'd take her good pocket-
book, and drive thirty miles to where the Long Island
Railroad began, to ride the train into town.

I have always carried a mythic New York in me, the
New York my mother inspired. She was, like
Chekhov's Olga, Irena, and Masha, always going back.
New York for my mother was sophisticated, witty,
tribal. It was loud talk, Chinese restaurants, smart
clothes, Brooklyn. It meant being a Jew without seeing the words in italics. For her, leaving New York
meant living in a vacuum with none of the above. In
the "country" she flagged, and in the absence of pavement, never found her footing. She was at her brightest at our city family get-togethers where a New Yorker
among New Yorkers she spat wise cracks, laughed till
she wiped the tears away, and insulted the hick ways of
our country neighbors. New York was the heart of her
world, but we lived too far away for her family or her
past to be anything but exotic to me. Even her Judaism
was exotically tied to duties for the dead. We lit candles
on the anniversary of her parents' death and occasionally went to Temple on Yom Kippur to pray for them.
The only event I remember that really translates the
euphoria of her New York Jewish childhood was at my
brother's Bar Mitzvah, which like most for boys of his
age and time, consisted of a brief temple ceremony,
followed by a catered dinner in a grand hall. I was
seven years old.

After the hors d'oeuvre smorgasbord of sliced der-
mas, beef franks in blankets, and the silverplated
tureens of chopped liver; after the sit-down dinner, the
Viennese dessert table and the Bar Mitzvah cake; the
caterers moved the food out and the parents of the new
man started to dance to "More than the Greatest Love
the World has Seen," and "When the Moon Hits Your
Eye Like a big Pizza Pie." During the dance, rocking
backwards on my chair, I gashed my head on a radiator.
I was concussed for several minutes while my father's
mother Goldie wailed that I had died. When the ambulance arrived, the entire family dressed in their finery, I
am told, ran alongside it for blocks. A satisfying image:

the women in their chiffons and high heels, their chignons coming undone; the men in their tight-fitting suits and all the children in shiny black shoes, like a Marc Chagall painting about us.

I am one of those bred to be a New Yorker, who has lived in self-imposed exile. Like a pioneer, or in less flattering terms—a colonial, I have adjusted to different climates and personnel, always carrying the idea of a superior home that cannot live in real air. My attitude would often bring out the worst in out-of-towners (carrying New York as I did, like the Irish priests carried writing in the Dark Ages). And it has taken me years to learn to mask myself. What is normal speech and body language in New York is often construed as bossy, pushy, anxious and neurotic in less confident towns. I have noticed that in smaller cities particularly, false modesty to an extreme degree, imposes a silent censorship. In these places one must be careful when describing accomplishments not to hurt feelings, or undermine the security of one's conversational partners. (Implying a provincialism to their beloved home is one of the fastest ways I know to get off on the wrong side of a new friend.) While, on the information highway we may all be residents of one great truck stop, there are still lingering human distinctions, and one of them is regionalism. This is not to say that I approve of the snobs who blithely invert Minneapolis and Indianapolis, or confuse an ignorant population with the residents of geographical location far from them ("Will it play in Peoria?"). I'm no urbanologist, but it seems to me, the larger the city, the bolder the braggadocio of its citizens. New Yorkers who find a bone scream it from the rooftops.

I have lived my life in orbit of New York. The irony of this is that while no other place feels like home, contemporary New York can't possibly measure up to its legend. Never having endured the long-term day-to-day there, I am ferociously loyal to it. I am a dream New Yorker: basking in its benefits, bearing none of its burdens, unlikely at this point ever to exchange myth for reality.

2 – Leaving Long Island

After my mother died and my father re-married, we moved to the suburbs. Only an hour's commute from town, Massapequa was one of the many bedroom communities that grew up with the population boom after the war. Architecturally divided between ex-ploded Levitown-style homes and wealthy ocean-side palazzos tinged with the mystery of the mafiosi, we called home matzo/pizza. Later, comic Jerry Seinfeld, a Massapequan himself, translated the town's name for history as "Indian for by the mall."

For me suburbia, malls, and cars held little interest. The Vietnam War was in full force, and the center of anti-war activity was New York City. At fifteen, I was a teeny-bopper commuting to town on the weekends to crash in Greenwich Village pads, share hash and march shoulder to shoulder with my hippie comrades. In such a grand city, every speech, every manifesto, every ges-ture was grand. I was used to large events: 200,000 people or more standing up in solidarity. Potent and arousing as they were, demonstrations only occupied so much time, there was still plenty of opportunity to hang around the Fillmore East and the Electric Circus; watch Godard movies; and pretend to bored sophistication in the Museum of Modern Art. I already knew I wanted to be a writer. I was writing for a high school underground paper oddly named *The New York Herald Tribune* (they'd folded and we'd claimed the name!). On the train in and out of the city, I was reading everything about the New York of J. D. Salinger, of Grace Paley, of Dutch last names, of Dorothy Day and Dorothy Parker; of jet-setters and social reformers, and I was eager to meet a real author. One afternoon, at the cafe next to MOMA, I caught the eye of a glittering human *bon bon* (black marshmallow hair, almond white lips and eyelashes long as her nose) whom I immediately recognized from the cover of her popular book. It was on the incorrect book list, decadent and bourgeois. A bad, sexy book, which I'd inhaled in a single wanton breath. Here was Jacqueline Sussann, author of *Valley of the Dolls,* and on her lap Fifi, or Mimi, or Didi, her toy poodle in its blinding jeweled collar.

"Jackie," I ventured.

She arched an elaborate brow.

"I just wanted to tell you, I *love* your writing."

"You're too young for my book," Jackie said, surprisingly practical. I have often wondered what she thought of her reading audience. For a time her flamboyant melodramas caught the trashy glamour of the age. They were devoured across the spectrum, hidden under covers and in cupboards by businessmen and underaged revolutionaries alike. That, I take for authorial breadth.

In 1968, when Columbia blew, too young to participate (non-college students and all "outside agitators" prohibited from entering the school grounds), I stood for hours staring ardently through the barred gates. I only wanted to get to college to go on strike. As my own schoolwork failed, I took a technical diploma and counted on my political poetry to get me into an arty school. Teenybopping weekends, city literature, and street life were building to the climax of my graduation and subsequent ascension into the life of a bona fide town dweller. Despite my grades, Fordham University had offered me a place in their urban studies program. And it was as if New York itself was offering me a seat at the table (maybe not the round table), but a situation in town with a future. Pondering my acceptance, the city loomed as a surprisingly heavy, certain, and static environment. I knew it would be my job to look beneath the pavement, to replace the legend with a microscopic examination of it. Day after day I would plod to work, take measurements, compare graphs, analyze statistics, announce findings, in the rain and the snow, in the grainy gray ant-like rush hour. I balked. Leaving New York was the only way I could preserve its poetry. I was seventeen.

I went to Europe when America was still the great imperialist war-mongering monster. Strangely, I was held responsible. The only thing considered worse than to be an American in Europe in the early 1970s was to be a New Yorker. New York had no cachet in the communes of Amsterdam and London among the wild hippie/politico crowd with whom I craved to connect. San Francisco was flowers in your hair, Chicago was rat-a-tat-tat Al Capone, but New York, New York was the belly of the beast. So I said I was Canadian.

I jettisoned New York and being Jewish around the same time. Perhaps it was a defensive measure against the casual anti-Semitism of my European companions. Some held attitudes that were chillingly pre-war. As though the war against the Jews had never happened, as if the war of their parents had just folded into utopian time. It was a sweet concept that could only be floated on the backs of many drugs. And the Irish, Italian, Dutch, British, French and German youths who shared those seventies communes sloughed off their past and their surnames as surely as I did. In the psychedelic night world, I changed my name to the organic and unrefined-sounding Buckwheat Groats, and affected a London accent.

I was living in an abandoned house in Camden Town; I'd joined the International Women's Itinerant Hobo's Union, and was lobbying anyone who would hold still for a moment about my views on the uselessness of national borders, passports and copyright. I'd gotten a job as a printer from some Spanish Civil War Veterans for the Black Flag Anarchist Press, and curiously I'd never felt so American. The language appeared the same, but the British usage was alarming me. One night, after watching Monty Python on the telly I saw a British chat show that I now realize helped me find my way back to New York. (I have to preface this by saying how I was at that point so deeply burrowed into the counterculture that the very concept of television blew my mind. I was like the tribal member of a cargo cult, spirits and demons were trying to communicate from a box!). Up on a cheesy platform, announced by pre-Beatle pop, in sixties aqua molded chairs, two gin-lit, mottled-faced gents with bad teeth who chain-smoked kept crossing and uncrossing their legs. They were reminiscing about a third colleague (a famous writer recently dead) and his secret love affair with a married "Jewess." Maybe it was the atmosphere, maybe it was the hash, but I found their use of that word at that moment a shock. I don't know how many nouns we English speakers have that end in *e-s-s*, but some seem rooted in a shadow vocabulary: adventuress, authoress, poetess. All rather archaic now, they imply a diminution of the activities they describe. While a devil-may-care adventurer might firm up into an explorer, and get his name inscribed on the walls of the London Geographic Society, adventuress connotes a seedy cloud of flop houses, prostitution, and con artistry. Authoress, too, seems an eternally deficient female who pens gothics for romantic girls and home-bound females with time to fritter and too little education. The word poetess fares only slightly better. Edna St. Vincent Millay was called poetess in her time, but she loomed above the word. Elizabeth Barrett Browning with her curly locks and floppy dog was more the type, but all her hard work seems to conflict with the *e-s-s*'s dismissive style. Perhaps only Colette artiste, vagabond, literary lioness, stretched out on pillows like an odalisque, could manage the language on her own terms: adventuress, authoress, poetess, but she didn't write in English.

Then there is "Jewess," not entirely out of use in the British press. Having sidestepped the subject previously by hiding under a new accent and a new name, at first I was merely indulging in a literary exercise. Was there such a person as a Moslemess? a Christianess? a Buddhistess? (Prioress just wasn't the same.) I supposed it could have been worse, the word could have been "Jewette" or "Jewtrix" (Jewelle on the other hand has a pretty ring). The fact is because the English dictionary defines Jewess as a Jewish woman or girl, by virtue of its existence, we are set apart. You can understand how it felt more than a little creepy. The way those guys were tossing off their words on television—tittering, while they innuendoe'd, sotto voce'd and double entendre'd their way through the litany of jolly birds their old mate had pulled was really pissing me off. Now I'd probably pay to hear those two exhausted aristos gossip about the lives of their pals, half of whom wrote brilliant books while the other half were spies. But back then, my brain was like a motor boat crossing the Atlantic. I thought, we name female animals: sheep are ewes; horses, mares; dogs, bitches. Words matter! Years later I read Laurens Van der Post, Jung's biographer, and he had much to say on the topic of meaning and emptiness, but one quote keeps coming back, "We feel it such a terrible crime in the West to counterfeit money;" he wrote, "but it should be a worse crime to counterfeit words."

When you are young, you go along, shedding your skin, trying things on, and then maybe a word, just one word, accidentally heard, diverts your path. You'd think from the fuss I'm making that I went on to become a rabbi. I didn't. What happened was, words started to coalesce in ways they hadn't before, meaning simply became more precious.

Perhaps it was only because the New Yorkers who got together for softball games on the Fourth of July, and dinners on Thanksgiving *advertised* that I took the next step back (not even the Californians *advertised*). Joining the exiles that November and hearing their complaints in our own beautiful tribal New Yorker's language, I experienced a reconversion. Canada is a beautiful country, an admirable sovereignty. My ancestors might have landed in Canada—it was always the luck of the draw for Eastern European refugees whether or not they sailed to New York, Montreal, or South Africa. But my grandparents landed on Ellis Island, so I still can conjure up the thrill tinged with apology that I felt that Thanksgiving. I felt welcomed back to the New World, sitting among other loud, extravagant people, some like me with large gestures and generous noses. Jewess-adventuress-authoress (or would-be). I was fast becoming the most hyphenated woman I knew. Far away in London that November I felt more of a New Yorker than ever.

3 – Jewish Geography

That's how it has been for me. The farther away, the more devoted I become. In New York on a visit I'm a rube. I don't know the subway system, I don't know where to eat, I get lost between East and West, and don't ask me about Fashion Avenue. I am a champion of the long-gone time. In Union Square, I imagine the gigan-

tic push and shove of the marches that ended there, pre-
ceded by the demonstrations of my father's day, when,
as a labor organizer for district 65—garment workers,
on the verge of the Chinese-Japanese War, he was
arrested for supporting Chinese self-determination.
Before he worked for the union he used to work for his
uncle, climbing up and sorting through mountains of
rags. My mother used to shop at Klein's, once a land-
mark department store across from Union Square. After
a demonstration she and her girlfriends might have run
over and tried on hats.

When I am in town now, first I go to the Strand
Bookstore, then I usually look for a bakery where they
still sell the black and white cookies of my youth. It is
not hard to discern the origin of the butter cookies we
used to buy "to bring something" for a hostess gift.
Those yellow drops dotted with jam or half dipped in
chocolate came right from the confectionery shops of
Germany and Austria. The Italian biscotti were of
equally obvious derivation. But where did the black
and white cookies come from? Lemony, cushioned and
the size of a personal pizza, the frosting split the cookie,
half white and half black. You could make something of
it being a symbol of the New York I grew up in—either
a shared New York or a divided one.

It is a truth universally acknowledged that there is no
place like home, but you can't go there again. My parents moved to Miami, sold the family house. Everyone I
knew in town has moved to the suburbs or lives in a flat
so small, the sofa is used for a filing cabinet. And New
York has gotten on without me. Though not well. And
here I will quote from a column published in the *Nation*
on January 23rd, 1995, written by Alexander Cockburn:

New York has about 1.8 million people on welfare. One out of
every four New Yorkers is a pauper, and in the Bronx the rate is
40 percent. A recent study by the Food and Hunger Hotline
shows that in 1979 there were thirty emergency soup kitchens
and food pantries in New York City serving about a million
meals per year. In 1991 there were 730, serving almost 30 million meals. Virtually all people seeking emergency food last
year—97 percent—owned or rented apartments; about a quarter of them had jobs. In 1989, 48,000 New Yorkers who were

not on welfare needed food stamps to avert hunger and malnutrition: five years later there were 81,000 such individuals.

Mayor Guiliani wants to gut the remaining social services, and Governor Pataki is positioning himself to be Lord High Executioner. Not for a minute have I forgotten that it is a privilege to *enjoy* New York. When I look at the baleful statistics, I can't help but wonder if it would have made a difference if I'd stuck around to take the measurements, compare the graphs, analyze the statistics, announce the findings. (The very idea that I could, seems very New York—not to be awed by size or noise or speed).

I am often asked why I don't live in New York. And I'm always stumped for an answer. Should I say I want a ticker tape parade, I'll go when they offer me an honorary doctorate at Columbia, or *The New Yorker* hires me on staff? I wonder if I'd stayed, would I have left by now? My expectations for the city remain very grand. Think for a minute of a New York Minute, a New York State of Mind, a New York Eggcream. What do people *mean* when they utter these words? That New York defines time, space, and fountain beverages? I am a New Yorker with many hyphenates, perched on the border with a view. Lately, when someone asks, why don't you live there? I look mysteriously into the distance and say, don't I?

———

LESLIE BRODY *was born in New York and, as her piece* "Jewish Geography" *attests, remains devoted to the city. She has lived and worked on the East Coast and in St. Paul, Minnesota. Before becoming involved in literary journalism, she wrote and adapted scripts for the stage.*

She has been a regular contributor to the Hungry Mind Review *and* Elle *magazine, as well as a writer for the* Washington Globe-World. *She recently finished her first novel.*

"Jewish Geography" was written for Leaving New York.

Mona Simpson

The Things We Do for Love

As any frequent flyer knows, all miles are not equal. A New York bound traveller from Los Angeles can arrive in less than five hours, and with the luck of the time change, comfortably go to sleep that night on eastern time. Going west is not so easy. The flight can take up to six and a half hours, depending on headwinds. And the odd disjuncture of arriving only three hours after you leave New York makes you feel all the more ravaged, as if the clock and light refuse to acknowledge your ordeal. In our mythology, going west has always been the more arduous journey. Going west meant foraging into the frontier, our own and last heart of darkness. East was synonymous with return.

Californians of my generation never made that original journey themselves. It was an ardor endured and commemorated by parents or grandparents or even great-great grandparents. Having built fortunes or at least lives on the frontier, having cultivated "the desert bloom," they nonetheless retain sufficient nostalgia and fretful insecurity to be happy to pay to have their children "finished" a few years in the East, at an Ivy League college or in an entry-level job in New York, the way earlier generations of Americans in Henry James' novels sent their sons and daughters to Europe. Of course, as anyone who remembers Isabel Archer knows, there is always a danger in the journey. As a friend's grandmother chided as he was packing to go off to college in New York, "If you go to live back east, you'll make friends back east. And then pretty soon you'll fall in love there in the East and you'll end up marrying an Easterner and staying there. You'll never come back."

The three girls I was closest to in high school, wanted more than anything to go "back east" for college, a goal each of them accomplished, and now, almost twenty years later, they are still "east." My circumstances were somewhat different. By the time I graduated from high school in California, I had already attended seven different schools and lived in many places. I went to Berkeley for college and I intended to stay. And I did stay, for two years after completing my degree, and only went to New York, more or less by accident.

During my junior year of college, I won a contest; the prize was work at a woman's magazine for a month in the spring. As my favorite of the eleven other "guest editors" once said, "the best part of the whole thing was finding out you got it." A sharp woman on a high floor of Condé Nast's Madison Avenue Building told me she could "place" a girl the first time she saw her. It was not hiring she did, but "matchmaking." She told me *Mademoiselle* or possibly *Vogue*. She said I would not be happy at *Glamour*. She said she could tell from my scarf.

I returned to Berkeley, convinced that New York, with its high heels and high prices and its truly terrifying subway, was not for me. (Everyone was talking that spring about the young woman who'd been trapped on the tracks before an oncoming train. Had she jumped? Was she pushed? No one seemed to know.) I applied to graduate schools, halfheartedly. I sent in my papers to Columbia only because a girl I knew from Berkeley was already there. But I wanted to go to Iowa. I thought I'd like Iowa because I'd grown up part of my childhood in Wisconsin. During Berkeley's winter and spring breaks, I took the Amtrak train and Greyhound bus to see my grandmother there. But my grandmother died in January of my senior year, and anyway, I didn't get into Iowa.

Columbia did accept me with a scholarship. To simply say I didn't go would be to deflate the drama of six months. I remember walking around the block with my boyfriend's hands locked over my wrists, as he told me again and again I was too young to understand what he understood, which was that long-distance relationships didn't work. In June, I called Columbia and said I couldn't come because I was in love. A conscientious administrator scribbled "in love" on the top of my file, a notation I much regretted two years later.

You see, I didn't especially want to go to New York City. It didn't hold any particular romance for me. I, and everyone else I knew, had read Joan Didion's *Slouching Towards Bethlehem* and her famous essay about New York. Sometimes, when life in the Bay Area was going so badly it seemed I really would *have* to go to New York, I'd re-read "Goodbye to All That" and try to borrow some of the romance she had found there. New dresses, parties, perfumes: her elegy of New York touched all the totems of my mother's youth, the post-war romance of real drinks and real clothes, the relentless identification with all the props and accoutrements of adulthood.

With the exception of things I'd found in my aunts' Wisconsin closets and my mother's wedding gown, which she'd shortened to cocktail length long after the divorce, I didn't even own a dress.

The two years:

The Bay Area boyfriend had plans for me. I was to do what he hadn't been smart enough to do when he was my age, which was to *get in on the ground floor*. I was supposed to put together a portfolio full of slogans such as Faulkner's famous Raid Kills Bugs and get hired by an ad agency.

But I had the idea that I would write journalism to support my short stories. And I did write articles, free-lance, at first for papers distributed in bars, but eventually also for the two San Francisco dailies. But I was slow. I'd take six or seven months to finish an article. What I was paid usually turned out to be less than gas money for reporting. Soon enough, I had to get a job writing press releases to support my journalism, which was supposed to be supporting my fiction. I was still young and dauntless in my mission of staying put, but in all this vast food chain, no one was eating any too well. And I was beginning to lose heart.

Everyone I knew in the Bay Area seemed to accept the idea that living here was worth massive downsizings in expectations. The brightest friend I had in college now worked for the post office, while teaching himself Greek by correspondence course at night. We all knew Ph.D.s who worked as waiters rather than leave. Whenever an administrative job opened in a local arts organization or radio station, legend had it that hundreds of applications poured in. I had no reason to suspect the legend: my applications had been among them. My boss, a laconic man who spent his best energies on his romantic life, said, "Well, I wanted to be a writer too and see, now my title is Senior Writer, so things work out."

Which was well enough on the good days. But I was no longer seeing the boyfriend who didn't believe in long-distance relationships, and the stories I sent weekly to *The New Yorker* were coming back again, almost weekly in the mail.

So I applied to graduate school again. I was sick of time cards. Classes—just the word began to hold an enchantment. "Go," one of my old teachers said, "the line will still be there, whether or not you're in it." In fact, that same teacher had been Joan Didion's teacher, when she was an undergraduate at Berkeley. I'd said something about her being shy, which I'd read in one of her essays. "She wasn't she when she was here," my teacher affirmed. "She stood up on her desk and said, 'I won a prize, I'm going to New York City!'"

I wrote to an editor at *The New Yorker* who'd once sent an encouraging rejection letter and asked if he thought I had the talent to be a writer. I believe I wrote a long letter setting out the whole lay of my life.

He wrote back a you-never-know kind of letter.

So I went.

I talked about leaving New York before I ever moved there. In *five years,* I promised myself I'd be back. One night near the beginning, it had been snowing for two days, but I'd been invited to a dinner party in the twenties and the dinner was still on. My best friend and I walked at five o'clock through the streets, among the rare hush, the great towering lights mocked by the deep snow stalling the wide avenues. We had boots and warm underwear, but still no real winter coats. Halfway there, we rented skis. The dinner was in a walkup. Artists and writers joked all night about poverty and sell-outs. I wished I could tell a story better at a dinner party, but I was happy.

Although, at the time, I talked about liking the seasons, weather in New York City seems to me now to resemble weather inside glass souvenir snowballs. I remember snow falling outside oversized arched windows, rain under umbrellas in the dash from awning to taxi, the smell of mud as the daffodils and crocuses began to come up in the park, late-night dinners downtown in summer, when you could walk at midnight in sleeveless shirts and just then feel the wind beginning to come up from the river.

I ended up borrowing from Joan Didion's romance after all. It turned out to be an idea older than both Joan Didion and my mother, a scenario supported by a life's worth of movies. I, too, fell in love with a city boy who wore hard shoes and suits and who always knew a place around the corner with white tablecloths where we could get a drink.

My friends were writers who had not yet published their books, graduate students working on their dissertations or painters who didn't have a regular gallery. We were the kind of poor that doesn't deserve pity because we were choosing poverty: our jobs were all part-time, so we could devote our best hours to the other thing that meant most to us. And we all had the sort of jobs that, though they paid little and offered no health insurance, came with perks: free tickets to concerts, operas, black-tie benefits, all the back-drop to young urban romance offered up by society in *War and Peace*. I always knew someone who either worked in the curatorial department or had a grant to do research on "drawings and paintings" and who could get me into museums on Mondays, when they were closed.

For a long time, I resisted New York the way one

might, resist a person who could overwhelm you. At the beginning I left parties early, if I didn't know people, if I saw drugs, if the boys seemed drunk or scary, if the girls seemed too pretty or even just because they were downtown and I could still take the subway home and save the cab money. But eventually, I adjusted without even noticing. My mother came to visit one spring and bought me a beautiful dress, a dress I wore often enough to be named "*the* dress" by a young editor I knew, himself a Westerner, who at the time dealt drugs to supplement his publishing salary. Eventually, the purple painter pants I used to wear with the red webbed belt, which my first New York boyfriend liked because they were too short, were replaced with evening clothes, going-out clothes, all black, which I wore with my grandmother's and great aunts' old costume jewelry. I worked in the sort of homey office where evening clothes were not uncommon, and the rest of the time we came in jeans. Because our own work was nowhere near being out in the world to represent us, we represented ourselves with opinions about everything. Every new short story in the *Atlantic Monthly,* every first novel by someone under forty, was scrutinized. We all had a strong opinion about Anselm Kiefer.

Few of my friends those years were married or living together. No one I knew in the city had a child. We all cared about love first and foremost, and often said so. We talked of little else. As much of our "free" time went to romance as it did to that pursuit of what allegedly meant most to us, but our romance was largely of the suffering variety. Often its object was elsewhere, in Israel, in California, or even on the Lower East Side and not speaking to us, but we took long walks in the melting snow of Riverside, lamenting our misfortune. We would occasionally meet new people, but we talked incessantly of the old: the girl who'd left to marry someone she loved less in Israel, the man who'd left his boyfriend to marry his hometown sweetheart back in Tennessee, the princess who returned to England and the boy who wore hard shoes and a suit and who now held a grudge. Sexualities were dexterous and confusing. Other people seemed to get married, have children, find jobs, get on with their lives elsewhere, while we were still single, working part-time and going to concerts, art openings, and taking walks to get out of our small apartments in New York. I now suspect we weren't really serious, or as serious as we believed we were, about our private lives. There was too much happiness in the coffee and just-out-of-the-oven muffins in my fifteenth-floor apartment, snow falling at the window. Later, when people began to publish their novels and sell their paintings, they left town. For the most part, they went home, or to far-flung new American cities where they'd been offered teaching jobs, which tended to come with health insurance and retirement benefits. Shortly after, many people married.

I stayed long enough to wear out not one, but two winter coats, and to outgrow even my intimidation by the Ivy League. I got over my outrage and amazement that there actually was such a thing as a social register and to understand that the term "self-made" here was often derogatory.

I ran every day, through all weather, in Riverside Park, up past the theological seminary and Grant's Tomb and then down again to the boat basin. It seems now that I ran with many generations of friends who all eventually moved. The girl with whom I ran and ate Sal and Carmine's pizza by the slice for supper on brownstone stoops moved to Brooklyn because the rent was cheaper. The photographer fell in love, left her husband, and went out west, only to eventually settle in Boston. Her sister won a fellowship to study Bernini's Towers in Rome. My last running friend went to Berkeley to finish her dissertation, but she says she'll be back by next fall.

After five years, I was still living in my one-bedroom apartment, which looked over a synagogue's rooftop school and a field of water towers and spires, all for four hundred and sixty dollars a month. The apartment had a kitchen that doubled as a hallway and a sink I had to reach back behind a pillar to get to, but I still cooked in it.

A writer friend gave me a daily journal to keep notes about the year my first book came out. I managed to make three entries, none of which made any reference to best-seller lists, reviews or foreign sales. In April, I included a draft of what I hoped would be a jaunty note to send on the birthday of the friend who held a grudge.

I also found a draft of a letter to the publisher of the magazine I worked for, in which I attempted to ask gracefully for health insurance. In the magazine's long and illustrious history I was apparently the first employee to ask for it. When I'd mentioned it to my boss the first time around, he said, "Well, no we couldn't do that," but if I got sick and had to go to the doctor, I should give his accountant the bill.

I stayed much longer than five years. I stayed twelve. For most of those twelve years I talked a lot about leaving, about going back. By now I'd been in New York longer than I'd lived anyplace else in my life. So the "back" was more mythic than perhaps it should have been.

After talking about leaving New York for more than a decade, I finally did, only in a rush and when I didn't want to. My husband was offered a job that was too good to refuse, we reasoned over and over. So we left, the baby in a corner bassinet of our apartment as the movers packed up our boxes.

We've been living since a year ago January in Los Angeles, the city most often compared to New York, and I can report that most of the clichés cited in the familiar litany are true. Life in California is more "casual" than in New York. With a wardrobe from either city, it is almost impossible not to feel entirely wrong in the other. A few months after I moved here, my niece flew down from San Francisco for her birthday, and I planned a theater evening. To my surprise, there is no theater district here. My attempt to find an atmospheric restaurant nearby landed us in a stunningly beautiful old Hollywood hotel, which had been recently renovated, with a severely stoned waiter who seemed stunned to find customers actually in need of a menu and eager to eat. At the play, a piece that had just moved from Broadway, most of the audience seemed to be wearing white drawstring pants. At intermission, chocolate-covered Häagen-Dazs popsicles were sold. It is probably also true that people drink less here. And for mysterious reasons, I've found that although New York is three hours later than California, I usually eat dinner at the same time as my husband's grandparents eat there.

There are fewer "seasons" here although there is considerably more "weather." Rain, always a source of charm and, at the very worst, ruined suede pumps in New York, virtually stops L.A. The Fox lot operates at half capacity, and a friend told me recently that half her morning meetings were cancelled when rain shorted out security gates, locking people inside their homes.

Friends in both cities ask us whether we worry about safety in the other. Despite the fact of crack vials in profusion every morning on the sidewalk outside our apartment and the recently opened halfway house for drug-addicted, HIV-positive schizophrenic men on my block, the truth is, we never felt frightened in New York. (Of course, we did not have a baby then, old enough to pick up and try to swallow crack vials.) Sometimes, a certain sordidness crept in: rats scooting out of park foliage at dusk with their strange scuttle like tin wind-up toys. We felt exasperated, being awakened the third or fourth night in a row by the bickering of an impromptu marketplace that had formed in Riverside Park outside our windows summer nights, a sort of emporium for the barter and trade of collected cans. But we nonetheless felt safe the way one does in New York, not from statistics or from a certifiably "good" neighborhood, but from crowds, from the knowledge that the fruit markets at the top of the subway stairs, open twenty-four hours a day, would attract students and dog-walkers, tons of people, at any time of day or night. Or maybe the kind of security I am talking about comes from memory and habit and luck, so far, having been on our side, from living in the same iffy neighborhood for twelve years with nothing bad happening to us and our friends. Here in Los Angeles, most of our neighbors' lawns support signs, warning intruders of security systems, including the threat: armed response.

If I'd come from anywhere else, these quiet streets might have the air of the 1950s, the aura of family life offered by *My Three Sons*. But because I've lived here before, as a teenager, which is to say as a member of the society who is the ultimate spy on family life, the empty lawns and drawn curtains and clean, vacant look of houses make me think of tan trim men in offices talking on telephones while wives slip into bed in the afternoon, the bottle of pills on the night table, from which a UCLA extension course catalogue has slipped off onto the floor, the TV murmuring across the room.

It's also probably true that Hollywood centers Los Angeles in the way that "Culture," in the derogatory sense of "high culture," dominates New York. Someone once said that because the light was variable in New York, New York became the center of painting, and because the light was constant in Los Angeles, Los Angeles became the center for moving pictures. Running recently with a director who considers himself "highbrow" as opposed to "mainstream," we talked about a young novelist, whose second novel the director had adapted for a movie. I asked whether he'd read her recent book which I preferred. "I started it," he replied, "but it wasn't a movie."

This may all amount to nothing except that we're new here and we miss our friends.

Anyway, I hear on the grapevine that Joan Didion and her husband moved back.

MONA SIMPSON, *whose first novel,* Anywhere but Here *(1987) earned high praise from writers and critics, was born in 1957 in Green Bay, Wisconsin. She received her undergraduate degree from the University of California at Berkeley and a master of fine arts from Columbia. She worked for the* PARIS REVIEW *from 1981 to 1986 and has taught at Bard College since 1988.*

Mona Simpson's stories have been selected for the Best American Short Stories of 1986, The Pushcart Press XI,

Best of the Small Presses, *and* 20 under 30. *Her short fiction has appeared in the* Paris Review, Ploughshares, The Iowa Review, *and the* North American Review. *Among her honors are a National Endowment for the Arts Fellowship, a Kellogg National Fellowship, and a Whiting Writers' Award. Her novel* The Lost Father *was published in 1992.*

She lived in New York City from 1981 through 1994. She now lives in California, but keeps a New York apartment and spends part of each year there.

Willie Morris

Farewell

While John Cowles, Jr., remained aloof in The Land of 10,000 Lakes, he more or less turned over his purview of *Harper's* to the elusive William S. Blair, now the magazine's president and chief executive officer. In mid-1970 the magazine formally became an operating division of the Star-Tribune Company, which in fiscal 1969 had turned a profit of many vast millions. We were beginning to hear reports that Jack Fischer, the editor emeritus, now age sixty, who was still writing his "Easy Chair" column but who rarely came to the office, was openly expressing grave distaste for the magazine in the city's publishing circles for its editorial content and writers, for the whole thrust and language of it, for its anti-Vietnam posture. What we did not know at the time was that his denunciations were being taken earnestly in Minnesota. A friend in the Century Club told me he had overheard Jack Fischer at an adjoining table with John Gunther and others being unqualifiedly critical of the publication's entire substance and approach.

Co-existence between Blair and me was at best uneasy; "I've had some sense of Willie's philosophy and mine being incompatible for some time," he said later. He was a cloud of doom and pessimism. The personal chemistry between the two of us had become an evil and destructive one. I had long suspected he was undercutting the editorial side at every opportunity among the proprietors with criticisms of the writers and their writings while protecting his own flanks—a not unfamiliar and indeed hoary tale. He was often suggesting *Harper's* become more a special-interest journal like *Ski Magazine*.

It was the fecund era for executives, and Blair eventually began turning out the memos. In the recession that was generally affecting American publishing, *Harper's* circulation, which had been rising by about 100,000 in four years, had dropped from 350,000 to 325,000, roughly the same as our competitor, *The Atlantic Monthly*. Advertising lineage was on the same level as the previous year but with a strained overall budget; although the total editorial costs of the magazine were no more than $250,000, Blair proposed dismissing either Bob Kotlowitz or Midge Decter. "It should be possible to get this magazine out with one editor-in-chief (yourself), one responsible senior editor (either Midge or Bob), and one junior editor," he declared in one such memo, with other reductions in secretaries, promotion, and office space. He criticized the amount of money being paid the contributing editors Halberstam, King, Corry, Frady, and Lapham under our contractual arrangement determined by the number of stories produced, questioned their productivity, and advocated drastic change in that set-up. In my reply I supported some of these reductions (though certainly not firing Kotlowitz or Decter, who were making $32,000 and $30,000 a year respectively), defended the editorial quality of the magazine, proposed as another economy measure that my salary of $37,500 and Blair's of $54,000 be reduced one-third (this not being agreed to), and defended the money paid the contributing editors and their prolific output. In his best financial year at *Harper's,* for instance, Halberstam had grossed $20,000 by writing seven tenthousand-word articles and another of twenty thousand words. Two others had produced more pieces than their contracts required. All were compensated more for writing for other magazines than for *Harper's*. Larry L. King was never paid more than $2,000 for a *Harper's* piece; *Life*, *Playboy*, *True*, *Cosmopolitan*, *West*, and *Saturday Evening Post* paid him much more. Among other contributors the magazine's commission for a standard article ranged from $1,000 to $1,500.

However, Norman Mailer would receive $10,000 for "The Prisoner of Sex," which the business side considered would be a good investment.

It had become clear to many of us that Blair had spent considerable money on promotion and readership surveys and polls and a new assistant publisher and was quick to blame editorial when circulation diminished. The story was by no means a new one. Yet the real question underlying all of this concerned the basic philosophy about the long-range and enduring future of the publication, and what it might or might not embody, say, in A.D. 1993.

Larry L. King, whose account of what was to ensue at *Harper's* in his book *None But a Blockhead: On Being a Writer* is an accurate one, wrote: "In retrospect, *Harper's* as we knew it was doomed early on. The Nixon recession of 1970–71 caused losses larger than had been anticipated, and Bill Blair was a bottom-line business type who cared no more for literary standards than a billygoat." King sometimes enjoyed paraphrasing his fellow Texan J. Frank Dobie in saying Blair valued good writing and reportage and fiction and poetry about as much as a razorback sow cared about Keats's "Ode on a Grecian Urn." Blair once referred to himself, in talking with King, as "the boss." "You're not *my* boss," King told him. "I'm not a goddamn accountant. I'm a writer. Morris is *my* boss."

I had long before discovered that John Cowles, Jr., was not exceptionally bright, and not very strong, and that somewhere beneath his phlegmatic exterior lay reclusive yet strongly evangelical compulsions, groping and inconsistent though they might have been. His uncle Russell, a reformed alcoholic, would tell Richard Broderick of the *Minnesota Monthly* that the Cowleses were "a dysfunctional family" given to "compulsive behavior." I would not learn for a long time, however, that beginning in that year, 1969, John Jr. was becoming seriously immersed in what later would be called the human potential movement. That year he attended a clinic for executives at Menninger's in Kansas called "Toward Understanding Man," from which he returned highly excited. From there he and his wife, Sage,

inevitably drifted into EST—the Erhard Seminars
Training—founded by the later-discredited entrepre-
neur Werner Erhard, who inspired confrontational ses-
sions conducted like boot camps with emphasis on
intense emotional experiences with the purpose of
stripping the faithful to the bone, tearing down their
"belief systems" and their guilts, shames, and insecuri-
ties. John Jr. said later that "it was like living in a house
and thinking you knew all the rooms and then suddenly
discovering that there were many more rooms in the
house and places you could go. The realm of possibilities expanded enormously." In addition to the EST
commitment, the Cowleses eventually joined other
human potential programs such as channeling, and the
Skinner Releasing Technique.

Robert Gottlieb, the chief editor at Knopf in those
days, who was bringing out some of the best books of
the decade, once suggested to me why magazine editors were so consistently anxious. No sooner had they
put one monthly issue to bed, for which they had
opened a vein, than they had to start in all over again on
another, which had to be better than the one before. In
that sense one's monthly magazine was not unlike the
cotton candy at the county fairs of one's childhood,
delicious and sweet but not lasting very long. It is an
occupational hazard.

A suicidal sense of perfection, not to mention the big
dare, will often be compounded by personal and professional faults, as in my case. In time's perspective I see
how bull-headed I was, and not a very good administrator or businessman. Midge Decter once remarked that a
magazine such as *Harper's* could never make any money,
but that the owners foolishly thought it could, and that
I should have confronted them with that reality at the
start. She was probably right, as she usually was—if I
had it all to do over again, I would have said: This magazine will never make money, you have all the money
you need anyway. Your corporation made so many millions last year, let's continue to put out a fine magazine
and keep the losses down: let's consider *Harper's* a luster
in the corporate crown. I believe I thought I was buying

time, with good writing and hard work and, yes, adrenaline, but I soon perceived that time would buy nothing: our owners had become fearful of the kind of magazine our labors had created, the no-holds-barred nature of it that surely was a challenge to what they themselves believed, but gave no indication beyond "specialization" of what it was they wanted. Perhaps there should have been a wave in my petulant brain that said *stroke them*, "kiss ass," but I could not do so. I had been schooled in newspaper journalism, in which the mentors and exemplars taught young editors then never to concern themselves with writing for the advertisers, or publishing what readers wanted to read, but to print the truth; there was always Pulitzer's claim on my wall. That, at least, was the old way, and it may have been vanishing. There was also something going far back in my very blood and heritage, of the bloodkin's irascibility and defeat and dispossession, that would not allow it, my very Southern pride, and distrust of inherited and entrenched absentee wealth and what has so often sprung from it, and its absence of any real comprehension of the complexities of this nation, and in this regard I suppose I was exceedingly ill-equipped for that job. But I have never once apologized for that pride, and never been ashamed of it, and never will be, and it is just such indigenous regional pride, admirable to some, abominable to others, that might someday help redeem the greater nation.

In the retrospect of time, I cannot help but believe that what was hotly simmering near the surface of things at *Harper's* much pertained to the Vietnam war, with all that that involved. The war dominated everything then. It was both substantive and symbolic. Every argument, every idea, every policy came back to it, and the new *Harper's* group was on one side, and the old group, represented by my predecessor John Fischer, was on the other. Everything in the larger society seemed at stake. Some of that showed in the tension I observed between Fischer and David Halberstam. In his "Easy Chair" columns Jack was continuing to take a strong pro-war position. I suspected that he was going off to his lunches at the Century Club to meet with his sources, whom he valued, his old friends in government and the foreign policy Establishment, the good people who represented the Washington view that the high Americans in Saigon were telling him the truth. Then, oddly, he would bring in the drafts of his columns and ask Halberstam to critique them. David had returned from his weeks in Vietnam in '67 on *Harper's* assignment and was darkly pessimistic about the war, and he continued to write as much. He remembered that Jack Fischer kept asking him for his suggestions but never once used any. Although no harsh words were ever spoken between these two very different men representing two irredeemably different American generations and outlooks, I could tell they personally despised each other, and when Halberstam advised Jack that his premises were wrong and that he was hedging the reality of our failure in Vietnam, this was only representative of the generational and political divisions taking place all over the country in those years in homes, businesses, everywhere. "We spoke in the same language," David recalled, "but we understood nothing that the other said."

"People were doing it all over town," a character in Wilfrid Sheed's *Office Politics,* his novel of the magazine business, observed, "—in all those great morose buildings on both sides of the street, it was plot, plot, plot." It was a wizened New York circumstance, to be repeated time and again as long as there are magazines, and people who run them. John Kennedy liked to improvise from *Ecclesiastes*: "A time to weep and a time to laugh, a time to mourn and a time to dance, a time to fish and a time to cut bait." JFK also knew there was a time to keep fishing. What were being made plain to me were these alternatives:

· Fold the magazine.
· Retrench and cut back circulation.
· Cut the budget in half, and fire most of the editors.
· Make *Harper's* more "specialized."

Someone else could do these things, but I was not the man; I genuinely thought we could make it, given time, with the kind of publication we then had, which was of some importance, I believed, to the social and cultural life of the nation. Who knows? Yet it was not difficult to see the handwriting on the wall. I myself did not handle the situation particularly well, but I see now how inevitable it all was.

"The American psyche of 1970," Steve Erickson wrote, "seemed split between those who hated and loved America simply—those who questioned everything about it, even what was good and reasonable; and those who served its authority and rules so blindly that not only their imaginations but their common sense became paralyzed," and in this regard the early months of the new decade extended the antagonisms of the Sixties. In addition to the continuing generational hostility, the war, the racial violence, the broader economic affluence which undergirded even the most calamitous strivings of the 1960s was giving way to high unemployment, inflation, and recession. "Not only is there no God," Woody Allen said, "but try getting a plumber on weekends." The anti-war movement, riven with factionalism and the simple debilitating reality of the broadening war itself, was beginning to sour. The Sixties party was pretty much over, with Watergate yet to come. But when Nixon's Republicans did poorly in the off-year elections, the background was set for the increasingly parapolitical tone of the Nixon realists, beginning with the founding, subsidized by large and often secret contributions, of the Citizens Committee for the Reelection of the President, of which much was destined to be heard.

The example of the older black civil rights movement was having a passionate impact now on a yet more widespread social revolution, a broadening change of contexts: the burgeoning women's movement in particular. And paralleling this were the accumulating demands for gay rights, Indian rights, single-issue causes, and the first effective beginnings of one of the most valuable and lasting endowments of Sixties protest, the environmental movement.

At *Harper's* the good moments remained. Marshall Frady had his three-part series "An American Innocent in the Middle East," where he found between Arabs and Israelis "a collision of two ages, a blind grappling of two dialectics, two realities, each barely comprehensible to the other." Pete Axthelm's *The City Game* examined basketball in New York, and how it offered escape to its boys, and the brief glory of being a hero. (*The City Game* was one of quite a few examples of the symbiosis between the magazine and Harper's Magazine Press, which we had established early on. Herman Gollob had asked Axthelm to write a book about the New York Knicks. He responded he would like to do a book which would combine the Knicks' championship season and the story of Harlem playground basketball. We made a deal calling for the book and a magazine first-serial excerpt.) Aaron Latham wrote on Scott Fitzgerald's last days in Hollywood, Blair Clark on General Westmoreland, Joseph Kraft on Henry Kissinger, John Bart Gerald on the Vietnam wounded, Harold Clurman on the contemporary theater, R. C. Padden on Las Vegas. Fiction by James Jones was set during the 1968 student revolution in Paris. Frank Conroy in the Empire Chinese had proposed to do a piece on Charles Manson and the most garish crime of the decade; he had been unable to get access to the prisoner and wished out of his own imaginings to delve Manson's masturbatory fantasies when thrown in jail, and this grew into "Manson Wins!" one of the most adventuresome extensions of the new journalism.

Jack Richardson wrote on the Ali versus Quarry fight in Atlanta:

It was a Klansman's nightmare, a recrudescence of the worst excesses of the South's post-bellum years. Inceding down Peachtree Street, spiritual and legendary Southern thoroughfare, were Muhammad Ali and his laughing entourage. They moved with loose, ambling confidence along this main street of Atlanta, as though each step were a gentle appropriation of a moment in history, a casual reclamation of a cultural manner that had been kept . . . in the corners of our society for a hundred years.

John Kenneth Galbraith wrote an account of a dinner at Averell Harriman's house in New York for Nikita Khrushchev with all the American power scions there, the Rockefellers and Rusks and McCloys and Sarnoffs and Finletters—and why on earth, Professor Galbraith asked himself, was *he* there, and on leaving, a distinctly city tableau:

Outside it was still daylight, a lovely autumn evening, and a large crowd of newspapermen and cameramen were waiting. I walked out with Tom Finletter. Several reporters sensed that we might be the soft underbelly of the Establishment and tried to pump us. We remained loyal—a sense of class solidarity is quickly acquired. But it was not quite complete. As we turned down 81st Street, Tom said, "Do you have any doubt as to who was the smartest man in there tonight?"

For several years Larry L. King had been trying unsuccessfully to write about his father. Many times I had attempted to get him to. "Goddammit, I'm intimidated," Larry kept saying. "I guess I just don't understand him well enough." I always agreed with his first point, but never his second. A couple of hours after his father's funeral in Midland, Texas, Larry telephone me. "I can write it now," he said. The result, which Bruce Cook of *The National Observer* called "quite simply the finest piece of magazine journalism I have ever read," proved also to be one of the most widely anthologized ever:

Now it was late afternoon. His sap suddenly ran low; he seemed more fragile, a tired old head with a journey to make; he dangerously stumbled on a curbstone. Crossing a busy intersection, I took his arm. Though that arm had once pounded anvils into submission, it felt incredibly frail. My children, fueled by youth's inexhaustible gases, skipped and cavorted fully a block ahead. Negotiating the street, The Old Man half laughed and half snorted: "I recollect helpin' you across lots of streets when you was little. Never had no notion that one day you'd be doin' the same for me." Well, I said. Well. Then: "I've helped that boy up there"—motioning toward my distant and mobile son—"across some few streets. Until now, it never once occurred that he may someday return the favor." "Well," The Old Man said, "he will if you're lucky."

Halberstam's piece "The End of a Populist" on Senator Albert Gore, Sr., and his final defeat in Tennessee because of his civil rights and anti-Vietnam stands dealt too with the son, Al Gore, Jr., who had just graduated from Harvard, militantly anti-war and not wanting to go into the Army, but faced with a big choice: to stay out and avoid the draft in Tennessee would cost the Senate one of its most outspoken doves. Al Jr.'s family told him to make his own decision, his mother even saying she would go to Canada with him:

Young Al called an uncle down in West Tennessee who questioned him on why he was so antiwar. "I guess," he said, "it's my Baptist religion." "I never knew there was anything in the Baptist religion against war," the uncle said. "What about the sixth commandment, thou shalt not kill," young Al answered. But the conversation had given young Al the feeling of what the campaign against his father would be like and he had decided to serve. Those who know the Senator suspect that he would not have minded at all running a campaign with a son who refused to go to Vietnam; that he would in fact have relished it—the drawing of the line, the ethic of it. Show Albert the grain, says a friend, so he can go against it.

Halberstam's explorations of the roots of the Vietnam war, of how and why we went there, continued with the career that reflected and powerfully influenced the nation's journey in the Sixties, from highest idealism and confidence to the deepest self-doubt, in "The Programming of Robert McNamara": "To say that something could not work, that it was beyond the reach of this most powerful country in the world, was to fail. He hated failure."

Two of the most striking projects in the declining months involved a pair of American originals, Bill Moyers and the undauntable Norman Mailer.

There were parallels between Bill Moyers's life and mine. We were almost exactly the same age. He was a small-town Southerner, having grown up in Marshall, Texas, near the Louisiana line, and he too had started working for newspapers as a teenager. We were classmates at the University of Texas. He was funny and a prankster, and hard-working: a forty-eight-hour week at Lady Bird Johnson's television station, and Sabbath sermons as a part-time Baptist preacher. We were different kinds of people: he less histrionic, shrewder and more pragmatic; I admired him enormously. His relationship with Lyndon Johnson, for whom he also worked, was son-to-father, but he left him during his Vice-Presidency to become deputy director of the new Peace Corps, and was instrumental in making that institution a vital force among the young people of the country. He was in Austin doing advance work for John Kennedy's trip through Texas when he heard of the assassination, chartered a small aircraft to Dallas, scribbled a note to Johnson outside the Presidential plane saying, "I'm here if you need me," which he gave to a Secret Service man, and soon was rushed aboard Air Force One. He was to remain with Johnson as a close advisor and then chief of the White House staff, where at age twenty-nine he was a principal architect of the programs of the Great Society, the highwater point of the LBJ Presidency. "I think he is a Texas-size man," Tom Wicker wrote of him at the time for *Harper's,* "in his great talent, his unflagging energy, the reach of his ideas, the depth of his dedication. There is nothing small about Moyers, including his ambition and where it may take him in the long years ahead perhaps only a Texan's imagination can conceive." Once early in his tenure Celia and I came down from the city to have dinner with Bill and his wife Judith in a restaurant near the White House. Later we walked there and wandered about on the deserted and darkened West Wing, like college kids on an outing, the slender and boyish Moyers flipping a light on here and there as we explored the Cabinet room and the Oval Office and the little rooms bordering the big ones, a strange and spooky midnight stillness pervading that place of history and endurance and power. He subsequently became press secretary at LBJ's insistence, resigning in '66. There were reports that he left because of his opposition to the war in Vietnam. "I'd like to claim to have been a prophet about the war early on," he told me much later, "but I'd be lying. I paid little attention to it while I was working on the domestic programs, and when I became press secretary, I accepted for a while the premises LBJ had embraced. Things were complex in that house of gray shadows. As the war claimed our resources, the President's time and energies as well as the budget, I became disillusioned, frustrated, and ineffective, torn by loyalty to him and my inability to make a difference."

After that, Moyers was publisher of *Newsday* on Long Island, the largest suburban daily in the United States, for over three years. He had transformed *Newsday* into one of the country's most exciting papers. Among other projects, he had persuaded Saul Bellow to cover the '67 war in the Middle East, and Daniel P. Moynihan to write on the urban uprisings, and he and his editorialists defended the peace marchers and antiwar activism of the late Sixties. On a television program, when the interviewer asked me what person my age did I think might someday make an outstanding President of the United States, I cited Bill Moyers, and explained why. The next day Moyers telephoned me.

"Okay," he asked, "what do you want?"

"I want the Court of St. James's," I said.

"You're not rich enough for that. I'll give you Haiti."

Bill's patron on Long Island, much as John Fischer had earlier been mine, was the wealthy Harry Guggenheim, the controlling owner in *Newsday,* and it was even rumored in New York circles familiar to me that Guggenheim intended someday to deed his majority interest to Moyers. It did not work out that way. Guggenheim became increasingly annoyed by his protégé's "left-wing sympathies" and sold the paper out from under him to the L.A. Times-Mirror Company. The Binghams offered Moyers the editorship of the *Louisville Courier-Journal,* but he did not like horse racing and mint juleps. I had known Bill for years, and when he lost it all at *Newsday* I felt for him, for what he was going through. David Halberstam and I asked him what his plans were; he did not know. We suggested he consider travelling extensively around the country on a bus for three months or so, stopping off at wherever his impulses told him to, and write about it for *Harper's.* He agreed on the spot. This was the origin of his brilliant "Listening to America."

"Listening to America" was a forty-five-thousand-word cover piece resulting from a thirteen-thousand-mile swing across the nation—"a troubled, spirited, inspired, frightened, complacent, industrious, selfish,

magnanimous, confused, spiteful, bewitching country"—capturing as few documents did the moods, fears,
and accents of that day, with its portraits of college
presidents, student radicals, American Legionnaires,
runaway kids, street people, union rebels, junkies,
country doctors, black spokesmen, unemployed executives, business leaders, hard-working cops, ordinary citizens (and also Groucho Marx)—all part of a narrative
rich in humor, sorrow, and understanding. Bill was
a joy to work with, funny, mischievous, curious, although I detected in him then a dejection about his
own life, surely having to do with losing *Newsday* after
the thrall and majesty of the White House. I felt that his
confrontation with hard-core reporting changed his
life. "No one really understands just how difficult it is
to write, do they?" he said to Marshall Frady and me
one day. The book from the experience published by
Herman Gollob and the Harper's Magazine Press
under the same title eventually became a bestseller.

People are more anxious and bewildered than
alarmed. They don't know what to make of it all: of
long hair and endless war, of their children deserting
their country, of congestion on their highways and
overflowing crowds in their national parks; of art that
does not uplift and movies that do not reach conclu-
sions; of intransigence in government and violence; of
politicians who come and go while problems plague
and persist; of being lonely surrounded by people, and
bored with so many possessions; of the failure of orga-
nizations to keep the air breathable, the water drink-
able, and man peaceable; of being poor. I left Houston
convinced that liberals and conservatives there shared
three basic apprehensions: they want the war to stop,
they do not want to lose their children, and they want
to be proud of their country. But it was the same everywhere.

There is a myth that the decent thing has almost
always prevailed in America when the issues were
clearly put to the people. It may not always happen. I
found among people an impatience, an intemperance,
an isolation which invites opportunists who promise
too much and castigate too many. And I came back

with questions. Can the country be wise if it hears no wisdom? Can it be tolerant if it sees no tolerance? Can the people I met escape their isolation if no one listens?

The people at Channel 13 in New York saw the piece, thought Moyers would be a suitable host for a series they were launching from around the country, and that was the beginning of his life in national television, for in truth it was his love of conversation that would be his greatest gift to that powerful and tainted medium. He would become one of America's freshest and most essential voices, dramatic as Edward R. Murrow, trustworthy as Walter Cronkite. "I know that trip redeemed my life," he told me years later, "caused me to want to put behind me all that establishment stuff that had reached out to seduce me at *Newsday*, and to be a real journalist. It not only helped me rediscover America, but myself as well."

To no avail we had been trying to get something else from Mailer. I called him to have lunch. He would like that, he said, but not to try to persuade him to write anything. We met at a restaurant called Spats with an ersatz Twenties motif on Thirty-third Street. After the second Bloody Mary he said, "I know you've got an idea, and I know what the idea is, and I've got the same idea." What was it? I asked. He told me, and he was right: the Women's Movement. He agreed to do it. Once again Midge Decter and I flew up to the Cape, to another wintry landscape by the water. I brought Muriel Oxenberg Murphy with me this time. Mailer had a new wife, Carol Stevens. As before, he had been working at a feverish pace. As he was finishing he said to me, "I may be handing you a hot one this time."

"The Prisoner of Sex" was the whole cover for the March 1971 issue, with the subtitle: "On women and men, liberation and subjection, the body, the spirit, and physical love." Midge wrote the introduction:

In devoting virtually our entire March issue to "The Prisoner of Sex"—Norman Mailer's bold analysis of the Women's Liberation Movement—the editors of *Harper's* wish to assert our belief that Women's Liberation is a development of possibly very great significance to the future of American society—

certainly this movement is showing itself to be a major force in the social and cultural atmosphere currently surrounding us. We believe, moreover, that no writer in America could have illuminated as Norman Mailer has the deep underlying issues raised by what may be—in the parlance of Women's Liberation itself—"the last of the revolutions." Far from being simply the preserve of an extreme or "elite" minority, as many people charge, and far from being merely the latest of the creations of more publicity, this new radical impulse to erase the body of our institutionalized distinctions as to sex touches nothing less than the very heart of our traditional arrangements for day-to-day human existence.

Our magazine from the start had amply dealt with the Movement in all its implications, and Mailer's essay confronted in all his characteristic wild humor and vitality the most mystifying and often threatening question of all: the individual and private relations between women and men—and sex itself.

"The Prisoner of Sex" issue sold more copies on the national newsstands than any single issue in the history of *Harper's*. It also proved to be my last as editor.

Now the days were winding down, the words of a sad song, to a precious few. I suppose now I knew these were waning days. Did I see the omen and refuse to look at it?

In late February, a week or so after the "Prisoner of Sex" issue came out, I went to Minneapolis for a meeting, having been the only editorial person so invited. John Cowles, Jr., and Blair were there, along with other executives. Blair read a twenty-one-page memo. The meeting lasted three and a half hours and dealt with money and editorial content, including criticism of editorial performances as they related to circulation, making *Harper's* more "specialized," and continuing the readership polls. Blair spoke at length on how the magazine had caught on only with "Eastern communicators." He advised dismissing all the contributing editors. The atmosphere was cold. Cowles backed Blair without reservation. One of the Minneapolis businessmen said, "No wonder it's such a failure. Who are you editing this magazine for? A bunch of hippies?"

The Mississippi bull-head was angry, more than he had ever been in his whole life. After the meeting I skipped lunch with the executives and booked a flight back to New York. I had some time to kill, walking about in the clean snow, white and immaculate on the streets of the clean, white, immaculate town, and went into a movie just then sweeping the country called *Love Story,* in which Ali McGraw delivered the line "Love is never having to say you're sorry," and then died, aptly matching my own mood.

On the long flight back it all came to a head for me. I knew in my deepest being I could no longer stay with the magazine, for this would involve acts of both public and private humiliation, not to mention the danger to the sturdier traditions of *Harper's*. In New York, against the advice of some of my friends, who counselled leaving room for compromise, I mailed my letter to Minneapolis. My statement to the press read:

I am resigning because of severe disagreements with the business management over the purpose, the existence and the survival of *Harper's Magazine* as a vital institution in American life. My mandate as its eighth editor in 120 years has been to maintain its excellence and its courage. With the contribution of many of this country's finest writers, journalists, poets and critics, I think we have succeeded.

It all boiled down to the money men and the literary men. And as always, the money men won.

The article in our current issue by Norman Mailer has deeply disturbed the magazine's owners. Mailer is a great writer. His work matters to our civilization.

I have given eight years of my life, four of them as editor in chief, to help make *Harper's* true to its finest traditions. I leave *Harper's* with an honorable conscience. It is at its most vital. It matters to the nation as it seldom has before. My resignation grieves my heart, but I am leaving as a protest against the calculated destruction of *Harper's*.

All writers, editors and journalists who care passionately about the condition of the written word in America should deplore with me the cavalier treatment by business management of America's oldest and most distinguished magazine. This is the saddest day of my life.

The only point I would alter in that statement was on the Mailer piece. It was not central to the issue, only part of it, less at that moment substantive than symbolic. As for the rest, many years have passed since then, and in the nature of things few except the surviving participants really remember or care, and there has been many another editorial crisis in that city in time's long interval, though none nearly so lucid and emotional and direct. Rereading those words now—in a place far away, on a yellowing clipping from the *Times* —strangely overcomes me anew with the emotion and the fear of that long-ago moment, as any of us who has experienced similar moments will know and remember, for other people I loved suffered from them too. But to this day I will hold them—because despite everything I was right.

Not long ago, the passions of these events muffled but still very real, a couple of my colleagues of that time and I, in the spirit of rounding out the story, pondered the question of John Cowles, Jr., of what had happened with him, and to a remarkable degree we agreed. A magazine taking off on a journey like ours, especially given the nature of those years, has a limited amount of powder it can use, no matter how successful "Steps of the Pentagon," or "My Lai," or the Bundy and McNamara profiles, or "The Prisoner of Sex," or the others. What the magazine was cumulatively demonstrating was that Cowles could not really control us, and that this began to work systematically against us.

By coincidence on the noon of the morning I mailed my resignation to Minneapolis, another of the endless happenstances of New York, I had a lunch appointment with my competitor, Bob Manning, the editor-in-chief of *The Atlantic Monthly*, down for the day from Boston. He was a very fine editor, and in our lengthy yet not unfriendly *mano a mano* we had gotten together occasionally over the years, just the two of us, to compare tales and complain of ownership and feel each other out, like old managers long around the hardball circuit. He consoled me in my melancholy. I apologized that lunch would have to be brief, since Bill Bradley of the Knicks had invited my son David Rae to work out with the team in Madison Square Garden and I had to meet

him there. "God, I'd love to go with you," my rival said.
"I like Bill Bradley. I've got an appointment with Dean
Rusk at the Century."

Later, in the big deserted Garden arena, I idled on a
front row and watched David shoot free throws with
Frazier, Reed, and Debusschere. I was just then losing
everything I ever wanted, I was thinking, and I was suf-
fused now with a terrible sorrow and guilt and short-
coming of the headstrong, emotions that would never
leave me for many years—and also with waves of the
most tender memory. As the echoes of the bouncing
basketballs resounded to the arched roof high above,
and my son weaved a fast-break with Barnett and
Bradley, I thought of my own father not long before his
death on gray winter afternoons long ago, stopping on
his way home from work to watch our high school
team practice in our cramped little gymnasium in
Yazoo. I half-expected him now. I would have wished
to talk with him. Down on the basketball court, the
practice was over and all the Knicks had retired to the
lockerroom except Bradley, who was at the free-throw
line giving David instructions. Immersed in my
thoughts, alone in my conjurings in that grand and
empty palace, I barely heard the footsteps coming my
way. Suddenly the editor-in-chief of the *Atlantic
Monthly* stood before me. "I cut Dean Rusk short," he
said. Then, pointing to the two figures on the court, he
asked: "Say, which one's Bradley?"

Later that day I had my last appointment as an editor, among the bizarre and notable hundreds of those
years in all the city's wide-swept settings, and this one
was with Gore Vidal, who had phoned in an agitated
mood and wanted to have a talk. I had resigned my
official position, and I had nothing else to do, so what
the hell? Vidal and I met in the King Cole Room of the
St. Regis, just down the hall from the little bar where
Bill Styron and I had convened that distant afternoon
when he had just finished his novel and conversed with
the Englishman who had had tea with Hitler. I had not
seen Gore Vidal since the winter's day at his house on
the frozen Hudson River, and his vehemence, which at
the moment seemed boundless, was over Mailer's "The

Prisoner of Sex," which he had just read and judged, on a number of counts, outrageous. "Break my icy exterior," Vidal had once said of himself, "and beneath you'll find ice water." He wanted to do a long rebuttal to Mailer and, lame duck though I was, I said why not? Besides, I enjoyed sitting there listening to his brilliant, amusing, dyspeptic critiques of the New York intellectual life. I suppose one could have done much worse than go out of the New York days *tête-à-tête* with Gore Vidal.

George Plimpton had been assigned by *Sports Illustrated* to cover the Ali-Frazier fight at the Garden that week, the first heavyweight championship to which he had ever been assigned, and he remembered sitting at ringside only seconds before the first-round bell with his notebooks and pens feeling very nervous. This had been billed as the Fight of the Century and the tension, Plimpton recalled, was extraordinary; a man a few rows down had just been carted off with a heart attack. Suddenly Norman Mailer came up and knelt next to Plimpton in the aisle. Plimpton could barely hear what Mailer was telling him: "George, we've got to get to John Cowles. Willie Morris has just resigned." Cowles had been Plimpton's roommate at Harvard. Plimpton remembers Norman's urgency, "as if he half-expected me to rush out to the nearest pay phone to call John Cowles." Plimpton replied, "Oh, God, Norman, I don't think I can do anything about this right now."

Any irrational thoughts I might have had about my resignation not being accepted, and for a brief time I actually must have thought it might not, were soon dissipated. The resignation was quickly announced without explanation by the Cowles organization. I learned of the acceptance from William S. Blair's secretary— "Oh, I'm so sorry you're leaving us." At the *Harper's* offices both Halberstam and King angrily confronted Blair with having told the *New York Times* that the magazine's contributing editors were overpaid and had not produced the number of pieces called for in their contracts. King had agreed on Blair's suggestion to confer with John Cowles, Jr., about the future of the magazine, and when Blair told other colleagues that the proud Texan was staying on, King called him a son-of-a-bitch and demanded he admit to having lied. "All Blair would admit was a 'misunderstanding,'" King wrote later. "I roundly cursed him, said I would have nothing to do with him the rest of my life and forbade him ever to speak to me again." That evening, in a party at Muriel Murphy's, I watched helplessly as King, sobbing and raging, delivered a kick to an antique chair, which shattered into many little pieces.

Shortly after that, there was a bitter, edgy meeting with John Cowles, Jr., who flew in from Minneapolis, and the other editors, Kotlowitz, Halberstam, King, Corry, Frady, John Hollander, and the newest addition, Lewis Lapham. Three of the number later described the event to me. Midge Decter had already resigned; telegrams arrived from Arthur Miller and William Styron. Lewis Lapham, who had not been with the magazine very long, went to Halberstam and said he wanted to be with them. David advised him that there was going to be blood over everyone and that he ought to stay as far away as possible, but Lapham told Halberstam and the others that the magazine had been the happiest professional experience of his life and that he wanted to support them.

The meeting began late at night and lasted three hours. The setting was the St. Regis, "in a chandeliered suit," the sweet-tongued Frady later noted, "that would have fair served for treaty-signing ceremonies at the Congress of Vienna, complete with a pageantry buffet of DeMillean splendor and various waiters and attendants padding about." Larry L. King said, "We were treated as buck privates in the rear ranks—lucky to escape court-martials," and that the event reminded him of the film clips of General MacArthur accepting the surrender of the Japanese on the *U.S.S. Missouri*. With the editors lined up in front of him on straight-backed chairs, from a yellow couch Cowles spoke at first from a prepared statement concerning the publication's decline in circulation and said that William Blair would be promoted to publisher, effective immediately, and that *Harper's* would go in "new directions." He spoke of readership survey polls showing the magazine should try something else, and that market and readership research should determine the stories the magazine should undertake. Larry L. King said, "If you can find one single god-damn self-respecting writer worth the ink of his by-line who'll work on terms like that, John, I'll kiss your ass till your nose bleeds." Halberstam asked Cowles to define the new directions the magazine should pursue, and what he was specifically objecting to, suggesting it was "the hottest book in the trade." Cowles replied, "A magazine can't live on favorable press notices and din-ner party conversation." He added, "Much of it bores me." Halberstam reminded him that he had pledged the editors five years to turn the magazine around, that in response from readers they had done so, and now he was "pulling the rug." Larry L. King would later write in *None But a Blockhead: On Being a Writer:*

Cowles said he just couldn't give it more time, that the maga-zine had become a cross to bear and that his father had urged him to sell it or padlock it "because it simply isn't worth the trouble." This cavalier dismissal of a magazine we loved and that had an honored history and tradition in American letters infuriated the brotherhood. We began to shout of money *Harper's* management had wasted in redesigning the maga-zine's binding, in remodelling Bill Blair's offices, in commis-sioning useless readership surveys, in buying *The Reporter's* circulation for huge sums when that magazine folded and then doing nothing to keep that circulation. Junior Cowles was offended that a scruffy bunch of writers would presume to question his business acumen, and the air grew chillier within the St. Regis.

The dissenters offered to find financing to purchase the magazine. It was not for sale, the owner replied, and William Blair would remain in charge and choose the new editor. The editors backed Bob Kotlowitz for that position. Cowles responded that Kotlowitz was on Blair's list, but added that he was sure Muhammad Ali was also. "Either we were speaking in Chinese and he was listening in English," Halberstam described the ses-sion to the newsweeklies, "or we were speaking in En-glish and he was listening in Chinese." Cowles began

enumerating all the things he disliked about the magazine. Halberstam asked him if there was anything he
liked about it and he said, No, there was not. "That, of
course, was it," Halberstam remembered. "We had
poured everything we had into the magazine for a long
time. We had *lived* that magazine, we were justifiably
proud of the product, the response on the part of the
readers and our professional peers was exceptional, and
here he was giving us a vote of no-confidence."

A strange thing happened. Lewis Lapham switched
sides and began agreeing with the owner. Yes, he said,
polling readers to ascertain what they wanted was a
great idea. "His behavior," Halberstam recalled,
"stunned us all."

John Corry said, "All right, John, are you telling us
that the magazine will change but you won't say in
what direction, and that Blair will remain in power?"
Cowles replied, "Yes, that's pretty much the case."
With that Larry L. King stood up. "Then fuck it,
there's no reason to stay here. I resign," and stormed
out of the chamber, followed rapidly by Kotlowitz,
Halberstam, Corry, and Hollander. Marshall Frady,
often gentlemanly in the manner of Ashley Wilkes in
Gone with the Wind, stayed behind. He remembered:
"I thought Cowles, who seemed a rather amiable and
mild-mannered if somewhat simple-witted chap, could
somehow be *reasoned* with. Which I was effusively trying to do, until I heard a bellow from the hallway,
'Frady, get on out here!' I mumbled to Cowles, 'Scuse
me now. I'm with them,' and bolted on out." All of
them subsequently resigned. The only one who stayed
behind was Lewis Lapham. (Lapham became the new
magazine editor, replacing Kotlowitz, and in due time
would be editor-in-chief. He told someone that it was
during the meeting in the St. Regis that he suddenly
realized he could have the entire magazine.) Someone
said to Hollander, the poetry editor, "This bunch of
owners won't care much for poetry now." In his letter
to Cowles Bob Kotlowitz said he was leaving because
"the heart has gone out of the magazine" and because
he did not think Blair should have the authority to pick
a new editor-in-chief.

John Fischer was brought back as interim editor. He immediately sent out a memo. What *Harper's* needed most, he said, was articles about the future. "We don't need articles about dead people. We don't need criticism of Henry James, or Proust, or William Dean Howells. We don't need articles about defeated politicians. We don't need nostalgic reminiscences of childhood. We need material about people who are on the way up, not on the way down."

As such things happen, the mass walkout was a media event. *Saturday Review:* "In issue after issue *Harper's* writers put their own lives on the line in passages of personal revealment and commitment [and] provided pieces of penetrating journalism." *Boston Globe*: "one of the very best magazines ever published in America." On and on. And none more touching to me, in these dreariest moments of my life, than the words of my colleagues and collaborators to the press. Midge Decter: "I cannot believe that in a country of two hundred million people—even during economic recessions—there isn't room for a good magazine like *Harper's*." Norman Mailer: "This is the most depressing event in American letters in many a year because *Harper's* had become the most adventurous of all magazines." Dave Halberstam: "Cowles did not understand what the excellence of the magazine stood for. It was an editorial *tour de force* with limited financial resources. He did not know the value of what he was sponsoring." He added: "We were a band of brothers."

The last day in my office, a Sunday when no one was there, I lingered for a long time at my old desk, remembering in the strange quiet the burnished morning of spring those years ago when I had sat there for the very first time with my youthful hopes and memories. In this moment I thought about my colleagues, and how proud and gratified I was that they had stood up to the magazine and for themselves and for me—but had I let *them* down?

I had to give a speech that night to the University of Texas Alumni in New York, and in the solitude I sat down and wrote it, a defense of my old student paper the *Daily Texan* against its most recent bouts with the censors. Later, at the alumni meeting in the Princeton Club Bill Moyers was to present me with a Texas Longhorn Award. "We have gathered together tonight," he said, in tones more sonorous than his youthful Baptist sermons must ever have been, "to honor a truly distinguished, gracious, and eminent American." He paused. "And after we finish with that, we're going to give a prize to Willie Morris."

Marshall Frady came back up from Atlanta on a special mission. He had journeyed to a Civil War shop at Kennesaw Mountain, where he bought a cavalry saber which had belonged to a young officer from Corinth, Mississippi. He had taken a flight for New York with the saber unsuccessfully disguised in bulkily wrapped butcher's paper, and it had taken, he reported to me, "no inconsiderable exertions of elaborate explanation to get it aboard the plane." A blizzard had settled over the northeastern coast, and the plane was diverted to Baltimore, and he had made it into Manhattan by train. He presented the handsome saber to me with a fine flourish of rhetoric at our same old table at the Empire Chinese. As the snow flurried on the darkened Madison Avenue outside, we talked of writing. Finally he had to leave. We shook hands, and then he, too, was gone.

Everything in life I have known to be true has come to me as a paradox. To me in this moment the most aching irony involved a reversal of the deepest emotions: almost overnight years before I had suddenly felt myself a "New Yorker," and now, just as swiftly, the city became large and hostile again. This, too, is a very American phenomenon, not an unfamiliar sensation to the many among us who arrive from elsewhere and appropriate the city's glitter and promise and then, sooner or later, confront in full, last measure its stalemates and subjugations. The magic and wonder and challenge give way, as sometimes they must in the miscreance and adventure of life, to pain and loss and reality.

"The city arouses us with the same forces by which it defeats us," Alfred Kazin wrote in our pages in those years. Even Scott Fitzgerald, lyricist of the New York

splendor, came to the misgiving that the city had eventually blighted and devastated the people he knew from
the Midwest, and that in the end it was "unreal, a
mirage, and distinctly treacherous." Perhaps I too had
not had the patience or the staying power for it. The
burning passion had given way to the uneasy suspicion
that I was now all emotionally burnt out. The high
whining screech of the garbage trucks on the turbulent
thoroughfares, the casual taunts and gesticulations on
the streets, the whole jarring thrust and parry of that
teeming life, served only to mock me now, and even the
lights of the skyscrapers seemed dim and craven. All
this, I suppose now, as with the very Sixties themselves,
had something to do with a loss of innocence. I never
picked up a *Harper's Magazine* again, sometimes even
averting my gaze when I saw one on a newsstand.

One thing I did know was that after nine years of
hard work on a publication, I was left with little money,
departing the city, just as I had first come to it, more or
less broke. Job offers came, of course. I thought about
newspaper work again and other magazines, but I had
had my organizational summit. I had given all of myself
to my magazine, and I felt there was nothing else com-
parable for me in an institutional way. I even responded
to a telegram from Sargent Shriver and met him for
lunch in the Four Seasons, where amid the wordly con-
sonance of the midday trade among the same tables
where I had so often entertained writing people we
talked lovingly of his brothers-in-law Jack and Bobby
Kennedy, and he wanted me to go to work writing
speeches for Senator Muskie of Maine, who was about
to seek the Democratic nomination for President so he
could run against Nixon. But nothing came of it, and I
knew anyway it was really about time to go.

So I packed my stuff and moved out the hundred
miles to eastern Long Island—the South Shore—the
vicinity I had grown to love, and settled in a wing of a
sprawling old house on an inlet of the ocean. It is an
axiom of existence that people will drop you. Also, that
it is exceedingly human to be curious about, and even
to enjoy, the travails of one's fellows, for the simple reason that this takes one's own mind away from one's

own sorrows and failures, but not for long, since one's own troubles will sooner or later win out again anyway. Nonetheless, normally the least paranoic of creatures, I imagined that half of Manhattan Island in that transitory instant was reveling in my headstrong, self-inflicted exile. I felt like the old horse set out to pasture must have felt, the fine white horse who had walked round and round in circles ten hours a day pulling the beam that provided the power for the presses of Harper & Brothers Publishers in the last century, who in retirement continued to walk round and round.

The South Shore is a place of bleak and procrastinating winters, of long nights and silences, and there was immense snow on the ground. In the snowy solitude I surveyed the frail wreck of ambition. The telephone never rang. I missed the perquisites and attentions of high station. It was strange to wake up in the morning and have no place, no office to go to, no salary to pay the bills. I had come to New York with a heart full of stars and hopes, and to have gone so high so fast, then down in a moment, was more than I had ever bargained for, as if I had somehow lost my reason for existing. I gazed interminably out the window upon the hushed landscapes, the frozen inlet, the Canada geese in V formation, trying to put things into some larger piece. To try to figure out anew who I really was, and to begin molding from this another life, was baffling and mysterious. Perhaps our greatest personal strengths, I see now, also entail and embrace our greatest weaknesses, and that we somehow have to reconcile these old secret human dichotomies through time, play them off against each other, comprehend them, seldom wanting others, even those we love the most, or those who love us, to recognize these weaknesses, but they come out sooner or later anyway, and that is likely just as well. I tried to explain to my son David what had happened, but in the moment I was not completely sure myself. "It's okay," he said. "I think I understand. Let's go to a ball game." I talked with Bill Moyers, who had been through the same himself. He reminded me I was thirty-seven years old, and to remember that I still owned a typewriter. I was not so much frightened as bereft.

From the bookcases I pulled out three books: *Huck Finn, Moby Dick, Go Down, Moses*. I had not been truly lonely in a long time, and it hurt. I took long walks in that sequestered terrain, past a derelict concrete pillbox or two built against the Nazis in the previous war, to the sand dunes in the snow and the desolate winter beach, the gulls and scurrying little terns, and as far as the eye could see the gray wintry Atlantic breakers. A lone fisherman said to me, "Take a boat from right where we stand and head due east and the first landfall is Portugal."

Was it my fault? Should I have always just been a writer, and never tried the editor's role? Should I have compromised with the owners? Had any of it been worth it? Hundreds upon hundreds of letters came from the magazine's subscribers, often eloquent, in- cluding a wonderful one from Cass Canfield, Sr. I tried to answer some of them, but there were far too many, and after a while I gave up. I do not even know where those letters are now, probably in a dusty corner of an abandoned attic in eastern Long Island.

A man has to search for the hope in the hurt. "In reality, nothing is as bad as it seems," Mary McCarthy once wrote, "or in logic ought to be," and the same emotions of a future Kenny Rogers tune kept going around in my head—"Got to know when to hold 'em, know when to fold 'em, know when to walk away"— and after a while I sat down and started writing a chil- dren's book, about childhood and adventure and frightening things in the South many years ago. Muriel, her daughter Julia, and David came out from the city on weekends. In front of the roaring fireplace, the snow again falling on the frozen pines and inlet, I would read to the kids what I had written that week.

"Go on," one or the other of them would ask when I finished.

"I can't," I would say. "That's all I've got for now."

"What happens next?"

"I don't know, but I'll sure find out."

Why would the hurt and anger and guilt, the tangi- ble and continual sense of loss, last so long, so far into my adulthood? Someday I would know. My magazine was a living thing to me, and leaving it was like death. And it was palpable and inherent and symbol to me of its place: ineluctable town, sinew and fabric, of youth and dreams.

————————

WILLIE MORRIS, *author and former editor-in-chief of* Harper's *magazine, was born in 1936 in Yazoo City, Mississippi, to a long-established clan of Mississippi Southerners. He attended the University of Texas in Austin and Oxford University in England before becoming editor of Austin's* Texas Observer *newspaper in the early 1960s.*

He went to New York in 1963 to accept an offer at Harper's, *where he worked as a writer and associate editor until 1967, when he became editor-in-chief. Willie Morris is only the eighth person in the magazine's 117-year history to hold that position. After leaving* Harper's *in 1971, he moved from Manhattan to the South Shore of Long Island.*

In 1980 Morris returned to his southern roots; he now lives and writes in Mississippi. Among his works are Yazoo, Good Old Boy, *and* North towards Home. *"Farewell" is excerpted from* New York Days *(1993).*

3

Lyrics of the City

Derek Walcott

A Village Life

(for John Robertson)

I

Through the wide, grey loft window,
I watched that winter morning my first snow
crusting the sill, puzzle the black,
nuzzling tom. Behind my back
a rime of crud glazed my cracked coffee cup,
a snowfall of torn poems piling up,
heaped by a rhyming spade.
Starved, on the prowl,
I was a frightened cat in that grey city.
I floated, a cat's shadow, through the black wool
sweaters, leotards, and parkas of the fire-haired,
snow-shouldered Greenwich Village *mädchen,*
homesick, my desire
crawled across snow
like smoke, for its lost fire.

All that winter I haunted
your house on Hudson Street, a tiring friend,
demanding to be taken in, drunk, and fed.
I thought winter would never end.

I cannot imagine you dead.
But that stare, frozen,
a frosted pane in sunlight,
gives nothing back by letting nothing in,
your kindness or my pity.
No self-reflection lies

within those silent, ice-blue irises,
whose image is some snow-locked mountain lake
in numb Montana.

And since that winter I have learnt to gaze
on life indifferently as through a pane of glass.

II

Your image rattled on the subway glass
is my own death mask in an overcoat;
under New York, the subterranean freight
of human souls, locked in an iron cell,
station to station cowed with swaying calm,
thunders to its end, each in its private hell,
each plumped, prime bulk still swinging by its arm
upon a hook. You're two years dead. And yet
I watch that silence spreading through our souls:
that horn-rimmed midget who consoles
his own deformity with Sartre on Genet.
Terror still eats the nerves, the Word
is gibberish, the plot Absurd.
The turnstile slots, like addicts, still consume
obols and aspirin, Charon in his grilled cell
grows vague about our crime, our destination.
Not all are silent, or endure
the enormity of silence; at one station,
somewhere off 33rd and Lexington,
a fur-wrapped matron screamed above the roar
of rattling iron. Nobody took her on,
we looked away. Such scenes
rattle our trust in nerves tuned like machines.
All drives as you remember it, the pace
of walking, running the rat race,
locked in a system, ridden by its rail,
within a life where no one dares to fail.
I watch your smile breaking across my skull,
the hollows of your face below my face
sliding across it like a pane of glass.
Nothing endures. Even in his cities
man's life is grass.
Times Square. We sigh and let off steam,
who should screech with the braking wheels, scream

like our subway-Cassandra, heaven-sent
to howl for Troy, emerge
blind from the blast of daylight, whirled
apart like papers from a vent.

III

Going away, through Queens we pass
a cemetery of miniature skyscrapers. The verge
blazes its rust, its taxi-yellow leaves. It's fall.
I stare through glass,
my own reflection there, at
empty avenues, lawns, spires, quiet
stones, where the curb's rim
wheels westward, westward, where thy bones . . .

Montana, Minnesota, your real
America, lost in tall grass, serene idyll.

Poet, playwright, director, and winner of a Nobel Prize for literature in 1992, DEREK WALCOTT *is not only widely recognized as a writer, but as a voice for Caribbean creativity and culture itself. Born in Castries, St. Lucia, in 1930, he founded the St. Lucia Arts Guild at the age of twenty. His first three volumes of poems were published in Trinidad between 1948 and 1953. Acclaim as a poet first came to him in the 1960s, with the publication of* In a Green Night, The Castaway, *and* The Gulf. *He followed these with an autobiographical poem,* Another Life, *and* Sea Grapes, The Star-Apple Kingdom, Selected Poetry, The Unfortunate Traveller, Midsummer, *and* Omeros.*

His plays mix folk-singing, dancing, and storytelling with colloquial speech and metaphor. Among his dozen or more dramatic works are Henry Christophe, Henri Dernier, The Dream on Monkey Mountain, O Babylon, Remembrance, *and* Pantomime.

Derek Walcott lived in New York as a Rockefeller Fellow in 1958. A member of the American Academy and Institute of Arts, he now teaches at Boston University. "A Village Life" appeared first in The Gulf (1969).*

Jean Valentine

3 A. M. *in New York*

FOR A.V.C.

I have been standing at the edge
of this green field all night.
My hand is sticky with sugar.

The village winks; it thinks it is
the muscle of the world. The heart.
The mouth.

The horse is standing across the field, near the fence.
He doesn't come any closer,
even in the dark, or run away.

Blood memory:
fixed on vacancy:
coming back and back for a sign

the flat of his coat
the shut out of his eye.

JEAN VALENTINE *was born in Chicago and earned her undergraduate degree from Radcliffe College. She has received numerous fellowships—including a Guggenheim —and awards from the National Endowment for the Arts, the Rockefeller Foundation, and the Bunting Institute.*

She teaches at Sarah Lawrence College and lives in New York City and Provincetown. Her most recent book of poetry is The River at Wolf. *"3 A.M. in New York" is from her collection* Ordinary Things, *published in 1974.*

Lucie Brock-Broido

Heartbeat

Let me be brief then
I will go on worshiping
the perfect mean lines, the light
on them visible only through the neon
signs of life, the parts which glow
all night when peaceful sorts are sleeping,
when the wanderers are still avenging
their insomnia in the dark
false hellebore red of poolhalls,
in the allnight pastel caves of laundromats,
in the wrong decade coffee shop in Ypsilanti
where even the manager can't lend the key
to the men's room,
                              I love
these things too, the self serve
filling station where a pale hand
sneaks out making silver
change, or the one dark palm
in the meat shop on Amsterdam & 110th
behind the curtain handing out
the little envelopes of *Heartbeat,*
                              I covet
these things too,
some third world after this one
& the one that goes hereafter,
in that world you will be important,
devoured by the fawns,
inscrutable Christmas rose, toxic
in your leather coat phase for a long time
worshiping the long blonde stains left
after light & after fire.

LUCIE BROCK-BROIDO *was born in Pittsburgh. She received her undergraduate education from Johns Hopkins and her master's from the Writing Seminars at Johns Hopkins. Her MFA is from Columbia. Brock-Broido has held poetry fellowships from the National Endowment for the Arts, the Fine Arts Work Center in Provincetown, and the Hoyns Fellowship from the University of Virginia. She was the Briggs-Copeland Lecturer in Poetry at Harvard and now is the associate professor of Poetry at the School of the Arts, Columbia. "Heartbeat" is taken from her first book,* A Hunger. *Her second collection of poems,* The Master Letters, *will be published by Knopf in the fall of 1995.*

Henri Cole

Une Lettre à New York

If it's spring in the city, have the marchers,
each one with a shrieking whistle, short-circuited the
    streets,
their cause as grave as the dirty cabs growling at their
    feet?
Is Paul Taylor at the City Center? Has my architecture-
grad-student-subtenant remembered Sting, a pet
    squirrel
whose appearance each May on the fire escape ledge
is as celebrated as our pink dogwood's flowering?
    Privileged
as she is, eating Arabian almonds all these years, if she's
    early
and hears me in the shower, she knows to come right in.
Will Joe, my Italian barber, still tell me what to do in
    life,
reading my moods in his mirror—his razor like a fruit
    knife
against the peach's flesh instead of the proud artist's
    chin?
Will a burglar have borrowed my red Schwinn from
    the rooftop,
the rusty chain foiling a smooth delirious escape?
With pompoms swinging on their skimmers like
    grapes,
does a Colombian troupe still serenade commuters
    stopped,
even in gray business suits, by a tug on the heart-
    strings,
the subway chasm converted into a dream of
    disembarking?

Does the beggar on my block, who says his name is
    Marx,
still wear a deeper tan than mine? Will souls of three
    sleeping
friends—May, Lola and Vladimir—visit in the evening,
arranging themselves in the ailanthus outside my window?
If they smile and blink as from some Broadway video,
it will be an urban bequest for those who could not say
    good-bye,
their numinous bodies dissolving then into July's fireflies,
whose lanterns alchemize my cheap paper shades into
    Chinese silk.
Each of you who writes reports illness, pain from love
    spilt,
or someone who's gone to the other side, yet correspon-
    dence tries
to be uplifting, disproving Judas who writes man's sad
    history.
Could he have been right who said there was earth and
    man
in the beginning, that we created God, that we created
    Heaven,
in our want or need for something more than awful
    elegy?
The little island wedged between three rivers,
from which our letters come and go, is the personification
    of hope.
The buildings are black and white like sonnets. And
    enveloped
in between, the first sweet cherries of the season are being
    delivered.

———————————

*Presently the Briggs-Copeland Lecturer in Poetry at Harvard
University, HENRI COLE has taught at the University of
Maryland, Yale, Columbia, and Reed College. Between 1982
and 1988 he directed the Academy of American Poets. Born in
1956 in Fukuoka, Japan, Henri Cole grew up in Virginia and
graduated from the College of William and Mary. He has
received graduate degrees from Columbia University and the
University of Wisconsin. He has won awards and fellowships*

from the National Endowment for the Arts, the Ingram Merrill Foundation, and the Amy Lowell Poetry Traveling Scholarship. In addition to numerous journals, his poetry has been published in three collections: The Marble Queen, The Zoo Wheel of Knowledge, *and* The Look of Things. *"Une Lettre à New York" is from his collection,* The Look of Things.

Li-Young Lee

The City in Which I Love You

> *I will arise now, and go*
> *about the city in the streets,*
> *and in the broad ways I will seek . . .*
> *whom my soul loveth.*
>
> SONG OF SONGS 3:2

And when, in the city in which I love you,
even my most excellent song goes unanswered,
and I mount the scabbed streets,
the long shouts of avenues,
and tunnel sunken night in search of you. . . .

That I negotiate fog, bituminous
rain ringing like teeth into the beggar's tin,
or two men jackaling a third in some alley
weirdly lit by a couch on fire, that I
drag my extinction in search of you. . . .

Past the guarded schoolyards, the boarded-up churches,
swastikaed
synagogues, defended houses of worship, past
newspapered windows of tenements, among the
    violated,
the prosecuted citizenry, throughout this
storied, buttressed, scavenged, policed
city I call home, in which I am a guest. . . .

A bruise, blue
in the muscle, you
impinge upon me.

As bone hugs the ache home, so
I'm vexed to love you, your body

the shape of returns, your hair a torso
of light, your heat
I must have, your opening
I'd eat, each moment
of that soft-finned fruit,
inverted fountain in which I don't see me.

My tongue remembers your wounded flavor.
The vein in my neck
adores you. A sword
stands up between my hips,
my hidden fleece sends forth its scent of human oil.

The shadows under my arms,
I promise, are tender, the shadows
under my face. Do not calculate,
but come, smooth other, rough sister.
Yet, how will you know me

among the captives, my hair grown long,
my blood motley, my ways trespassed upon?
In the uproar, the confusion
of accents and inflections,
how will you hear me when I open my mouth?

Look for me, one of the drab population
under fissured edifices, fractured
artifices. Make my various
names flock overhead,
I will follow you.
Hew me to your beauty.

Stack in me the unaccountable fire,
bring on me the iron leaf, but tenderly.
Folded one hundred times and
creased, I'll not crack.
Threshed to excellence, I'll achieve you.

But in the city
in which I love you,
no one comes, no one
meets me in the brick clefts;
in the wedged dark,

no finger touches me secretly, no mouth
tastes my flawless salt,
no one wakens the honey in the cells, finds the humming
in the ribs, the rich business in the recesses;
hulls clogged, I continue laden, translated

by exhaustion and time's appetite, my sleep abandoned
in bus stations and storefront stoops,
my insomnia erected under a sky
cross-hatched by wires, branches,
and black flights of rain. Lewd body of wind

jams me in the passageways, doors slam
like guns going off, a gun goes off, a pie plate spins
past, whizzing its thin tremolo,
a plastic bag, fat with wind, barrels by and slaps
a chain-link fence, wraps it like clung skin.

In the excavated places,
I waited for you, and I did not cry out.
In the derelict rooms, my body needed you,
and there was such flight in my breast.
During the daily assaults, I called to you,

and my voice pursued you,
even backward
to that other city
in which I saw a woman
squat in the street

beside a body,
and fan with a handkerchief flies from its face.
That woman
was not me. And
the corpse

lying there, lying there
so still it seemed with great effort, as though
his whole being was concentrating on the hole
in his forehead, so still
I expected he'd sit up any minute and laugh out loud:

that man was not me;
his wound was his, his death not mine.
And the soldier
who fired the shot, then lit a cigarette:
he was not me.

And the ones I do not see
in cities all over the world,
the ones sitting, standing, lying down, those
in prisons playing checkers with their knocked-out teeth:
they are not me. Some of them are

my age, even my height and weight;
none of them is me.
The woman who is slapped, the man who is kicked,
the ones who don't survive,
whose names I do not know;

they are not me forever,
the ones who no longer live
in the cities in which
you are not,
the cities in which I looked for you.

The rain stops, the moon
in her breaths appears overhead.
The only sound now is a far flapping.
Over the National Bank, the flag of some republic
    or other
gallops like water or fire to tear itself away.

If I feel the night
move to disclosures or crescendos,
it's only because I'm famished
for meaning; the night
merely dissolves.

And your otherness is perfect as my death.
Your otherness exhausts me,
like looking suddenly up from here
to impossible stars fading.
Everything is punished by your absence.

Is prayer, then, the proper attitude
for the mind that longs to be freely blown,
but which gets snagged on the barb
called *world,* that
tooth-ache, the actual? What prayer

would I build? And to whom?
Where are you
in the cities in which I love you,
the cities daily risen to work and to money,
to the magnificent miles and the gold coasts?

Morning comes to this city vacant of you.
Pages and windows flare, and you are not there.
Someone sweeps his portion of sidewalk,
wakens the drunk, slumped like laundry,
and you are gone.

You are not in the wind
which someone notes in the margins of a book.
You are gone out of the small fires in abandoned lots
where human figures huddle,
each aspiring to its own ghost.

Between brick walls, in a space no wider than my face,
a leafless sapling stands in mud.
In its branches, a nest of raw mouths
gaping and cheeping, scrawny fires that must eat.
My hunger for you is no less than theirs.

At the gates of the city in which I love you,
the sea hauls the sun on its back,
strikes the land, which rebukes it.
What ardor in its sliding heft,
a flameless friction on the rocks.

Like the sea, I am recommended by my orphaning.
Noisy with telegrams not received,
quarrelsome with aliases,
intricate with misguided journeys,
by my expulsions have I come to love you.

Straight from my father's wrath,
and long from my mother's womb,
late in this century and on a Wednesday morning,
bearing the mark of one who's experienced
neither heaven nor hell,

my birthplace vanished, my citizenship earned,
in league with stones of the earth, I
enter, without retreat or help from history,
the days of no day, my earth
of no earth, I re-enter

the city in which I love you.
And I never believed that the multitude
of dreams and many words were vain.

Born in 1957 in Jakarta, Indonesia, of Chinese parents,
LI-YOUNG LEE *spent his first seven years traveling from
Indonesia to Hong Kong, Macau, Japan, and eventually to
the United States, where his family settled. He studied at
the University of Pittsburgh, the University of Arizona,
and the State University of New York, Brockport. Li-Young
Lee now lives in Chicago with his wife and two children.*

*Among his honors are a Guggenheim Fellowship, as well
as grants from the Illinois Arts Council, the Pennsylvania
Council on the Arts, and the National Endowment for
the Arts. His first collection of poetry,* Rose *(1986), won
the Delmore Schwartz Memorial Poetry Award, and his
second collection,* The City in Which I Love You, *was the
1990 Lamont Poetry Selection. In 1995, he published* The
Winged Seed, *an autobiographical work of prose exploring
his family's history.*

*"The City in Which I Love You" is from the collection of
the same title.*

4

The City – Affectionate Shadows

Anne Waldman

A Phonecall from Frank O'Hara

That all these dyings may be life in death

I was living in San Francisco
My heart was in Manhattan
It made no sense, no reference point
Hearing the sad horns at night,
fragile evocations of female stuff
The 3 tones (the last most resonant)
were like warnings, haiku-meuzzins at dawn
The call came in the afternoon
"Frank, is that really you?"

I'd awake chilled at dawn
in the wooden house like an old ship
Stay bundled through the day
sitting on the stoop to catch the sun
I lived near the park whose deep green
over my shoulder made life cooler
Was my spirit faltering, grown duller?
I want to be free of poetry's ornaments,
its duty, free of constant irritation,
me in it, what was grander reason
for being? Do it, why? (Why, Frank?)
To make the energies dance etc.

My coat a cape of horrors
I'd walk through town or
impending earthquake. Was that it?
Ominous days. Street shiny with
hallucinatory light on sad dogs,

too many religious people, or a woman
startled me by her look of indecision
near the empty stadium
I walked back spooked by
my own darkness
Then Frank called to say
"What? Not done complaining yet?
Can't you smell the eucalyptus,
have you never neared the Pacific?
'While frank and free / call for
musick while your veins swell'"
he sang, quoting a metaphysician
"Don't you know the secret, how to
wake up and see you don't exist, but
that does, don't you see phenomena
is so much more important than *this*?
I always love *that*."
"Always?" I cried, wanting to believe him
"Yes." "But say more! How can you if
it's sad & dead?" "But that's just it!
If! It isn't. It doesn't want to be
Do you want to be?" He was warming to his song
"Of course I don't have to put up with as
much as you do these days. These *years*.
But I do miss the color, the architecture,
the talk. You know, it *was* the life!
And dying is such an insult. After all
I was in love with breath and I loved
embracing those others, the lovers,
with my *body*." He sighed & laughed
He wasn't quite as I'd remembered him
Not less generous, but more abstract
Did he even have a voice now, I wondered
or did I think it up in the middle
of this long day, phone in hand now
dialing Manhattan

―――――――

ANNE WALDMAN, *author of more than thirty published
pamphlets, chapbooks, and collections of poetry, grew up in
New York City and graduated from Bennington College in*

Vermont. Between 1966 and 1978 she was assistant director and director of the Poetry Project at St. Mark's-in-the-Bowery Church. In 1974, with Allen Ginsberg, she founded the Jack Kerouac School of Disembodied Poetics at the Naropa Institute in Boulder, Colorado.

Anne Waldman also "performs" her poetry, often in collaboration with dancers and musicians. She is a two-time winner of the Heavyweight Championship Poetry Bout in Taos, New Mexico. Currently she directs the Department of Writing and Poetics at the Naropa Institute.

"A Phonecall from Frank O'Hara" is from her collection Helping the Dreamer.

Pam Houston

Sometimes You Talk About Idaho

You've come, finally, to a safe place. It could be labeled *safe place,* marquee-style in bright glittering letters. You've put the time in to get there. You've read all the books. You have cooked yourself elaborate gourmet meals. You have brought home fresh-cut flowers. You love your work. You love your friends. It's the single life in the high desert. No booze, no drugs. It isn't just something you tell yourself. It's something you believe.

The man you admire most in the world calls you and asks you out to lunch. He is your good father, the one you trust, the one you depend on. The only one, besides your agent and the editors, who still sees your work.

You have lunch with him often because he is honest and rare, and because he brings a certain manic energy to your life. He is the meter of your own authenticity. The way his eyes drop when you say even the most marginally ingenuous thing. He lives in a space you can only pretend to imagine. When he talks about his own life there seem to be no participants and no events, just a lot of energy moving and spinning and changing hands. It's dizzying, really; sex becomes religion, and religion becomes art.

Sometimes you talk about Idaho: the smell of spruce trees, the snap of a campfire, the arc of a dry fly before it breaks the surface of the water. Idaho is something he can speak about concretely.

He always asks about your love life. No, you say, there's no one at all.

"The problem," he says, "with living alone is that

you have to go so far away to the place you can do your work, and when you're finished there's no one there to tell you whether or not you've gotten back."

Your good father smiles a smile of slight embarrassment, which is as uncomfortable as new shoes on his soft face. He has a friend, he says, that he'd like you to meet.

"He is both smart and very masculine," your good father says, something in his voice acknowledging that this is a rare combination because he wants you to know he's on your side here. "Our friendship," he says, "is ever new."

"Imagine a first date," your good father says, "where you don't have to watch your vocabulary. Imagine a man," he says, "who might be as intense as you."

Your good father's friend lives in Manhattan, twenty-two hundred miles from the place you've learned to call home. He's a poet, a concert pianist, a soap opera star. He's translated plays from five different Native American languages. He's an environmentalist, a humanist, he's hard to the left.

"He's been through a lot of self-evaluation. He wants a relationship," your good father says, "and he's a dog person. Now that you fly back to New York so often, it could be just the right thing."

You watch him wait for your reaction. You look at the lines that pain has made on his face and realize that you love your good father more than anyone you have slept with in the last five years. You would do anything he told you to do.

"Sounds like fun," you say, without blinking. You are pure nonchalance. A relationship, you've decided, is not something you need like a drug, but a journey, a circumstance, a choice you might make on a particular day.

"My friend loves the mountains, and the desert," your good father says. "He comes out here as often as he can. His real name is Evan, but he's played the same part on the soap for so many years now, everyone we know just calls him Tex."

"Tex?" you say.

"I didn't tell you," he says. "My friend plays a cowboy." Your good father smiles his embarrassed smile. "That's the best part."

You fly to the East Coast on an enormous plane that is mostly empty. You watch the contours of the land get steadily greener, badlands to prairies to cornfields, till the clouds close your view and water runs off the wing.

Somehow you have lived to be twenty-nine years old without ever having gone on a blind date. You don't let yourself admit it, but you are excited beyond words.

You let your mother dress you. She lives in New Jersey and is an actress and you think it's her privilege. She makes you do the following things you are not accustomed to doing: wear foundation, curl your eyelashes, part your hair on the side. Even the Mona Lisa, she says, doesn't look pretty with her hair parted in the middle. She gives you her car so you don't have to take the bus into New York, and in exchange you leave her a phone number where she can reach you. She promises not to call.

It's a little dislocating in New Jersey, where there are cars on the road at all hours and it never really gets dark at night. On the freeway, four miles outside of Newark, you see a deer walking across a cement overpass that's been planted with trees. This seems more amazing to you than it probably is. A sign from your homeland, safe passage, good luck.

It works. You make it through the improbable fact of the Lincoln Tunnel and it doesn't cave in. You find a twenty-four-hour garage four blocks from Moran's Seafood, the meeting place for your date. On the way there you see a woman who looks very happy carrying a starfish in a translucent Tupperware bowl. You only have to walk down one street that scares you a little bit. You get to the restaurant first, and your wide-eyed reflection in the glass behind the bar startles you a little. You resist the urge to tell the bartender that you have a blind date.

When he walks in the door there's no mistaking him. He's the soap opera star with the umbrella, the strong back and shoulders, the laugh lines America loves. As he scans the bar it occurs to you for the first time to wonder what kind of a sales job your good father has done on him about you. Then you are shaking hands, then he is picking up your umbrella, one arm hooked in yours guiding you to the table for two.

It is only awkward for the first ten minutes. He is a great mass of charisma moving forward to ever more entertaining subjects. You are both so conscious of keeping the conversation going that you don't look at the menu till the waiter has come back for the fifth time.

Of all the things on the menu, you pick the only one that's difficult to pronounce. You have just passed a fluency exam in French that is one of the requirements of your Ph.D., but saying *en papillote* to the waiter is something that is beyond your power to do. So you describe the dish in English and when the waiter has watched you suffer to his satisfaction, he moves his pen and nods his head.

During dinner, you cover all the required topics for first dates in the nineties: substance abuse, failed marriage, hopes, dreams, and aspirations. You talk about your dogs so much he gets confused and thinks they are your children. He uses emotion words when he talks, sometimes more than one in a sentence: *ache, frightened, rapture*. And something else: He is listening, not only to the words you are saying, but to your rhythms, your reverberations, he picks them up like a machine. Something in his manner is so much like your good father that a confusion which is not altogether unpleasant settles in behind your heart.

Between the herbal tea and the triple fudge decadence he's ordered so that you can have one bite, he reaches across the table and takes your hand in both of his. Then he calls you a swell critter.

You feel a hairline fracture easing through your structure the way snow separates before an avalanche on a too-warm winter day. Something in the air smells a little like salvation, and you breathe deeper every minute but you can't fill your lungs. When all the tables are empty and every restaurant employee is staring at you in disgust, you finally let go of his hand.

Then you go walking. One end of Chelsea to the

other, all the time circumventing the block with your garage. He knows about the architecture. He reads from the historic plaques. He shows you nooks and crannies, hidden doorways, remnants of the Latinate style.

It's been raining softly for the hours since dinner and you can feel your hair creeping back over to its comfortable middle part. You smile at him like the Mona Lisa, and he looks as though he's going to kiss you, but doesn't. Then the sky opens up and you duck into a café for more herbal tea.

The café is crowded and the streets are full of people and it makes no sense to you when he tells you it's three o'clock in the morning. You can't possibly, he says, drive all the way back to New Jersey tonight. It's your first real chance to size him up and you do. From the empty next table your good father gives you a wink. "It would be foolish," you say, "to drive in the middle of the night."

When you look back on this date it's the cab ride you'll remember. Broadway going by in a wild blur of green lights, the tallest buildings all lit up like daytime. Your driver and another in a cab next to yours hang heads out their windows and converse at fifty miles an hour in a tongue that sounds a little like Portuguese, a little like music. It's pure unburdened anticipation: you both know sex is imminent, but you don't yet hold the fact of it in your hand. You are laughing and leaning against him. You are watching yourself on the giant screen, western woman finds daytime cowboy in the big city, where even if it wasn't raining, you couldn't see a single star.

His building is a West Side co-op, a name that sounds happy to you, like a place where everyone should get along. In his apartment there are the black-and-white photos you expected, the vertical blinds, the tiny kitchen and immense workplace, the antique roll-top desk.

Some tea without caffeine? he says. And you nod. You count. This is your eleventh cup of herbal tea today. You have never done a first date without alcohol. Now you know why.

You watch him move around the room like a soap opera star. Take one: western woman's seduction: a smile, a touch, a glance. You're still waiting for the big one-liner when he starts kissing you, his hand cupped around your chin, one on the back of your head. Procter and Gamble Industries has taught him how to do this. "Slowly now," the director says, "a little softer. Turn the chin, turn the chin, we can't see her face." You aren't fooling anybody. It's way better than TV.

"Let's forget the herbal tea," he says, which is a disappointment. You want to see the script. You want to make a big red X over that line and write in another, but he has your hand and is leading you to the bedroom with the queen-size bed and the wrought-iron headboard with the sunset over the mountains and there are so many things to think about. Like how many days since your last period and the percentage of people in New York with AIDS, and what you can say to make him realize, if it matters anymore, that going to bed on first dates is not something you do with great regularity. Something needs to be said here, not exactly to defend your virtue, but to make it clear that the act needs to be meaningful, to make it matter, not for all time or forever but for right now, because that's what you've decided it needs to be with sex—after discarding all those other requirements over the years—something that matters right now.

"I'm feeling a little strange," you begin, and you realize this isn't just about you but you're testing him to see if he'll let you talk. "I seem to be violating my own code of dating," you say. "If I have one, that is. I mean, I wanted to come here with you, I didn't want this to end just now, and then we have this other person in common, and because we both love him, there's this closeness between us, this trust which may be totally inappropriate, and so," you wind up, "I'm just feeling a little strange."

This is what happens, you realize, when you begin to get mentally healthy. Instead of letting yourself be whisked silently off to bed you feel compelled to say a lot of mostly incoherent things in run-on sentences.

"I know how you feel," he says. "Me too. But I want

this closeness. I don't want you to go back home without us having had it."

It's not exactly a declaration, but it's good enough for you. You fall into the ocean that banks the sunset over mountains. It's a thunderstorm in the desert. It's warm wind on snow. You lose count of orgasms under the smoky city lighting, first streetlight and then daylight, the contours always changing.

"Having fun?" he says, at one point or another. And you nod because fun is one of the things you are having.

He does something to the back of your neck that is closer, more intimate, somehow, even than having him inside you. You read an article once on craniosacral massage, where the body's task of pumping blood to the brain is performed by another person, giving the patient's body the closest thing it's ever had to total rest.

At eight-thirty your mother calls and you take a break long enough to mumble a few words into the phone. "I'm perfectly safe," you tell her, and laugh all the way back to the bedroom at the absurdity of your lie.

It is noon before you emerge, still not having slept, your body feeling numb and tingling and drenched, weightless, rain-soaked, rejuvenated.

But like it or not, it's the next day. You both have appointments. He kisses you twice. "Dinner?" he says. "It'll be late," you say. "That's okay," he says, "call me."

You go to meeting after meeting, and finally to a party with people who mean everything to your career. You are wearing the same clothes as yesterday, walking a little tender, and bowlegged as a bear. Your editor, by some miracle of perception, takes your hand and doesn't let it go all night, even when you are involved in two separate conversations.

Later, you call the soap opera star. He tries to give you directions. "You," he says, "are on the East Side. I am on the West Side."

You tell him you've been to New York before. You hang up.

On the way to his house you get lost. It is raining the kind of rain it never rains in the high desert. A saturating rain where the air spaces between the raindrops contain almost as much moisture as the raindrops themselves.

You drive your mother's car through running canals deeper than your wheel wells. You have never been to this part of Manhattan before. Street after street bears a name you don't recognize. Dark figures loom in dark doorways, and the same series of parks seems to have you boxed in. Your defroster can't keep up with your anxiety. Then suddenly you are back on Broadway. You find his house.

"I had a learning experience," you say. What should have taken fifteen minutes has taken an hour and a half. He isn't angry, but he takes the keys from your hand. Together you look for an open garage.

"Dinner?" he says. You shake your head either no you haven't had it or no you don't want it.

"If you're not sleeping," he says, "you need to eat." The two of you look like war-zone survivors. You both try to be charming and fail. Even the simplest conversation is beyond your power. Finally you eat in silence. You fall into bed. It's sleep you both need, but there's the fact of what's insatiable between you. All night you keep reaching, tumbling, waiting for the bell to ring to let you know you've found each other, to let you know it's okay to sleep.

In what seems like minutes, it's time to say goodbye, way too early, not even light out, dusky gray New York morning, clear or cloudy, who can tell without the stars? He has to go to the studio and put on his cowboy boots and court somebody named Hannah, so that all of America can sigh.

"So is Tex nice?" you say, sleepy-eyed as he kisses you goodbye.

"Darlin'," he says, "they don't come any nicer than Tex. Drop the keys in the mail slot. Take care."

When he's gone the phone rings and the machine gets it. Past experience has taught you to expect a woman's voice, but it's your good father, wanting Evan to tell him how everything went. You imagine your good father in the desert, bright sunshine, sage and warm wind. When you hear his laugh crackle over the answering machine your dislocation is complete.

You wander around New York until your lunch date. One of the polished magazines you have written a few short pieces for wants to sent you to Yugoslavia. This is not something you can immediately comprehend. They keep talking about it, airfare and train passes and what time of year is the most beautiful, and even though they have said they want you to go you keep thinking, But why are they saying this to me?

It's Wednesday, a matinee day, so you stand in line to get half-priced tickets to a musical, even though you pre-fer drama, but you know you aren't up for anything that requires you to think. You pick the wrong musical any-way. The first words delivered onstage are "Love changes everything," and it's downhill from there. You leave feeling like you've been through three and a half hours of breath work. On the way up Fifty-seventh Street you realize a valuable and frightening thing: Today you want to be in love more than you want any-thing; the National Book Award, say, or a Pulitzer Prize.

You've left something at the soap opera star's apart-ment; a contact lens, a computer disk, your forty-dollar Oscar de la Renta underwear. It takes several phone calls to determine a time to retrieve them. He is short on the phone, on the other line to a director in London, and you realize you've stepped across some kind of a boundary into his space. You have forgotten how New Yorkers can be about their space. You are overly hard on yourself. Where you live, there is plenty of space. There is so much goddam space you can hardly believe it. Finally, it's the doorman who lets you into his empty apartment.

And then you go home, on another enormous air-plane, and sit next to a fat woman who is reading a book called *Why Women Confuse Love with Sex*. It's not her you're mad at, but you glare at her so she won't speak to you because you know that anything—any-thing—anybody says to you will make you cry and cry.

For two days you catch up on sleep and expect him to call. On the third day you come to your senses enough to go hiking, to get out into the landscape that heals you. There is a dynamic in the desert that you understand perfectly: the dry, dry earth and the plants designed to live almost forever without the simple and basic ingredients they need the most. After five days you know he isn't going to call, which is okay, because out of the rubble you carried back from the city you have resurrected your independence. Your work surrounds you like a featherbed and things almost go back to how they were before. But now desire grows inside you like a plant, a big green leafy thing that has been fed only once, but now that it's growing, it won't be still. You sit in your own house and talk to your dogs. More often than not, you answer back.

Your good father calls and asks you out to breakfast. It's an early appointment but you get up even earlier to bathe and dress. It's breakfast at Howard Johnson's but you wear what you wore at Moran's. You even curl your eyelashes. You tell your good father that Evan was everything he said he would be. You run down the weekend with more facts than innuendo. He gets the picture. He is, he says, a lonely man himself.

You tell him about the leafy thing in your stomach, how you have detached it from Evan, how your desire has become something you own, after all. When you get to that part, tears spring into your eyes. It's your turn to give the performance, and its authenticity doesn't make it any less theatrical. It's honesty you are striving for, and still, you're a little bigger than life. Your good father's eyes tell you you've succeeded, and yet your motives are too suspect for even you to explore. You choose to boil it down to what's simple: You perform for your good father because you love him. Anything else is beside the point. Your good father reaches across the table and takes your hand in both of his. "Evan will call you," he says. "I know him. He will."

You wonder what Evan has said to your good father on the phone. You wonder why there's no word for the opposite of lonely. You wonder if there's a difference between whatever might be truth and a performance that isn't a lie. In your life right now, you can't find one.

―――――――――

PAM HOUSTON, *who received her Ph.D. from the University of Utah, won the 1993 Western States Book Award for her collection,* Cowboys Are My Weakness.

She has published stories in Mirabella, Mademoiselle, *and the* Mississippi Review. *Her nonfiction has appeared in* Elle, Outside, *and the* New York Times.

Pam Houston has worked as a hunting guide in Alaska and is a licensed river guide in Creede, Colorado. She now divides her time between Creede and Oakland, California. She edited Women on Hunting, *published in 1994 by Ecco Press.*

"Sometimes You Talk About Idaho" is from Cowboys Are My Weakness.

Truman Capote

A House on the Heights

I live in Brooklyn. By Choice.

Those ignorant of its allures are entitled to wonder why. For, taken as a whole, it *is* an uninviting community. A veritable veldt of tawdriness where even the *noms de quartiers* aggravate: Flatbush and Flushing Avenue, Bushwick, Brownsville, Red Hook. Yet, in the greenless grime-gray, oases do occur, splendid contradictions, hearty echoes of healthier days. Of these seeming mirages, the purest example is the neighborhood in which I am situated, an area known as Brooklyn Heights. Heights, because it stands atop a cliff that secures a sea-gull's view of the Manhattan and Brooklyn bridges, of lower Manhattan's tall dazzle and the ship-lane waters, breeding river to bay to ocean, that encircle and seethe past posturing Miss Liberty.

I'm not much acquainted with the proper history of the Heights. However, I *believe* (but please don't trust me) that the oldest house, the oldest still extant and functioning, belongs to our back-yard neighbors, Mr. and Mrs. Philip Broughton. A silvery gray, shingle-wood Colonial shaded by trees robustly leafed, it was built in 1790, the home of a sea captain. Period prints, dated 1830, depict the Heights area as a cozy port bustling with billowed sails; and, indeed, many of the section's finer houses, particularly those of Federal design, were first intended to shelter the families of shipmasters. Cheerfully austere, as elegant and other-era as formal calling cards, these houses bespeak an age of able servants and solid fireside ease; of horses in musical harness (old rose-brick carriage houses abound hereabouts; all now, naturally, transformed into pleasant, if rather doll-pretty, dwellings); invoke specters of bearded seafaring fathers and bonneted stay-at-home wives: devoted parents to great broods of future bankers and fashionable brides. For a century or so that is how it must have been: a time of tree-shrouded streets, lanes limp with willow, August gardens brimming with bumblebees and herbaceous scent, of ship horns on the river, sails in the wind, and a country-green meadow sloping down to the harbor, a cow-grazing, butterflied meadow where children sprawled away breezy summer afternoons, where the slap of sleds resounded on December snows.

Is that how it was? Conceivably I take too Valentine a view. However it be, my Valentine assumes the stricter aspect of a steel engraving as we mosey, hand in hand, with Henry Ward Beecher, whose church once dominated the spiritual life of the Heights, through the latter half of the last century. The great Bridge, opened in 1883, now balanced above the river; and the port, each year expanding becoming a more raucous, big-business matter, chased the children out of the meadow, withered it, entirely whacked it away to make room for black palace-huge warehouses tickly with imported tarantulas and reeking of rotten bananas.

By 1910, the neighborhood, which comprises sly alleys and tucked-away courts and streets that sometimes run straight but also dwindle and bend, had undergone fiercer vicissitudes. Descendants of the Reverend Beecher's stiff-collared flock had begun removing themselves to other pastures; and immigrant tribes, who had first ringed the vicinity, at once infiltrated en masse. Whereupon a majority of what remained of genteel old stock, the sediment in the bottom of the bottle, poured forth from their homes, leaving them to be demolished or converted into eyesore-seedy rooming establishments.

So that, in 1925, Edmund Wilson, allowing a paragraph to what he considered the dead and dying Heights, disgustedly reported: "The pleasant red and pink brick houses still worthily represent the generation of Henry Ward Beecher; but an eternal Sunday is on them now; they seem sunk in a final silence. In the streets one may catch a glimpse of a solitary well-dressed old gentleman moving slowly a long way off; but in general the respectable have disappeared and only the vulgar survive. The empty quiet is broken by the shouts of shrill Italian children and by incessant mechanical pianos in dingy apartment houses, accompanied by human voices that seem almost as mechanical as they. At night, along unlighted streets, one gives a wide berth to drunkards that sprawl out across the pavement from the shadow of darkened doors; and I have known a dead horse to be left in the road—two blocks from the principal post office and not much more from Borough Hall—with no effort made to remove it, for nearly three weeks."

Gothic as this glimpse is, the neighborhood nevertheless continued to possess, cheap rents aside, some certain appeal brigades of the gifted—artists, writers—began to discover. Among those riding in on the initial wave was Hart Crane, whose poet's eye, focusing on his window view, produced *The Bridge*. Later, soon after the success of *Look Homeward, Angel,* Thomas Wolfe, noted prowler of the Brooklyn night, took quarters: an apartment, equipped with the most publicized icebox in literature's archives, which he maintained until his "over-growed carcass" was carried home to the hills of Carolina. At one time, a stretch of years in the early forties, a single, heaven knows singular, house on Middagh Street boasted a roll call of residents that read: W. H. Auden, Richard Wright, Carson McCullers, Paul and Jane Bowles, the British composer Benjamin Britten, impresario and stage designer Oliver Smith, an authoress of murder entertainments—Miss Gypsy Rose Lee, and a Chimpanzee accompanied by Trainer. Each of the tenants in this ivory-tower boarding house contributed to its upkeep, lights, heat, the wages of a general cook (a former Cotton Club chorine), and all were present at the invitation of the owner, that very original editor, writer, *fantaisiste,* a gentleman with a guillotine tongue, yet benevolent and butter-hearted, the late, the justly lamented George Davis.

Now George is gone; and his house too: the necessities of some absurd civic project caused it to be torn down during the war. Indeed, the war years saw the neighborhood slide to its nadir. Many of the more substantial old houses were requisitioned by the military, as lodgings, as jukebox canteens, and their rural-reared, piney-woods personnel treated them quite as Sherman did those Dixie mansions. Not that it mattered; not that anyone gave a damn. No one did; until, soon after the war, the Heights commenced attracting a bright new clientele, brave pioneers bringing brooms and buckets of paint: urban, ambitious young couples, by and large midrung in their Doctor-Lawyer-Wall Street-Whatever careers, eager to restore to the Heights its shattered qualities of circumspect, comfortable charm.

For them, the section had much to offer: roomy big houses ready to be converted into private homes suitable for families of old-fashioned size; and such families are what these young people either had made or were making at stepladder rates. A good place to raise children, too, this neighborhood where the traffic is cautious, and the air has clarity, a seaside tartness; where there are gardens for games, quiet stoops for amusing; and where, above all, there is the Esplanade to roller-skate upon. (Forbidden: still the brats do it.) While far from being a butterflied meadow, the Esplanade, a wide terrace-like walk overlooking the harbor, does its contemporary best to approximate that playing pasture of long-gone girls and their brothers.

So, for a decade and longer, the experiment of reviving the Heights has proceeded: to the point where one is tempted to term it a *fait accompli*. Window boxes bloom with geraniums; according to the season, green foliated light falls through the trees or gathered autumn leaves burn at the corner; flower-loaded wagons wheel by while the flower seller sings his wares; in the dawn one occasionally hears a cock crow, for there is a lady with a garden who keeps hens and a rooster. On winter nights, when the wind brings the farewell callings of boats outward bound and carries across rooftops the chimney smoke of evening fires, there is a sense, evanescent but authentic as the firelight's flicker, of time come circle, of ago's sweeter glimmerings recaptured.

Though I'd long been acquainted with the neighborhood, having now and then visited there, my closer association began two years ago when a friend bought a house on Willow Street. One mild May evening he asked me over to inspect it. I was most impressed; exceedingly envious. There were twenty-eight rooms, high-ceilinged, well proportioned, and twenty-eight workable, marble-manteled fireplaces. There was a beautiful staircase floating upward in white, swan-simple curves to a skylight of sunny amber-gold glass. The floors were fine, the real thing, hard lustrous timber; and the walls! In 1820, when the house was built, men knew how to make walls—thick as a buffalo, immune to the mightiest cold, the meanest heat.

French doors led to a spacious rear porch reminiscent of Louisiana. A porch canopied, completely submerged, as though under a lake of leaves, by an ancient but admirably vigorous vine weighty with grapelike bunches of wisteria. Beyond, a garden: a tulip tree, a blossoming pear, a perched black-and-red bird bending a feathery branch of forsythia.

In the twilight, we talked, my friend and I. We sat on the porch consulting Martinis—I urged him to have one more, another. It got to be quite late, he began to see my point: Yes, twenty-eight rooms *were* rather a lot; and yes, it seemed only *fair* that I should have some of them.

That is how I came to live in the yellow brick house on Willow Street.

Often a week passes without my "going to town," or "crossing the bridge," as neighbors call a trip to Manhattan. Mystified friends, suspecting provincial stagnation, inquire: "But what do you *do* over there?" Let me tell you, life can be pretty exciting around here. Remember Colonel Rudolf Abel, the Russian secret agent, the biggest spy ever caught in America, head of the whole damned apparatus? Know where they nabbed him? Right here! smack on Fulton Street! Trapped him in a building between David Semple's fine-foods store and Frank Gambuzza's television repair shop. Frank, grinning as though he'd done the job himself, had his picture in *Life;* so did the waitress at the Music Box Bar, the colonel's favorite watering hole. A peevish few of us couldn't fathom why our pictures weren't in *Life* too. Frank, the Music Box Bar girl, they weren't the only people who knew the colonel. Such a gentleman-like gentleman: one would never have *supposed.* . . .

I confess, we don't catch spies every day. But most days are supplied with stimulants: in the harbor some exotic freighter to investigate; a bird of strange plumage resting among the wisteria; or, and how exhilarating an occurrence it is, a newly arrived shipment at Knapp's. Knapp's is a set of shops, really a series of storerooms resembling caverns, clustered together on Fulton near Pineapple Street. The proprietor—that is too modest a designation for so commanding a figure—the czar, the Aga Khan of these paradisal emporiums is Mr. George Knapp, known to his friends as Father.

Father is a world traveler. Cards arrive: he is in Seville, now Copenhagen, now Milan, next week Manchester, everywhere and all the while on a gaudy spending spree. Buying: blue crockery from a Danish castle. Pink apothecary jars from an old London pharmacy. English brass, Barcelona lamps, Battersea boxes, French paperweights, Italian witch balls, Greek icons, Venetian blackamoors, Spanish saints, Korean cabinets; and junk, glorious junk, a jumble of ragged dolls, broken buttons, a stuffed kangaroo, an aviary of owls under a great glass bell, the playing pieces of obsolete games, the paper moneys of defunct governments, an ivory umbrella cane *sans* umbrella, crested chamber pots and mustache mugs and irreparable clocks, cracked violins, a sundial that weighs seven hundred pounds, skulls, snake vertebrae, elephants' hoofs, sleigh bells and Eskimo carvings and mounted swordfish, medieval milkmaid stools, rusted firearms and flaking waltz-age mirrors.

Then Father comes home to Brooklyn, his treasures trailing after him. Uncrated, added to the already perilous clutter, the blackamoors prance in the marvelous gloom, the swordfish glide through the store's Atlantic-depth dusk. Eventually they will go: fancier *antiquaires,* and anonymous mere beauty lovers, will come, cart them away. Meanwhile, poke around. You're certain to find a plum; and it may be a peach. That paperweight— the one imprisoning a Baccarat dragonfly. If you want it, take it now: tomorrow, assuredly the day after, will see it on Fifty-Seventh Street at quintuple the tariff.

Father has a partner, his wife Florence. She is from Panama, is handsome, fresh-colored and tall, trim enough to look well in the trousers she affects, a woman of proud posture and, vis-à-vis customers, of nearly eccentric curtness, take-it-or-go disdain—but then, poor soul, she is under the discipline of not being herself permitted to sell, even quote a price. Only Father, with his Macaulayan memory, his daz- zling ability to immediately lay hold of any item in the dizzying maze, is so allowed. Brooklyn-born, water- front-bred, always hatted and usually wearing a wet cold cigar, a stout, short, round powerhouse with one arm, with a strutting walk, a rough-guy voice, shy ner- vous sensitive eyes that blink when irritation makes him stutter, Father is nevertheless an aesthete. A tough aesthete who takes no guff, will not quibble over his evaluations, just declares: "Put it down!" and, "Get it Manhattan half the money, I give it yuh free." They are an excellent couple, the Knapps. I explore their museum several times a week, and toward October, when a Franklin stove in the shape of a witch hut warms the air and Florence serves cider accompanied by a damp delicious date-nut bread she bakes in dis- carded coffee-cans, never miss a day. Occasionally, on these festive afternoons, Father will gaze about him, blink-blink his eyes with vague disbelief, then, as though his romantic accumulations were closing round him in a manner menacing, observe: "I got to be crazy. Putting my heart in a fruitcake business like this. And the *investment.* The money alone! Honest, in your honest opinion, wouldn't you say I'm crazy?"

Certainly not. If, however, Mrs. Cornelius Oost- huizen were to beg the question—

It seems improbably that someone of Mrs. Oost- huizen's elevation should have condescended to distin-

guish me with her acquaintance. I owe it all to a pound
of dog meat. What happened was: the butcher's boy
delivered a purchase of mine which, by error, included
hamburger meant to go to Mrs. O. Recognizing her
name on the order slip, and having often remarked her
house, a garnet-colored château in mood remindful of
the old Schwab mansion on Manhattan's Riverside
Drive, I thought of taking round the package myself,
not dreaming to meet the fine lady, but, at most, ambitious for a moment's glance into her fortunate preserve. Fortunate, for it boasted, so I'd had confided
to me, a butler and staff of six. Not that this is
the Height's sole *maison de luxe:* we are blessed with
several exponents of limousine life—but unarguably,
Mrs. O. is *la regina di tutti.*

Approaching her property, I noticed a person in Per-
sian lamb very vexedly punching the bell, pounding a
brass knocker. "God damn you, Mabel," she said to the
door; then turned, glared at me as I climbed the steps—
a tall intimidating replica of frail unforbidding Miss
Marianne Moore (who, it may be recalled, is a Brooklyn lady too). Pale lashless eyes, razor lips, hair a silver
fuzz. "Ah, *you.* I know you," she accused me, as behind
her the door was opened by an Irish crone wearing an
ankle-length apron. "So. I supposed you've come to
sign the petition? Very good of you, I'm sure." Mum-
bling an explanation, muttering servile civilities, I conveyed the butcher's parcel from my hands to hers; she,
as though I'd tossed her a rather rotten fish, dangled it
gingerly until the maid remarked: "Ma'am, 'tis Miss
Mary's meat the good lad's brought."

"Indeed. Then don't stand there, Mabel. Take it."
And, regarding me with a lessening astonishment that I
could not, in her behalf, reciprocate: "Wipe your boots,
come in. We will discuss the petition. Mabel, send
Murphy with some Bristol and biscuit. . . . Oh? At the
dentist's! When I *asked* him *not* to tamper with that
tooth. What hellish nonsense," she swore, as we passed
into a hatrack-vestibule. "Why didn't he go to the hyp-
notist, as I told him? Mary! Mary! Mary," she said when
now appeared a friendly nice dog of cruel pedigree:
spaniel *cum* chow attached to the legs of a dachshund,

"I believe Mabel has your lunch. Mabel, take Miss Mary to the kitchen. And we will have our biscuits in the Red Room."

The room, in which red could be discerned only in a bowl of porcelain roses and a basket of marzipan strawberries, contained velvet-swagged windows that commanded a pulse-quickening prospect: sky, skyline, far away a wooded slice of Staten Island. In other respects, the room, a heavy confection, cumbersome, humorless, a hunk of Beidermeier pastry, did not recommend itself. "It was my grandmother's bedroom; my father preferred it as a parlor. Cornelius, Mr. Oosthuizen, died here. Very suddenly: while listening at the radio to the Roosevelt person. An attack. Brought on by anger and cigars. I'm sure you won't ask permission to smoke. Sit down. . . . Not there. There, by the window. Now here, it *should* be here, somewhere, in this drawer? Could it be upstairs? Damn Murphy, horrid man always meddling with my—no, I have it: the petition."

The document stated, and objected to, the plans of a certain minor religious sect that had acquired a half-block of houses on the Heights which they planned to flatten and replace with a dormitory building for the benefit of their Believers. Appended to it were some dozen protesting signatures; the Misses Seeley had signed, and Mr. Arthur Veere Vinson, Mrs. K. Mackaye Brownlowe—descendants of the children in the meadow, the old-guard survivors of *their* neighborhood's evilest hours, those happy few who regularly attended Mrs. O.'s black-tie-sit-downs. She wasted no eloquence on the considerable merit of their complaint; simply, "Sign it," she ordered, a Lady Catherine de Brough instructing a Mr. Collins.

Sherry came; and with it an assembly of cats. Scarred battlers with leprous fur and punch-drunk eyes. Mrs. O., motioning toward the least respectable of these, a tiger-striped marauder, told me: "This is the one you may take home. He's been with us a month, we've put him in splendid condition, I'm sure you'll be devoted. Dogs? What *sort* of dogs have you? Well, I don't approve the pure breeds. Anyone will give *them* a home. I took Miss Mary off the street. And Lovely

Louise, Mouse and Sweet William—my dogs, all my cats, too, came off the streets. Look below, there in the garden. Under the heaven tree. Those markings: graves are what you see, some as old as my childhood. The seashells are goldfish. The yellow coral, canaries. That white stone is a rabbit; that cross of pebbles: my favorite, the first Mary—angel girl, went bathing in the river and caught a fatal chill. I used to tease Cornelius, Mr. Oosthuizen, told him, ha-ha, told him I planned to put him there with the rest of my darlings. Ha-ha, he wasn't amused, not at all. So, I mean to say, your having dogs doesn't signify: Billy here has such spirit, *he* can hold his own. No, I insist you have him. For I can't keep him much longer, he's a disturbing influence; and if I let him loose, he'll run back to his bad old life in the St. George alley. I wouldn't want *that* on my conscience if I were you."

Her persuasions failed; in consequence our parting was cool. Yet at Christmas she sent me a card, a Cartier engraving of the heaven tree protecting the bones in its sad care. And once, encountering her at the bakery, where we both were buying brownies, we discussed the impudent disregard her petition had received: alas, the wreckers had wrecked, the brethren were building. On the same occasion, she shame-on-you informed me that Billy the cat, released from her patronage, had indeed returned to the sinful ways of the St. George alley.

The St. George alley, adjoining a small cinema, is a shadowy shelter for vagrants: wino derelicts wandered over the bridge from Chinatown and the Bowery share it with other orphaned, gone-wild creatures: cats, as many as minnows in a stream, who gather in their greatest numbers toward nightfall; for then, as darkness happens, strange-eyed women, not unlike those black-clothed fanatics who haunt the cat arenas in Rome, go stealing through the alley with caressing hisses and sacks of crumbled salmon. (Which isn't to suggest that Mrs. O. is one who indulges in this somehow unhealthy hobby: regarding animals, her actions, while perhaps a bit overboard, are kindly meant, and not untypical of the Heights, where a high percentage of the pet population has been adopted off the streets.

Astonishing, really, the amount of lost strays who roam their way into the neighborhood, as though instinct informed them they'd find someone here who couldn't abide being followed through the rain, but would, instead, lead them home, boil milk, and call Dr. Wasserman, Bernie, our smart-as-they-come young vet whose immaculate hospital resounds with the music of Bach concertos and the barkings of mending beasts.)

Just now, in connection with these notes, I was hunting through a hieroglyphic shambles I call my journal. Odd, indeed the oddest, jottings—a majority of which conceal from me their meanings. God knows what "Thunder on Cobra Street" refers to. Or "A diarrhea of platitudes in seventeen tongues." Unless it is intended to describe a most tiresome local person, a linguist terribly talkative in many languages though articulate in none. However, "Took T&G to G&T" does make sense.

The first initials represent two friends, the latter a restaurant not far away. You must have heard of it, Gage & Tollner. Like Kolb's and Antoine's in New Orleans, Gage & Tollner is a last-century enterprise that has kept in large degree its founding character. The shaky dance of its gaslight chandeliers is not a period-piece hoax; nor do the good plain marble-topped tables, the magnificent array of gold-edge mirrors, seem sentimental affectations—rather, it is a testament to the seriousness of the proprietors, who have obliged us by letting the place stay much as it was that opening day in 1874. One mightn't suppose it, for in the atmosphere there is none of the briny falderal familiar to such aquariums, but the specialty is sea food. The best. Chowders the doughtiest down-Easter must approve. Lobsters that would appease Nero. Myself, I am a soft-shelled-crab *aficionado:* a plate of sautéed crabs, a halved lemon, a glass of chilled Chablis: most satisfactory. The waiters, too, dignified but swift-to-smile Negroes who take pride in their work, contribute to the goodness of Gage & Tollner; on the sleeves of their very laundered jackets they sport military-style chevrons awarded according to the number of years each has served; and, *were* this the Army, some would be generals.

Nearby, there is another restaurant, a fraction less distinguished, but of similar vintage and virtually the same menu: Joe's—Joe being, by the way, an attractive young lady. On the far fringes of the Heights, just before Brooklyn becomes Brooklyn again, there is a street of Gypsies with Gypsy cafés (have your future foretold and be tattooed while sipping tankards of Moorish tea); there is also an Arab-Armenian quarter sprinkled with spice-saturated restaurants where one can buy, hot from the oven, a crusty sort of pancake frosted with sesame seed—once in a while I carry mine down to the waterfront, intending to share with the gulls; but, gobbling as I go, none is ever left. On a summer's evening a stroll across the bridge, with cool winds singing through the steel shrouds, with stars moving about above and ships below, can be intoxicating, particularly if you are headed toward the roasting-pork, sweet-and-sour aromas of Chinatown.

Another journal notation reads, "At last a face in the ghost hotel!" Which means: after months of observation, in all climates at all hours, I'd sighted someone in a window of a haunted-seeming riverfront building that stands on Water Street at the foot of the Heights. A lonely hotel I often make the destination of my walks: because I think it romantic, in aggravated moments imagine retiring there, for it is as secluded as Mt. Athos, remoter than the Krak Chevalier in the mountains of wildest Syria. Daytimes the location, a dead-end Chiricoesque piazza facing the river, is little disturbed; at night, not at all: not a sound, except foghorns and a distant traffic whisper from the bridge which bulks above. Peace, and the shivering glow of gliding-by tugs and ferries.

The hotel is three-storied. Sunstruck scraps of reflected river-shine, and broken, jigsaw images of the bridge waver across the windows; but beyond the glass nothing stirs: the rooms, despite contradictory evidence, milk bottles on sills, a hat on a hook, unmade beds and burning bulbs, appear unoccupied: never a soul to be seen. Like the sailors of the *Marie Celeste,* the guests, hearing a knock, must have opened their doors to a stranger who swallowed them whole. Could it be, perhaps it *was*, the stranger himself that I saw?—"At last a face in the ghost hotel!" I glimpsed him just the once, one April afternoon one cloudless blue day; and he, a balding man in an undershirt, hurled up a window, flexed hairy arms, yawned hugely, hugely inhaled the river breeze—was gone. No, on careful second thought, I will never set foot in that hotel. For I should either be devoured or have my mystery dispelled. As children we are sensitive to mystery: locked boxes, whisperings behind closed doors, the what-thing that lurks yonder in the trees, waits in every stretch between street lamps; but as we grow older all is too explainable, the capacity to invent pleasurable alarm recedes: too bad, a pity—throughout our lives we ought to believe in ghost hotels.

Close by the hotel begins a road that leads along the river. Silent miles of warehouses with shuttered wooden windows, docks resting on the water like sea spiders. From May through September, *la saison pour la plage,* these docks are diving boards for husky raga-muffins—while perfumed apes, potentates of the waterfront but once dock-divers themselves, cruise by steering two-toned (banana-tomato) car concoctions. Crane-carried tractors and cotton bales and unhappy cattle sway above the holds of ships bound for Bahia, for Bremen, for ports spelling their names in Oriental calligraphy. Provided one has made waterfront friends, it is sometimes possible to board the freighters, carouse and sun yourself: you may even be asked to lunch—and I, for one, am always quick to accept, embarrassingly so if the hosts are Scandinavian: they always set a superior table from larders brimming with smoked "taste thrills" and iced aquavit. Avoid the Greek ships, however: very poor cuisine, no liquor served except *ouzo*, a sickly licorice syrup; and, at least in the opinion of this pan-handler, the grub on French freighters by no means meets the standards one might reasonably expect.

The tugboat people are usually good for a cup of coffee, and in wintry weather, when the river is tossing surf, what joy to take refuge in a stove-heated tug cabin and thaw out with a mug of the blackest Java. Now and again along the route minuscule beaches occur, and once, it was around sunset on a quiet Sunday, I saw on one of them something that made me look twice, and twice more: still it seemed a vision. Every kind of sailor is common enough here, even saronged East Indians, even the giant Senegalese, their onyx arms afire with blue, with yellow tattooed flowers, with saucy torsos and garish *graffiti* (Je t'aime, Hard Luck, Mimi Chang, Adios Amigo). Runty Russians, too—one sees them about, flap-flapping in their pajama-like costumes. But the barefooted sailors on the beach, the three I saw reclining there, profiles set against the sundown, seemed mythical as mermen: more exactly, mermaids— for their hair, striped with albino streaks, was lady-length, a savage fiber falling to their shoulders; and in their ears gold rings glinted. Whether plenipotentiaries from the pearl-floored palace of Poseidon or mariners merely, Viking-tressed seamen out of the Gothic North languishing after a long and barberless voyage, they are included permanently in my memory's curio cabinet: an object to be revolved in the light that way and this, like those crystal lozenges with secretive carvings sealed inside.

After consideration, "Thunder on Cobra Street" does become decipherable. On the Heights there is no Cobra Street, though a street exists that suits the name, a steep downhill incline leading to a dark sector of the dockyards. Not a true part of the Heights neighborhood, it lies, like a serpent at the gates, on the outmost periphery. Seedy hangouts, beer-sour bars and bitter candy stores mingle among the eroding houses, the multifamily dwellings that architecturally range from time-blackened brownstone to magnified concepts of Mississippi privy.

Here, the gutters are acrawl with Cobras; that is, a gang of "juvenile" delinquents: COBRA, the word is stamped on their sweat shirts, painted, sometimes in letters that shine with a fearful phosphorescence, across the backs of their leather jackets. The steep street is within their ugly estate, a bit of their "turf," as they term it; an infinitesimal bit, for the Cobras, a powerful cabala, cast owning eyes on acres of metropolitan terrain. I am not brave—*au contraire;* quite frankly these fellows, may they be twelve years old or twenty, set my heart thumping like a sinner's at Sunday meeting. Nevertheless, when it has been a matter of convenience to pass through this section of their domain, I've compelled my nerves to accept the challenge.

On the last venture, and perhaps it will remain the last, I was carrying a good camera. The sun was unseen in a sky that ought to either rumble or rain. Rackety children played skip-rope, while a lamppost-lot of idle elders looked on, dull-faced and drooping: a denim-painted, cowboy-booted gathering of Cobras. Their eyes, their asleep sick insolent eyes, swerved on me as I climbed the street. I crossed to the opposite curb; then *knew*, without needing to verify it, that the Cobras had uncoiled and were sliding toward me. I heard them whistling; and the children hushed, the skip-rope ceased swishing. Someone—a pimpled purple birth-mark bandit-masked the lower half of his face—said, "Hey yuh, Whitey, lemmeseeduhcamra." Quicken one's step? Pretend not to hear? But every alternative seemed explosive. "Hey, Whitey, hey yuh, takemuh-pitchawantcha?"

Thunder salvaged the moment. Thunder that rolled, crashed down the street like a truck out of control. We all looked up, a sky ripe for storm stared back. I shouted, "Rain! Rain!" and ran. Ran for the Heights, that safe citadel, that bourgeois bastion. Tore along the Esplanade—where the nice young mothers were racing their carriages against the coming disaster. Caught my breath under the thrashing leaves of troubled elms, rushed on: saw the flower-wagon man struggling with his thunder-frightened horse. Saw, twenty yards ahead, then ten, five, then none, the yellow house on Willow Street. Home! And happy to be.

———————

Novelist and short-story writer TRUMAN CAPOTE *(1924-84) was born in New Orleans but moved to New York City in 1942, where he got a job with* The New Yorker. *His short story "Miriam" won the O. Henry Award in 1946, and his first novel,* Other Voices, Other Rooms, *was published in*

1948. This was followed by two books set in the South, A Tree of Night and Other Stories *(1949) and* The Grass Harp *(1951),* The Muses Are Heard *(1956), and a romantic comedy about life in New York,* Breakfast at Tiffany's *(1958).*

In 1966 he published another collection of stories, A Christmas Memory, *as well as* In Cold Blood, *his monumental investigation of the senseless murder of a Kansas family by two young men. Collections of his journalistic pieces include* Local Color *(1950),* Selected Writings *(1963),* The Dogs Bark *(1973), and* Music for Chameleons *(1981).*

"A House on the Heights" is from The Selected Writings of Truman Capote.

John Updike

Accumulation

Busbound out of New York
through New Jersey,
one sees a mountain of trash,
a hill of inhuman dimension, with trucks
filing up its slopes like ants
and filing down empty, back to the city
for more.
Green plastic flutters from the mountain's sides,
and flattened tin glints through the fill
that bulldozer treads have tamped
in swatches like enormous cloth.
One wonders, does it have a name,
this hill,
and has any top been set
to its garbagy growing?

Miles pass.
A cut by the side of the eight-
lane concrete highway
(where spun rubber and dripped oil
accumulate)
has exposed a great gesture of shale —
sediment hardened, coarse page by page,
then broken and swirled like running water,
then tipped and infolded by time,
and now cut open like a pattern of wood
when grain is splayed to make a butterfly.
Gray aeons stand exposed in this gesture,
this half-unfurling
on the way to a fuller unfurling

wherein our lives will have been of less moment
than grains of sand tumbled back and forth
by the solidifying tides.

Our past
lies at the end of this journey.
The days bringing each their detritus,
the years minute by minute have lifted
us free of our home,
that muck whose every particle—
the sidewalk cracks, the gravel alleys—
we hugged to our minds as matrix,
a cozy ooze.
What mountains we are,
all impalpable, and
perishable as tissue
crumpled into a ball and tossed upon the flames!
Lives, piled upon lives.
The faces outside the stopped bus window
have the doughy, stoic look of those
who grew up where I did,
ages ago.

———————

Novelist, short-story writer, poet, and twice winner of a
Pulitzer Prize, JOHN UPDIKE was born in 1932 in
Shillington, Pennsylvania. He moved to New York in 1955 to
work for The New Yorker as a "Talk of the Town" reporter
and then to Massachusetts, to concentrate on fiction and
poetry and to raise a family.

John Updike's first book of verse, The Carpentered Hen,
was published in 1958. The first of the Rabbit novels, Rabbit
Run, appeared in 1960. Then came Rabbit Redux, Rabbit
Is Rich, and Rabbit at Rest. The latter two received
Pulitzers. Rabbit Is Rich also won a National Book Critics'
Circle Award and a National Book Award. Updike also won
a 1963 National Book Award for The Centaur.

Updike's books of poetry include Telephone Poles, The
Dance of the Solids, and Facing Nature.

The poem "Accumulation" was published in his 1985
collection Facing Nature.

Jamaica Kincaid

Putting Myself Together

Last Halloween, my daughter—her name is Annie; she is ten years old—decided that the scary person she wanted to impersonate was the Countess Dracula, and so, without even knowing whether there ever was such a creature, I set out to make her a costume. I bought yards of gray and black lace, some black satin ribbon, and black thread. I stitched the black and gray lace together by hand to make a cape, and ran the black satin ribbon through a hem I had made along the neckline. The cape pleased her very much: I could see that from the way she twisted and turned while standing in front of the looking glass. Underneath the cape she wore an old black dress of mine that I had grown too fat to fit into any longer. She painted her face white, then blackened the area around her eyes with a pencil made for that purpose, drew long lines of red from the corner of her mouth to under her chin with my lipstick, and colored her lips with lipstick of another shade.

She also wore a hat—a black hat, made of corded velvet, that was flat and round, like a dinner plate. It had a tassel in the center—a piece of the corded velvet that had been deliberately unravelled by its maker. There was an elastic band that ran from one side to the other and was worn under the chin or tucked under the hairline in back, for anchoring the hat on the head. My daughter wore the band tucked under a bun I had made of her hair in the back. She did not scare anyone; she looked very beautiful. My daughter lives in a small village in a small state, and, when she stepped out to trick-

or-treat, the neighbors greeted her with enthusiasm. Her hat, especially, was admired.

That hat was one I used to wear all the time. I bought it at a store that sold old clothes, but I cannot remember if it was a store called Early Halloween and owned by a woman named Joyce, or a store called Harriet Love and owned by a woman named Harriet Love, or a store whose name I can't remember but which was owned by a woman named Enid. This was many years ago; I must have been twenty-five when I bought it, because I remember wearing it on my twenty-sixth birthday. I was born in 1949. My twenty-sixth birthday was the birthday when I felt old and used up—I had left home when I was sixteen, and ten years in a young life is a long time—and someone had taken me to dinner at a restaurant called the SoHo Charcuterie. While eating some absurd combination of food (or so it then struck me; no doubt it would seem quite ordinary now), I wondered aloud whether, at my advanced age, I would ever have any new relationships to look forward to.

I lived in New York. It was not the forbidding place then that it has become to me now. I was not afraid in those days. I used to tell perfect strangers how they should behave in public—that is, if I saw them misbehaving in public. My hat was firmly strapped in place. I was invulnerable. And if, for my interference, they threatened to kill me, I would inform them that killing me was not a proper response. None of them killed me; they only threatened to do so.

I had found a place to live near Bellevue Hospital, in a small apartment above a restaurant. The exhaust fan of the restaurant was just outside the window that I slept next to, on a lumpy rollout bed. The noise the exhaust fan made felt like such an injustice that I went to the owner of the restaurant to ask if he could be more considerate and close his restaurant earlier in the evening. The restaurant was owned by a family who came from somewhere in Asia. He did not say yes, he did not say no; everything went on just as it had done before.

I had no money. In the middle of the night, the landlord would call me up to demand the back months' rent. After a while, I did not answer the phone so late at night. I looked for a job, but I was not qualified to do anything respectable. On Sunday afternoons, I worked in a place where people rented bicycles. I changed my name, and started telling people I knew that I was a writer. This declaration went without comment. In this apartment, I slept with a man who used to buy me dinner. I liked fish of every kind, but I never ate much, no matter how hungry I had been when I sat down. When I went out with him, it was only to eat fish. Most of what we did together was inside the apartment, and that was soon over. In the middle of kissing me and doing other things, he would ask me to tell him of the other people I had kissed, but the list was so short then that he soon lost interest in kissing me and doing the other things. If only he had waited—for the list would become long and varied. So long and varied that if I met him today I would not be able to identify his face or any other part of him.

Soon I moved to an apartment on West Twenty-second Street. It was on the third floor; the walk up was tiring, but perhaps was good for me. The apartment was at the front of the building; it had two rooms and a small kitchen, which could hold no more than two people at once. The bathroom had a porcelain bathtub, and I used to lie in it and give myself coffee enemas. I don't remember who recommended such a thing to me; I do remember that once the coffee was too hot and I burned my bottom all the way up inside.

I slept on the floor in one of the rooms, because I could not afford a bed. I slept at first on newspapers and then on an old mattress I found on the street; someone gave me sheets, though I no longer remember who. I know that I slept more comfortably on the mattress than I did on the newspapers. The other room was empty except for a large old office desk, an old typewriter, and books that were piled on the floor. I was hungry; I could not afford to eat much real food. In the refrigerator I kept yogurt, a tin of brewer's yeast, orange juice, powdered skim milk, and many different kinds of vitamins; in the freezer compartment I kept slices of bananas. It was the refrigerator of someone who lived alone.

Below me lived a man who talked to himself: he had been in a war, and after that he never worked again—only talked to himself. On the ground floor, a man and a woman lived in the apartment they'd had since they were married, sometime in the nineteen-twenties. How the landlord wished them dead, for they paid a low rent. At first, the landlord had no luck at all: then the husband died, and the wife was very sad. I know she was very sad because she told me so. I don't know what became of her; I lost interest. Nothing happened to me as a result of all this.

In the New York days of my twenties, the streets were wide and open and always sunny, not narrow and closed and dark, the way they are now when I walk down the same streets. When I lived in the house on Twenty-second Street, I used to get up late in the morning—so late that the morning was by then quite stale, on the brink of being another time of day altogether. Then I would parade around the apartment without my clothes on, and I would bathe and, if it was the right day of the week, take my enema. I would have a small meal of something liquid, for I still would not and could not satisfy my appetite—any of my appetites. And then, finally, I would put on some clothes. This was not done carelessly.

I was very thin, because I had no money to eat properly, and because what little money I had I used to buy clothes. Being very thin, however, I looked good in clothes. I loved the way I looked all dressed up. I bought hats, I bought shoes, I bought stockings and garter belts to hold them up, I bought handbags, I bought suits, I bought blouses, I bought dresses, I bought skirts, and I bought jackets that did not match the skirts. I used to spend hours happily buying clothes to wear. Of course, I could not afford to buy my clothes in an actual store, a department store. Instead, they came from used-clothing stores, and they were clothes of a special kind, stylish clothes from a long-ago time—twenty or thirty or forty years earlier. They were clothes worn by people who were alive when I had not been;

by people who were far more prosperous than I could imagine being. As a result, it took me a long time to get dressed, for I could not easily decide what combination of people, inconceivably older and more prosperous than I was, I wished to impersonate that day. It was sometimes hours after I started the process of getting dressed that I finally left my house and set off into the world.

My world at that time was a restaurant, someone else's apartment, or any other place where I had agreed to meet a friend; the location was almost never chosen by me. One rainy day in spring, I left my house after my elaborate dressing ritual, and when I was two blocks away from my house and two blocks away from the subway a wind came and blew my hat off my head. My hat, the one made of black corded velvet, landed in the gutter. When I picked it up, it was wet and dirty. That was a moment in my life when I could not take much more of sad realities: I turned around and walked home, and when I got there I took off my clothes and lay down on my bed. When my friends called to inquire why they would not be seeing me that day, I only repeated, again and again, the words "Because my hat fell into the gutter."

The day that the wind blew my hat into the gutter, my hair was not in its natural state, which would have been black and long and thick and tightly curled. I had left it tightly curled but I had made it short and blond. Had I worn this hat with my hair in its natural state, I would have been wearing it with sincerity, with good intentions; I would have meant the hat to be a hat. But this was not so at all. With my hair in its natural state, such a hat—a style of hat that had been popular when my mother was a young woman—would not have appealed to me. For, really, it was impractical for a modern woman, suitable only as a costume. To wear such a hat, I needed to transform my hair. And should I say that transforming my hair was a way of transforming myself? I had no consciousness of such things then.

I did not know then that I had embarked on something called self-invention, the making of a type of person that did not exist in the place where I was born—a place far away from New York and with a climate quite unlike the one that existed in New York. I wanted to be a writer; I was a person with opinions, and I wanted them to matter to other people. I can admit that about myself as I was then; I cannot admit it about myself as I am now. It was just when I had despaired of ever becoming a writer that I applied for a secretarial position at the magazine *Mademoiselle*. I was twenty-four years old. To my job interview I wore a very short skirt, a nylon blouse under which I wore no brassiere, red shoes with very high heels and white anklets, and no hat to cover my short-cropped blond hair. *Mademoiselle* did not hire me. The people I talked to there had been so kind and sweet toward me, both on the phone and in person, that it took me a very long time to understand that they would never hire me. I wondered if it was my shoes and the anklets, or perhaps my hair. I was speaking of these things to a friend, wondering out loud why had I not been offered a job at *Mademoiselle* when the people there seemed to like me so much, and he said, But how could I have applied to a place like that—didn't I know that they never hired black girls? And I thought, But how was I to know that I was a black girl? I never pass myself in a corridor and say, I am a black girl. I never see myself coming toward me as I come round a bend and say, There is that black girl coming toward me. How was I really to know such a thing?

This life went on, this life of being young and in New York. I wondered if I would be young forever; I wondered if I would live in New York forever. Neither prospect gave me pleasure. What did I yearn for? In the New York of my youth, the evenings were too long, no matter what the time of year was. What I did with some people I knew was to drink. What I did with other people was to go and buy drugs from a man who kept a Physicians' Desk Reference on a table in his very pleasant living room. We would sit on his comfortable sofa and order drugs. He would present us with a tray of tablets, small and in many colors—it reminded me of going to a shop in my childhood, where I would stand behind a counter and gaze at the jars full of sweets,

sweets I was too poor to afford more than one or two of. In this man's pleasant living room, we would gaze upon his tray of colorful tablets, and we would decide which ones to buy on the basis of our attraction to the colors, and then look up the results they were expected to give in the Physicians' Desk Reference. On a day we were not visiting him, he was taken away by the police, and I have not heard of him since.

There were other ways of filling those long evenings. The list of the people who kissed me and did other things with me became so long that now I cannot remember the names on it. And though I remember many faces, I cannot say with certainty whose face I allowed to kiss me and do other things to me, and whose face I stood with in the dark before we shook hands and said good night. It was always in the dark, at night. There was a reason for that, perhaps practical, perhaps not; to give a reason now, I would have to make it up. Sometimes I meet people who say to me that they knew me well very long ago, and I can only wonder, How well could that have been? Sometimes I meet people who tell me they knew me in those days and they mention an event. I can remember the event, but I cannot remember them. At least, I don't recognize their faces; perhaps I would recognize other parts of them. But even the act of recollection is exhausting. My youth was exhausting, it was dangerous, and it is a miracle that I grew out of it unscathed.

Really, the list of those who went in and out of my bed was not so long; it was only a long list when compared with the sad facts regarding a part of my upbringing. I was brought up to marry one man and to have children with this one man, and this one man would be the only man to go in and out of my bed. It was understood that this one man would go in and out of the bed of many other women and have many children with them, which is not to say that he would have been a father to them any more than he would have been a husband to me. The person I had become, the person I had made myself into, did not place an obligation on anyone I allowed into my bed. But this was not without its snags and inconveniences. So many people are not as pleasing to look at in the light of the sun as they are to look at by the light of a lamp. It would happen that some of them left their smell with me, and it took the smell of many others to get rid of the one smell. It would happen that I would wake up, my throat raw from hours of gasping, my tongue sore from being fastened between my teeth, suppressing cries of ecstasy or boredom.

One year, I created a Halloween costume for myself by buying a dozen and a half bananas made of plastic (the sort used in some homes as a centerpiece for the dining table), stringing them together so that they made a skirt of sorts, and then tying the whole thing around my waist. I wore nothing underneath, had nothing to cover the rest of my body except an old fur coat that I had bought in an old-fur-coat store for thirty dollars. When I arrived at the party, of course, I removed the coat. The hair on the other parts of my body was not the same color as the hair on my head. I wore no hat to conceal this; it was not a detail that concerned me. And the evening passed, joining the other long evenings that were so exhausting to fill. What did I want? Did I know? I was twenty-five, I was twenty-six, I was twenty-seven, I was twenty-eight. At thirty, I was married.

———

JAMAICA KINCAID, *born Elaine Potter Richardson on the Caribbean island of Antigua, moved to New York in 1965 to work as an au pair. She later studied photography at the New School for Social Research and at Franconia College in New Hampshire. In 1973 she published "When I Was Seventeen" in* Ingenue *magazine and changed her name to Jamaica Kincaid. The following year the first of her many "Talk of the Town" pieces appeared in* The New Yorker. *She joined* The New Yorker *staff in 1976.*

Among her published works are Annie John, A Small Place, *and* Lucy. Autobiography of My Mother *will be published in the fall of 1995. "Putting Myself Together" is an autobiographical essay published in* The New Yorker *in 1995.*

5

My Heart Was in Manhattan

Henry James

The American Scene: New York Revisited

I

The single impression or particular vision most answering to the greatness of the subject would have been, I think, a certain hour of large circumnavigation that I found prescribed, in the fulness of the spring, as the almost immediate crown of a return from the Far West. I had arrived at one of the transpontine stations of the Pennsylvania Railroad; the question was of proceeding to Boston, for the occasion, without pushing through the terrible town—why "terrible," to my sense, in many ways, I shall presently explain—and the easy and agreeable attainment of this great advantage was to embark on one of the mightiest (as appeared to me) of train-bearing barges and, descending the western waters, pass round the bottom of the city and remount the other current to Harlem; all without "losing touch" of the Pullman that had brought me from Washington. This absence of the need of losing touch, this breadth of effect, as to the whole process, involved in the prompt floating of the huge concatenated cars not only without arrest or confusion, but as for positive prodigal beguilement of the artless traveller, had doubtless much to say to the ensuing state of mind, the happily-excited and amused view of the great face of New York. The extent, the ease, the energy, the quantity and number, all notes scattered about as if, in the whole business and in the splendid light, nature and science were joyously romping together, might have been taking on again, for their symbol, some collective presence of great circling and plunging, hovering and perching seabirds, white-winged images of the spirit, of the restless freedom of the Bay. The Bay had always, on other opportunities, seemed to blow its immense character straight into one's face—coming "at" you, so to speak, bearing down on you, with the full force of a thousand prows of steamers seen exactly on the line of their lon-gitudinal axis; but I had never before been so conscious of its boundless cool assurance or seemed to see its genius so grandly at play. This was presumably indeed because I had never before enjoyed the remarkable adventure of taking in so much of the vast bristling promontory from the water, of ascending the East River, in especial, to its upper diminishing expanses.

Something of the air of the occasion and of the mood of the moment caused the whole picture to speak with its largest suggestion; which suggestion is irre-sistible when once it is sounded clear. It is all, absolutely, an expression of things lately and currently *done,* done on a large impersonal stage and on the basis of inordinate gain—it is not an expression of any other matters whatever; and yet the sense of the scene (which had at several previous junctures, as well, put forth to my imagination its power) was commanding and thrilling, was in certain lights almost charming. So it befell, exactly, that an element of mystery and wonder entered into the impression—the interest of trying to make out, in the absence of features of the sort usually supposed indispensable, the reason of the beauty and the joy. It is indubitably a "great" bay, a great harbour, but no one item of the romantic, or even of the pic-turesque, as commonly understood, contributes to its effect. The shores are low and for the most part depressingly furnished and prosaically peopled; the islands, though numerous, have not a grace to exhibit, and one thinks of the other, the real flowers of geogra-phy in this order, of Naples, of Capetown, of Sydney, of Seattle, of San Francisco, of Rio, asking how if *they* justify a reputation, New York should seem to justify one. Then, after all, we remember that there are reputa-tions and reputations; we remember above all the imaginative response to the conditions here presented may just happen to proceed from the intellectual

extravagance of the given observer. When this personage is open to corruption by almost any large view of an
intensity of life, his vibrations tend to become a matter
difficult even for *him* to explain. He may have to confess that the group of evident facts fails to account by
itself for the complacency of his appreciation. Therefore it is that I find myself rather backward with a perceived sanction, of an at all proportionate kind, for the
fine exhilaration with which, in this free wayfaring relation to them, the wide waters of New York inspire me.
There is the beauty of light and air, the great scale of
space, and, seen far away to the west, the open gates of
the Hudson, majestic in their degree, even at a distance,
and announcing still nobler things. But the real appeal,
unmistakably, is in that note of vehemence in the local
life of which I have spoken, for it is the appeal of a particular type of dauntless power.

The aspect the power wears then is indescribable; it
is the power of the most extravagant of cities, rejoicing,
as with the voice of the morning, in its might, its for-
tune, its unsurpassable conditions, and imparting to
every object and element, to the motion and expression
of every floating, hurrying, panting thing, to the throb
of ferries and tugs, to the plash of waves and the play of
winds and the glint of lights and the shrill of whistles
and the quality and authority of breeze-borne cries—all,
practically, a diffused, wasted clamour of *detonations*—
something of its sharp free accent and, above all, of its
sovereign sense of being "backed" and able to back. The
universal *applied* passion struck me as shining unprece-
dentedly out of the composition; in the bigness and
bravery and insolence, especially, of everything that
rushed and shrieked; in the air as of a great intricate
frenzied dance, half merry, half desperate, or at least half
defiant, performed on the huge watery floor. This
appearance of the bold lacing-together, across the
waters, of the scattered members of the monstrous
organism—lacing as by the ceaseless play of an enormous system of steam-shuttles or electric bobbins (I
scarce know what to call them), commensurate in form
with their infinite work—does perhaps more than anything else to give the pitch of the vision of energy. One

has the sense that the monster grows and grows, flinging abroad its loose limbs even as some unmannered young giant at his "larks," and that the binding stitches must for ever fly further and faster and draw harder; the future complexity of the web, all under the sky and over the sea, becoming thus that of some colossal set of clockworks, some steel-souled machine-room of brandished arms and hammering fists and opening and closing jaws. The immeasurable bridges are but as the horizontal sheaths of pistons working at high pressure, day and night, and subject, one apprehends with perhaps inconsistent gloom, to certain, to fantastic, to merciless multiplication. In the light of this apprehension indeed the breezy brightness of the Bay puts on the semblance of the vast white page that awaits beyond any other perhaps the black overscoring of science.

Let me hasten to add that its present whiteness is precisely its charming note,the frankest of the signs you recognize and remember it by. That is the distinction I was just feeling my way to name as the main ground of its doing so well, for effect, without technical scenery. There are great imposing ports—Glasgow and Liverpool and London—that have already their page blackened almost beyond redemption from any such light of the picturesque as can hope to irradiate fog and grime, and there are others, Marseilles and Constantinople say, or, for all I know to the contrary, New Orleans, that contrive to abound before everything else in colour, and so to make a rich and instant and obvious show. But memory and the actual impression keep investing New York with the tone, predominantly, of summer dawns and winter frosts, of sea-foam, of bleached sails and stretched awnings, of blanched hulls, of scoured decks, of new ropes, of polished brasses, of streamers clear in the blue air; and it is by this harmony, doubtless, that the projection of the individual character of the place, of the candour of its avidity and the freshness of its audacity, is most conveyed. The "tall buildings," which have so promptly usurped a glory that affects you as rather surprised, as yet, at itself, the multitudinous sky-scrapers standing up to the view, from the water, like extravagant pins in a cushion already over-planted, and stuck in as in the dark, anywhere and any-how, have at least the felicity of carrying out the fairness of tone, of taking the sun and the shade in the manner of towers of marble. They are not all of marble, I believe, by any means, even if some may be, but they are impu-dently new and still more impudently "novel"—this in common with so many other terrible things in Amer-ica—and they are triumphant payers of dividends; all of which uncontested and unabashed pride, with flash of innumerable windows and flicker of subordinate gilt attributions, is like the flare, up and down their long, narrow faces, of the lamps of some general permanent "celebration."

You see the pin-cushion in profile, so to speak, on passing between Jersey City and Twenty-third Street, but you get it broadside on, this loose nosegay of archi-tectural flowers, if you skirt the Battery, well out, and embrace the whole plantation. Then the "American beauty," the rose of interminable stem, becomes the token of the cluster at large—to that degree that, posi-tively, this is all that is wanted for emphasis of your final impression. Such growths, you feel, have confessedly arisen but to be "picked," in time, with a shears; nipped short off, by waiting fate, as soon as "science," applied to gain, has put upon the table, from far up its sleeve, some more winning card. Crowned not only with no history, but with no credible possibility of time for history, and consecrated by no uses save the commercial at any cost, they are simply the most piercing notes in that concert of the expensively provisional into which your supreme sense of New York resolves itself. They never begin to speak to you, in the manner of the builded majesties of the world as we have heretofore known such—towers or temples or fortresses or palaces—with the authority of things of permanence or even of things of long dura-tion. One story is good only till another is told, and sky-scrapers are the last word of economic ingenuity only till another word be written. This shall be possibly a word of still uglier meaning, but the vocabulary of thrift at any price shows boundless resources, and the con-sciousness of that truth, the consciousness of the finite, the menaced, the essentially *invented* state, twinkles

ever, to my perception, in the thousand glassy eyes of
these giants of the mere market. Such a structure as the
comparatively windowless bell-tower of Giotto, in Florence, looks supremely serene in its beauty. You don't
feel it to have risen by the breath of an interested passion
that, restless beyond all passions, is for ever seeking
more pliable forms. Beauty has been the object of its creator's idea, and, having found beauty, it has found the
form in which it splendidly rests.

Beauty indeed was the aim of the creator of the spire
of Trinity Church, so cruelly overtopped and so barely
distinguishable, from your train-bearing barge, as you
stand off, in its abject helpless humility; and it may of
course be asked how much of this superstition finds
voice in the actual shrunken presence of that laudable
effort. Where, for the eye, is the felicity of simplified
Gothic, of noble pre-eminence, that once made of this
highly-pleasing edifice the pride of the town and the
feature of Broadway? The answer is, as obviously, that
these charming elements are still there, just where they
ever were, but that they have been mercilessly deprived
of their visibility. It aches and throbs, this smothered
visibility, we easily feel, in its caged and dishonoured
condition, supported only by the consciousness that
the dishonour is not fault of its own. We commune
with it, in tenderness and pity, through the encum-
bered air; our eyes, made, however unwillingly, at
home in strange vertiginous upper atmospheres, look
down on it as on a poor ineffectual thing, an architectural object addressed, even in its prime aspiration, to
the patient pedestrian sense and permitting thereby a
relation of intimacy. It was to speak to me audibly
enough on two or three other occasions—even through
the thick of that frenzy of Broadway just where Broadway receives from Wall Street the fiercest application of
the maddening lash; it was to put its tragic case there
with irresistible lucidity. "Yes, the wretched figure I am
making is as little as you see my fault—it is the fault of
the buildings whose very first care is to deprive
churches of their visibility. There are but two or three—
two or three outward and visible churches—left in New
York 'anyway,' as you must have noticed, and even they

are hideously threatened: a fact at which no one, indeed, appears to be shocked, from which no one draws the least of the inferences that stick straight out of it, which every one seems in short to take for granted either with remarkable stupidity or with remarkable cynicism." So, at any rate, they may still effectively communicate, ruddy-brown (where not browny-black) old Trinity and any pausing, any attending survivor of the clearer age—and there is yet more of the bitterness of history to be tasted in such a tacit passage, as I shall presently show.

Was it not the bitterness of history, meanwhile, that on that day of circumnavigation, that day of highest intensity of impression, of which I began by speaking, the ancient rotunda of Castle Garden, viewed from just opposite, should have lurked there as a vague nonentity? One had known it from far, far back and with the indelibility of the childish vision—from the time when it was the commodious concert-hall of New York, the firmament of long-extinguished stars; in spite of which extinction there outlives for me the image of the infant phenomenon Adelina Patti, whom (another large-eyed infant) I had been benevolently taken to hear: Adelina Patti, in a fan-like little white frock and "pantalettes" and a hussar-like red jacket, mounted on an armchair, its back supporting her, wheeled to the front of the stage and warbling like a tiny thrush even in the nest. Shabby, shrunken, barely discernible to-day, the ancient rotunda, adjusted to other uses, had afterwards, for many decades, carried on a conspicuous life—and it was the present remoteness, the repudiated barbarism of all this, foreshortened by one's own experience, that dropped the acid into the cup. The sky-scrapers and the league-long bridges, present and to come, marked the point where the age—the age for which Castle Garden could have been, in its day, a "value"—had come out. That in itself was nothing—ages do come out, as a matter of course, so far from where they have gone in. But it had done so, the latter half of the nineteenth century, in one's own more or less immediate presence; the difference, from pole to pole, was so vivid and concrete that no single shade of any one of its aspects was lost.

This impact of the whole condensed past at once produced a horrible, hateful sense of personal antiquity.

Yet was it after all that those monsters of the mere
market, as I have called them, had more to say, on the
question of "effect," than I had at first allowed?—since
they are the element that looms largest for me through
a particular impression, with remembered parts and
pieces melting together rather richly now, of "down-
town" seen and felt from the inside. "Felt"—I use that
word, I dare say, all presumptuously, for a relation to
matters of magnitude and mystery that I could begin
neither to measure nor to penetrate, hovering about
them only in magnanimous wonder, staring at them as
at a world of immovably-closed doors behind which
immense "material" lurked, material for the artist, the
painter of life, as we say, who shouldn't have begun so
early and so fatally to fall away from possible initia-
tions. This sense of a baffled curiosity, an intellectual
adventure forever renounced, was surely enough a state
of feeling, and indeed in presence of the different half-
hours, as memory presents them, at which I gave
myself up both to the thrill of Wall Street (by which I
mean that of the whole wide edge of the whirlpool),
and the too accepted, too irredeemable ignorance, I am
at a loss to see what intensity of response was wanting.
The imagination might have responded more if there
had been a slightly less settled inability to understand
what every one, what any one, was really doing; but the
picture, as it comes back to me, is, for all this foolish
subjective poverty, so crowded with its features that I
rejoice, I confess, in not having more of them to handle. No open apprehension, even if it be as open as a
public vehicle plying for hire, can carry more than a certain amount of life, of a kind; and there was nothing at
play in the outer air, at least, of the scene, during these
glimpses, that didn't scramble for admission into mine
very much as I had seen the mob seeking entrance to an
up-town or a down-town electric car fight for life at
one of the apertures. If it had been the final function of
the Bay to make one feel one's age, so, assuredly, the
mouth of Wall Street proclaimed it, for one's private
ear, distinctly enough; the breath of existence being

taken, wherever one turned, as that of youth on the run and with the prize of the race in sight, and the new landmarks crushing the old quite as violent children stamp on snails and caterpillars.

The hour I first recall was a morning of winter drizzle and mist, of dense fog in the Bay, one of the strangest sights of which I was on my way to enjoy; and I had stopped in the heart of the business quarter to pick up a friend who was to be my companion. The weather, such as it was, worked wonders for the upper reaches of the buildings, round which it drifted and hung very much as about the flanks and summits of emergent mountain-masses—for, to be just all round, there *was* some evidence of their having a message for the eyes. Let me parenthesize, once for all, that there are other glimpses of this message, up and down the city, frequently to be caught; lights and shades of winter and summer air, of the literally "finishing" afternoon in particular, when refinement of modelling descends from the skies and lends the white towers, all new and crude and commercial and over-windowed as they are, a fleeting distinction. The morning I speak of offered me my first chance of seeing one of them from the inside—which was an opportunity I sought again, repeatedly, in respect to others; and I became conscious of the force with which this vision of their prodigious working, and of the multitudinous life, as if each were a swarming city in itself, that they are capable of housing, may beget, on the part of the free observer, in other words of the restless analyst, the impulse to describe and present the facts and express the sense of them. Each of these huge constructed and compressed communities, throbbing, through its myriad arteries and pores, with a single passion, even as a complicated watch throbs with the one purpose of telling you the hour and the minute, testified overwhelmingly to the *character* of New York—and the passion of the restless analyst, on his side, is for the extraction of character. But there would be too much to say, just here, were this incurable eccentric to let himself go; the impression in question, fed by however brief an experience, kept overflowing the cup and spreading in a wide waste of speculation. I must dip into these depths, if it prove possible, later on; let me content myself for the moment with remembering how from the first, on all such ground, my thought went straight to poor great wonder-working Emile Zola and *his* love of the human aggregation, the artificial microcosm, which had to spend itself on great shops, great businesses, great "apartment-houses," of inferior, of mere Parisian scale. His image, it seemed to me, really asked for compassion—in the presence of this material that his energy of evocation, his alone, would have been of a stature to meddle with. What if *Le Ventre de Paris,* what if *Au Bonheur des Dames,* what if *Pot-Bouille* and *L'Argent,* could but have come into being under the New York inspiration?

The answer to that, however, for the hour, was that, in all probability, New York was not going (as it turns such remarks) to produce both the maximum of "business" spectacle and the maximum of ironic reflection of it. Zola's huge reflector got itself formed, after all, in a far other air; it had hung there, in essence, awaiting the scene that was to play over it, long before the scene really approached it in scale. The reflecting surfaces, of the ironic, of the epic order, suspended in the New York atmosphere, have yet to show symptoms of shining out, and the monstrous phenomena themselves, meanwhile, strike me as having, with their immense momentum, got the start, got ahead of, in proper parlance, any possibility of poetic, of dramatic capture. That conviction came to me most perhaps while I gazed across at the special sky-scraper that overhangs poor old Trinity to the north—a south face as high and wide as the mountain-wall that drops the Alpine avalanche, from time to time, upon the village, and the village spire, at its foot; the interest of this case being above all, as I learned, to my stupefaction, in the fact that the very creators of the extinguisher are the church-wardens themselves, or at least the trustees of the church property. What was the case but magnificent for pitiless ferocity?—that inexorable law of the growing invisibility of churches, their everywhere reduced or abolished *presence,* which is nine-tenths of their

virtue, receiving thus, at such hands, its supreme consecration. This consecration was positively the greater
that just then, as I have said, the vast money-making
structure quite horribly, quite romantically justified
itself, looming through the weather with an insolent
cliff-like sublimity. The weather, for all that experience,
mixes intimately with the fulness of my impression;
speaking not least, for instance, of the way "the state of
the streets" and the assault of the turbid air seemed all
one with the look, the tramp, the whole quality and
allure, the consummate monotonous commonness, of
the pushing male crowd, moving in its dense mass—
with the confusion carried to chaos for any intelligence,
any perception; a welter of objects and sounds in which
relief, detachment, dignity, meaning, perished utterly
and lost all rights. It appeared, the muddy medium, all
one with every other element and note as well, all the
signs of the heaped industrial battle-field, all the sounds
and silences, grim, pushing, trudging silences too, of
the universal will to move—to move, move, move, as
an end in itself, an appetite at any price.

In the Bay, the rest of the morning, the dense raw
fog that delayed the big boat, allowing sight but of the
immediate ice-masses through which it thumped its
way, was not less of the essence. Anything blander, as a
medium, would have seemed a mockery of the facts of
the terrible little Ellis Island, the first harbour of refuge
and stage of patience for the million or so of immigrants annually knocking at our official door. Before
this door, which opens to them there only with a hundred forms and ceremonies, grindings and grumblings
of the key, they stand appealing and waiting, mar-
shalled, herded, divided, subdivided, sorted, sifted,
searched, fumigated, for longer or shorter periods—the
effect of all which prodigious process, an intendedly
"scientific" feeding of the mill, is again to give the
earnest observer a thousand more things to think of
than he can pretend to retail. The impression of Ellis
Island, in fine, would be—as I was to find throughout
that so many of my impressions would be—a chapter
by itself; and with a particular page for recognition of
the degree in which the liberal hospitality of the emi-

nent Commissioner of this wonderful service, to whom I had been introduced, helped to make the interest of the whole watched drama poignant and unforgettable. It is a drama that goes on, without a pause, day by day and year by year, this visible act of ingurgitation on the part of our body politic and social, and constituting really an appeal to amazement beyond that of any sword-swallowing or fire-swallowing of the circus. The wonder that one couldn't keep down was the thought that these two or three hours of one's own chance vision of the business were but as a tick or two of the mighty clock, the clock that never, never stops—least of all when it strikes, for a sign of so much winding-up, some louder hour of our national fate than usual. I think indeed that the simplest account of the action of Ellis Island on the spirit of any sensitive citizen who may have happened to "look in" is that he comes back from his visit not at all the same person that he went. He has eaten of the tree of knowledge, and the taste will be for ever in his mouth. He had thought he knew before, thought he had the sense of the degree in which it is his American fate to share the sanctity of his American consciousness, the intimacy of his American patriotism, with the inconceivable alien; but the truth had never come home to him with any such force. In the lurid light projected upon it by those courts of dismay it shakes him—or I like at least to imagine it shakes him—to the depths of his being; I like to think of him, I positively *have* to think of him, as going about ever afterwards with a new look, for those who can see it, in his face, the outward sign of the new chill in his heart. So is stamped, for detection, the questionably privileged person who has had an apparition, seen a ghost in his supposedly safe old house. Let not the unwary, therefore, visit Ellis Island.

The after-sense of that acute experience, however, I myself found, was by no means to be brushed away; I felt it grow and grow, on the contrary, wherever I turned: other impressions might come and go, but this affirmed claim of the alien, however immeasurably alien, to share in one's supreme relation was everywhere the fixed element, the reminder not to be dodged. One's supreme relation, as one had always put it, was one's relation to one's country—a conception made up so largely of one's countrymen and one's countrywomen. Thus it was as if, all the while, with such a fond tradition of what these products predominantly were, the idea of the country itself underwent something of that profane overhauling through which it appears to suffer the indignity of change. Is not our instinct in this matter, in general, essentially the safe one—that of keeping the idea simple and strong and continuous, so that it shall be perfectly sound? To touch it overmuch, to pull it about, is to put it in peril of weakening; yet on this free assault upon it, this readjustment of it in *their* monstrous, presumptuous interest, the aliens, in New York, seemed perpetually to insist. The combination there of their quantity and their quality—that loud primary stage of alienism which New York most offers to sight—operates, for the native, as their note of settled possession, something they have nobody to thank for; so that *un*settled possession is what we, on our side, seem reduced to—the implication of which, in its turn, is that, to recover confidence and regain lost ground, we, not they, must make the surrender and accept the orientation. We must go, in other words, *more* than half-way to meet them; which is all the difference, for us, between possession and dispossession. This sense of dispossession, to be brief about it, haunted me so, I was to feel, in the New York streets and in the packed trajectiles to which one clingingly appeals from the streets, just as one tumbles back into the streets in appalled reaction from *them*, that the art of beguiling or duping it became an art to be cultivated—though the fond alternative vision was never long to be obscured, the imagination, exasperated to envy, of the ideal, in the order in question; of the luxury of some such close and sweet and *whole* national consciousness as that of the Switzer and the Scot.

II

My recovery of impressions, after a short interval, yet with their flush a little faded, may have been judged to involve itself with excursions of memory—memory directed to the antecedent time—reckless almost to extravagance. But I recall them to-day, none the less, for that value in them which ministered, at happy moments, to an artful evasion of the actual. There was no escape from the ubiquitous alien into the future, or even into the present; there was an escape but into the past. I count as quite a triumph in this interest an unbroken ease of frequentation of that ancient end of Fifth Avenue to the whole neighbourhood of which one's earlier vibrations, a very far-away matter now, were attuned. The precious stretch of space between Washington Square and Fourteenth Street had a value, had even a charm, for the revisiting spirit—a mild and melancholy glamour which I am conscious of the difficulty of "rendering" for new and heedless genera-tions. Here again the assault of suggestion is too great; too large, I mean, the number of hares started, before the pursuing imagination, the quickened memory, by this fact of the felt moral and social value of this com-paratively unimpaired morsel of the Fifth Avenue her-itage. Its reference to a pleasanter, easier, hazier past is absolutely comparative, just as the past in question itself enjoys as such the merest courtesy-title. It is all recent history enough, by the measure of the whole, and there are flaws and defacement enough, surely, even in its appearance of decency of duration. The tall building, grossly tall and grossly ugly, has failed of an admirable chance of distinguished consideration for it, and the dignity of many of its peaceful fronts has succumbed to the presence of those industries whose foremost need is to make "a good thing" of them. The good thing is doubtless being made, and yet this lower end of the once agreeable street still just escapes being a wholly bad thing. What held the fancy in thrall, however, as I say, was the admonition, proceeding from all the facts, that values of this romantic order are at best, anywhere, strangely relative. It was an extraordinary statement on the subject of New York that the space between Four-teenth Street and Washington Square *should* count for "tone," figure as the old ivory of an overscored tablet.

True wisdom, I found, was to let it, to make it, so count and figure as much as it would, and charming assistance came for this, I also found, from the young good-nature of May and June. There had been neither assistance nor good-nature during the grim weeks of mid-winter; there had been but the meagre fact of a discomfort and an ugliness less formidable here than elsewhere. When, toward the top of the town, circulation, alimentation, recreation, every art of existence, gave way before the full onset of winter, when the upper avenues had become as so many congested bottlenecks, through which the wine of life simply refused to be decanted, getting back to these latitudes resembled really a return from the North Pole to the Temperate Zone: it was as if the wine of life had been poured for you, in advance, into some pleasant old punch-bowl that would support you through the temporary stress. Your condition was not reduced to the endless vista of a clogged tube, of a thoroughfare occupied as to the narrow central ridge with trolley-cars stuffed to suffocation, and as to the mere margin, on either side, with snow-banks resulting from the cleared rails and offering themselves as a field for all remaining action. Free existence and good manners, in New York, are too much brought down to a bare rigour of marginal relation to the endless electric coil, the monstrous chain that winds round the general neck and body, the general middle and legs, very much as the boa-constrictor winds round the group of the Laocoon. It struck me that when these folds are tightened in the terrible stricture of the snow-smothered months of the year, the New York predicament leaves far behind the anguish represented in the Vatican figures. To come and go where East Eleventh Street, where West Tenth, opened their kind short arms was at least to keep clear of the awful hug of the serpent. And this was a grace that grew large, as I have hinted, with the approach of summer, and that made in the afternoons of May and of the first half of June, above all, an insidious appeal. There, I repeat, was the delicacy, there the mystery, there the wonder, in especial, of the unquenchable intensity of the impressions received in childhood. They are made then once for all, be their intrinsic beauty, interest, importance, small or great; the stamp is indelible and never wholly fades. This in fact gives it an importance when a lifetime has intervened. I found myself intimately recognizing every house my officious tenth year had, in the way of imagined adventure, introduced to me—incomparable master of ceremonies after all; the privilege had been offered since to millions of other objects that had made nothing of it, that had gone as they came; so that here were Fifth Avenue corners with which one's connection was fairly exquisite. The lowered light of the days' ends of early summer became them, moreover, exceedingly, and they fell, for the quite northward perspective, into a dozen delicacies of composition and tone.

One could talk of "quietness" now, for the shrinkage of life so marked, in the higher latitudes of the town, after Easter, the visible early flight of that "society" which, by the old custom, used never to budge before June or July, had almost the effect of clearing some of the streets, and indeed of suggesting that a truly clear New York might have an unsuspected charm or two to put forth. An approach to peace and harmony might have been, in a manner, promised, and the sense of other days took advantage of it to steal abroad with a ghostly tread. It kept meeting, half the time, to its discomfiture, the lamentable little Arch of Triumph which bestrides these beginnings of Washington Square— lamentable because of its poor and lonely and unsupported and unaffiliated state. With this melancholy monument it could make no terms at all, but turned its back to the strange sight as often as possible, helping itself thereby, moreover, to do a little of the pretending required, no doubt, by the fond theory that nothing hereabouts was changed. Nothing *was*, it could occasionally appear to me—there was no new note in the picture, not one, for instance, when I paused before a low house in a small row on the south side of Waverley Place and lived again into the queer mediæval costume (preserved by the daguerreotypist's art) of the very little boy for whom the scene had once embodied the pangs and pleasure of a dame's small school. The dame must have been Irish, by her name, and the Irish tradition, only intensified and coarsened, seemed still to possess the place, the fact of the survival, the sturdy sameness, of which arrested me, again and again, to fascination. The shabby red house, with its mere two storeys, its lowly "stoop," its dislocated ironwork of the forties, the early fifties, the record, in its face, of blistering summers and of the long stages of the loss of self-respect, made it as consummate a morsel of the old liquor-scented, heated-looking city, the city of no pavements, but of such a plenty of politics, as I could have desired. And neighbouring Sixth Avenue, overstraddled though it might be with feats of engineering unknown to the primitive age that otherwise so persisted, wanted only, to carry off the illusion, the warm smell of the bakery on the corner of Eighth Street, a blessed repository of doughnuts, cookies, cream-cakes and pies, the slow passing by which, on returns from school, must have had much in common with the experience of the ship-men of old who came, in long voyages, while they tacked and hung back, upon those belts of ocean that are haunted with the balm and spice of tropic islands.

These were the felicities of the backward reach, which, however, had also its melancholy checks and snubs; nowhere quite so sharp as in presence, so to speak, of the rudely, the ruthlessly suppressed birth-house on the other side of the Square. That was where the pretence that nearly nothing was changed had most to come in; for a high, square, impersonal structure, proclaiming its lack of interest with a crudity all its own, so blocks, at the right moment for its own success, the view of the past, that the effect for me, in Washington Place, was of having been amputated of half my history. The grey and more or less "hallowed" University building—wasn't it somehow, with a desperate bravery, both castellated and gabled?—has vanished from the earth, and vanished with it the two or three adjacent houses, of which the birthplace was one. This was the snub, for the complacency of retrospect, that, whereas the inner sense had positively erected there for its private contemplation a commemorative mural tablet, the very wall that should have borne this inscription had been smashed as for demonstration that tablets, in New York, are unthinkable. And I have had

indeed to permit myself this free fantasy of the hypothetic rescued identity of a given house—taking the
vanished number in Washington Place as most perti-
nent—in order to invite the reader to gasp properly
with me before the fact that we not only fail to remember, in the whole length of the city, one of these frontal
records of birth, sojourn, or death, under a celebrated
name, but that we have only to reflect an instant to see
any such form of civic piety inevitably and for ever
absent. The form is cultivated, to the greatly quickened
interest of street-scenery, in many of the cities of
Europe; and is it not verily bitter, for those who feel a
poetry in the noted passage, longer or shorter, here and
there, of great lost spirits, that the institution, the
profit, the glory of any such association is denied in
advance to communities tending, as the phrase is, to
"run" preponderantly to the sky-scraper? Where, in
fact, is the point of inserting a mural tablet, at any legi-
ble height, in a building certain to be destroyed to
make room for a sky-scraper? And from where, on the
other hand, in a façade of fifty floors, does one "see" the
pious plate recording the honour attached to one of the
apartments look down on a responsive people? We
have but to ask the question to recognize our necessary
failure to answer it as a supremely characteristic local
note—a note in the light of which the great city is projected into its future as, practically, a huge, continuous
fifty-floored conspiracy against the very idea of the
ancient graces, those that strike us as having flourished
just in proportion as the parts of life and the signs of
character have *not* been lumped together, not been
indistinguishably sunk in the common fund of mere
economic convenience. So interesting, as object-
lessons, may the developments of the American gregarious ideal become; so traceable, at every turn, to the
restless analyst at least, are the heavy footprints, in the
finer texture of life, of a great commercial democracy
seeking to abound supremely in its own sense and having none to gainsay it.

Let me not, however, forget, amid such contempla-
tions, what may serve here as a much more relevant
instance of the operation of values, the price of the as

yet undiminished dignity of the two most southward of the Fifth Avenue churches. Half the charm of the prospect, at that extremity, is in their still being there, and being as they are; this charm, this serenity of escape and survival positively works as a blind on the side of the question of their architectural importance. The last shade of pedantry or priggishness drops from your view of that element; they illustrate again supremely your grasped truth of the *comparative* character, in such conditions, of beauty and of interest. The special standard they may or may not square with signifies, you feel, not a jot: all you know, and want to know, is that they are probably menaced—some horrible voice of the air has murmured it—and that with them will go, if fate overtakes them, the last cases worth mentioning (with a single exception), of the modest felicity that sometimes used to be. Remarkable certainly the state of things in which mere exemption from the "squashed" condition can shed such a glamour; but we may accept the state of things if only we can keep the glamour undispelled. It reached its maximum for me, I hasten to add, on my penetrating into the Ascension, at chosen noon, and standing for the first time in presence of that noble work of John La Farge, the representation, on the west wall, in the grand manner, of the theological event from which the church takes its title. Wonderful enough, in New York, to find one's self, in a charming and considerably dim "old" church, hushed to admiration before a great religious picture; the sensation, for the moment, upset so all the facts. The hot light, outside, might have been that of an Italian *piazzetta;* the cool shade, within, with the important work of art shining through it, seemed part of some other-world pilgrimage—all the more that the important work of art itself, a thing of the highest distinction, spoke, as soon as one had taken it in, with that authority which makes the difference, ever afterwards, between the remembered and the forgotten quest. A rich note of interference came, I admit, through the splendid window-glass, the finest of which, unsurpassably fine, to my sense, is the work of the same artist; so that the church, as it stands, is very nearly as commemorative a

monument as a great reputation need wish. The deeply
pictorial windows, in which clearness of picture and
fulness of expression consort so successfully with a tone
as of magnified gems, did not strike one as looking into
a yellow little square of the south—they put forth a different implication; but the flaw in the harmony was,
more than anything else, that sinister voice of the air of
which I have spoken, the fact that one *could* stand there,
vibrating to such impressions, only to remember the
suspended danger, the possibility of the doom. Here
was the loveliest cluster of images, begotten on the
spot, that the preoccupied city had ever taken thought
to offer itself; and here, to match them, like some black
shadow they had been condemned to cast, was this particular prepared honour of "removal" that appeared to
hover about them.

One's fear, I repeat, was perhaps misplaced—but
what an air to live in, the shuddering pilgrim mused, the
air in which such fears are not misplaced only when we
are conscious of very special reassurances! The vision of
the doom that does descend, that had descended all
round, was at all events, for the half-hour, all that was
wanted to charge with the last tenderness one's memory
of the transfigured interior. Afterwards, outside, again
and again, the powers of removal struck me as looming,
awfully, in the newest mass of multiplied floors and
windows visible at this point. *They,* ranged in this terrible recent erection, were going to bring in money—and
was not money the only thing a self-respecting structure
could be thought of as bringing in? Hadn't one heard,
just before, in Boston, that the security, that the sweet
serenity of the Park Street Church, charmingest, there,
of aboriginal notes, the very light, with its perfect position and its dear old delightful Wren-like spire, of the
starved city's eyes, had been artfully practised against,
and that the question of saving it might become, in the
near future, acute? Nothing, fortunately, I think, is so
much the "making" of New York, at its central point, for
the visual, almost for the romantic, sense, as the Park
Street Church is the making, by its happy coming-in, of
Boston; and, therefore, if it were thinkable that the
peculiar rectitude of Boston might be laid in the dust,

what mightn't easily come about for the reputedly less austere conscience of New York? Once such questions had obtained lodgment, to take one's walks was verily to look at almost everything in their light; and to commune with the sky-scraper under this influence was really to feel worsted, more and more, in any magnanimous attempt to adopt the æsthetic view of it. I may appear to make too much of these invidious presences, but it must be remembered that they represent, for our time, the only claim to any consideration other than merely statistical established by the resounding growth of New York. The attempt to take the æsthetic view is invariably blighted sooner or later by their most salient characteristic, *the* feature that speaks loudest for the economic idea. Window upon window, at any cost, is a condition never to be reconciled with any grace of building, and the logic of the matter here happens to put on a particularly fatal front. If quiet interspaces, always half the architectural battle, exist no more in such a structural scheme than quiet tones, blest breathing-spaces, occur, for the most part, in New York conversation, so the reason is, demonstrably, that the building can't afford them. (It is by very much the same law, one supposes, that New York conversation cannot afford stops.) The building can only afford lights, each light having a superlative value as an aid to the transaction of business and the conclusion of sharp bargains. Doesn't it take in fact acres of window-glass to help even an expert New Yorker to get the better of another expert one, or to see that the other expert one doesn't get the better of *him?* It is easy to conceive that, after all, with this origin and nature stamped upon their foreheads, the last word of the mercenary monsters should not be their address to our sense of formal beauty.

Still, as I have already hinted, there was always the case of the one other rescued identity and preserved felicity, the happy accident of the elder day still ungrudged and finally legitimated. When I say ungrudged, indeed, I seem to remember how I had heard that the divine little City Hall had *been* grudged, at a critical moment, to within an inch of its life; had but just escaped, in the event, the extremity of grudging. It lives on securely, by the mercy of fate—lives on in the delicacy of its beauty, speaking volumes again (more volumes, distinctly, than are anywhere else spoken) for the exquisite truth of the *conferred* value of interesting objects, the value derived from the social, the civilizing function for which they happened to find their opportunity. It is the opportunity that gives them their price, and the luck of there being, round about them, nothing greater than themselves to steal it away from them. They strike thus, virtually, the supreme note, and—such is the mysterious play of our finer sensibility!—one takes this note, one is glad to work it, as the phrase goes, for all it is worth. I so work the note of the City Hall, no doubt, in speaking of the spectacle there constituted as "divine"; but I do it precisely by reason of the spectacle taken *with* the delightful small facts of the building: largely by reason, in other words, of the elegant, the gallant little structure's situation and history, the way it has played, artistically, ornamentally, its, has held out for the good cause, through the long years, alone and unprotected. The fact is it has been the very centre of that assault of vulgarity of which the innumerable mementos rise within view of it and tower, at a certain distance, over it; and yet it has never parted with a square inch of its character, it has forced them, in a manner, to stand off. I hasten to add that in expressing thus its uncompromised state I speak of its outward, its æsthetic character only. So, at all events, it has discharged the civilizing function I just named as inherent in such cases—that of representing, to the community possessed of it, all the Style the community is likely to get, and of making itself responsible for the same.

The consistency of this effort, under difficulties, has been the story that brings tears to the eyes of the hovering kindly critic, and it is through his tears, no doubt, that such a personage reads the best passages of the tale and makes out the proportions of the object. Mine, I recognize, didn't prevent my seeing that the pale yellow marble (or whatever it may be) of the City Hall has lost, by some late excoriation, the remembered charm of its old surface, the pleasant promiscuous patina of time; but the perfect taste and finish, the reduced yet ample scale, the harmony of parts, the just proportions, the modest classic grace, the living look of the type aimed at, these things, with gaiety of detail undiminished and "quaintness" of effect augmented, are all there; and I see them, as I write, in that glow of appreciation which made it necessary, of a fine June morning, that I should somehow pay the whole place my respects. The simplest, in fact the only way, was, obviously, to pass under the charming portico and brave the consequences: this impunity of such audacities being, in America, one of the last of the lessons the repatriated absentee finds himself learning. The crushed spirit he brings back from European discipline never quite rises to the height of the native argument, the brave sense that the public, the civic building is his very own, for any honest use, so that he may tread even its most expensive pavements and staircases (and very expensive, for the American citizen, these have lately become,) without a question asked. This further and further unchallenged penetration begets in the perverted person I speak of a really romantic thrill: it is like some assault of the dim seraglio, with the guards bribed, the eunuchs drugged and one's life carried in one's hand. The only drawback to such freedom is that penetralia it is so easy to penetrate fail a little of a due impressiveness, and that if stationed sentinels are bad for the temper of the freeman they are good for the "prestige" of the building.

Never, in any case, it seemed to me, had any freeman made so free with the majesty of things as I was to make on this occasion with the mysteries of the City Hall—even to the point of coming out into the presence of the Representative of the highest office with which City Halls are associated, and whose thoroughly gracious condonation of my act set the seal of success upon the whole adventure. Its dizziest intensity in fact sprang precisely from the unexpected view opened into the old official, the old so thick-peopled local, municipal world: upper chambers of council and state, delightfully of their nineteenth-century time, as to design and ornament, in spite of rank restoration; but replete,

above all, with portraits of past worthies, past celebrities and city fathers, Mayors, Bosses, Presidents, Gov-
ernors, Statesmen at large, Generals and Commodores
at large, florid ghosts, looking so unsophisticated now,
of years not remarkable, municipally, for the absence of
sophistication. Here were types, running mainly to
ugliness and all bristling with the taste of their day and
the quite touching provincialism of their conditions, as
to many of which nothing would be more interesting
than a study of New York annals in the light of their
personal look, their very noses and mouths and com-
plexions and heads of hair—to say nothing of their
waistcoats and neckties; with such colour, such sound
and movement would the thick stream of local history
then be interfused. Wouldn't its thickness fairly become
transparent? since to walk through the collection was
not only to see and feel so much that had happened, but
to understand, with the truth again and again inim-
itably pointed, why nothing could have happened otherwise; the whole array thus presenting itself as an
unsurpassed demonstration of the real reasons of
things. The florid ghosts look out from their exceedingly gilded frames—all that *that* can do is bravely done
for them—with the frankest responsibility for everything; their collective presence becomes a kind of copi-
ous tell-tale document signed with a hundred names.
There are few of these that at this hour, I think, we particularly desire to repeat; but the place where they may
be read is, all the way from river to river and from the
Battery to Harlem, the place in which there is most of
the terrible town.

III

If the Bay had seemed to me, as I have noted, most to
help the fond observer of New York aspects to a sense,
through the eyes, of embracing possession, so the part
played there for the outward view found its match for
the inward in the portentous impression of one of the
great caravansaries administered to me of a winter afternoon. I say with intention "administered": on so assidu-
ous a guide, through the endless labyrinth of the
Waldorf-Astoria was I happily to chance after turning

out of the early dusk and the January sleet and slosh into permitted, into enlightened contemplation of a pandemonium not less admirably ordered, to all appearance, than rarely intermitted. The seer of great cities is liable to easy error, I know, when he finds this, that or the other caught glimpse the supremely significant one — and I am willing to preface with that remark my confession that New York told me more of her story at once, then and there, than she was again and elsewhere to tell. With this apprehension that she was in fact fairly shrieking it into one's ears came a curiosity, corresponding, as to its kind and its degree of interest; so that there was nought to do, as we picked our tortuous way, but to stare with all our eyes and miss as little as possible of the revelation. That harshness of the essential conditions, the outward, which almost any large attempt at the amenities, in New York, has to take account of and make the best of, has at least the effect of projecting the visitor with force upon the spectacle prepared for him at this particular point and of marking the more its sudden high pitch, the character of violence which all its warmth, its colour and glitter so completely muffle. There is violence outside, mitigating sadly the frontal majesty of the monument, leaving it exposed to the vulgar assault of the street by the operation of those dire facts of absence of margin, of meagreness of site, of the brevity of the block, of the inveteracy of the near thoroughfare, which leave "style," in construction, at the mercy of the impertinent cross-streets, make detachment and independence, save in the rarest cases, an insoluble problem, preclude without pity any element of court or garden, and open to the builder in quest of distinction the one alternative, and the great adventure, of seeking his reward in the sky.

Of their licence to pursue it there to any extent whatever New Yorkers are, I think, a trifle too assertively proud; no court of approach, no interspace worth mention, ever forming meanwhile part of the ground-plan or helping to receive the force of the breaking public wave. New York pays at this rate the penalty of her primal topographic curse, her old inconceivably bourgeois scheme of composition and distribution, the uncorrected labour of minds with no imagination of the future and blind before the opportunity given them by their two magnificent water-fronts. This original sin of the longitudinal avenues perpetually, yet meanly intersected, and of the organized sacrifice of the indicated alternative, the great perspectives from East to West, might still have earned forgiveness by some occasional departure from its pettifogging consistency. But, thanks to this consistency, the city is, of all great cities, the least endowed with any blest item of stately square or goodly garden, with any happy accident or surprise, any fortunate nook or casual corner, any deviation, in fine, into the liberal or the charming. That way, however, for the regenerate filial mind, madness may be said to lie—the way of imagining what might have been and putting it all together in the light of what so helplessly is. One of the things that helplessly are, for instance, is just this assault of the street, as I have called it, upon any direct dealing with our caravansary. The electric cars, with their double track, are everywhere almost as tight a fit in the narrow channel of the roadway as the projectile in the bore of a gun; so that the Waldorf-Astoria, sitting by this absent margin for life with her open lap and arms, is reduced to confessing, with a strained smile, across the traffic and the danger, how little, outside her mere swing-door, she can do for you. She seems to admit that the attempt to get at her may cost you your safety, but reminds you at the same time that any good American, and even any good inquiring stranger, is supposed willing to risk that boon for her. "*Un bon mouvement*, therefore: you must make a dash for it, but you'll see I'm worth it." If such a claim as this last be ever justified, it would indubitably be justified here; the survivor scrambling out of the current and up the bank finds in the amplitude of the entertainment awaiting him an instant sense as of applied restoratives. The amazing hotel-world quickly closes round him; with the process of transition reduced to its minimum he is transported to conditions of extraordinary complexity and brilliancy, operating— and with proportionate perfection—by laws of their own and expressing after their fashion a complete scheme of life. The air swarms, to intensity, with the *characteristic*, the characteristic condensed and accumulated as he rarely elsewhere has had the luck to find it. It jumps out to meet his every glance, and this unanimity of its spring, of all its aspects and voices, is what I just now referred to as the essence of the loud New York story. That effect of violence in the whole communication, at which I thus hint, results from the inordinate mass, the quantity of presence, as it were, of the testimony heaped together for emphasis of the wondrous moral.

The moral in question, the high interest of the tale, is that you are in presence of a revelation of the possibilities of the hotel—for which the American spirit has found so unprecedented a use and a value; leading it on to express so a social, indeed positively an æsthetic ideal, and making it so, at this supreme pitch, a synonym for civilization, for the capture of conceived manners themselves, that one is verily tempted to ask if the hotel-spirit may not just *be* the American spirit most seeking and most finding itself. That truth—the truth that the present is more and more the day of the hotel—had not waited to burst on the mind at the view of this particular establishment; we have all more or less been educated to it, the world over, by the fruit-bearing action of the American example: in consequence of which it has been opened to us to see still other societies moved by the same irresistible spring and trying, with whatever grace and ease they may bring to the business, to unlearn as many as possible of their old social canons, and in especial their old discrimination in favour of the private life. The business for them—for communities to which the American ease in such matters is not native—goes much less of itself and produces as yet a scantier show; the great difference with the American show being that in the United States every one is, for the lubrication of the general machinery, practically in everything, whereas in Europe, mostly, it is only certain people who are in anything; so that the machinery, so much less generalized, works in a smaller, stiffer way. This one caravansary makes the American case vivid, gives it, you feel, that quantity of illustration which renders the place a new thing under the sun. It is an expression of the gregarious state breaking down every barrier but two—one of which, the barrier consisting of the high pecuniary tax, is the immediately obvious. The other, the rather more subtle, is the condition, for any member of the flock, that he or she—in other words especially she—be presumably "respectable," be, that is, not discoverably anything else. The rigour with which any appearance of pursued or desired adventure is kept down—adventure in the florid sense of the word, the sense in which it remains an euphemism—is not the least interesting note of the whole immense promiscuity. Protected at those two points the promiscuity carries, through the rest of the range, everything before it.

It sat there, it walked and talked, and ate and drank, and listened and danced to music, and otherwise revelled and roamed, and bought and sold, and came and went there, all on its own splendid terms and with an encompassing material splendour, a wealth and variety of constituted picture and background, that might well feed it with the finest illusions about itself. It paraded through the halls and saloons in which art and history, in masquerading dress, muffled almost to suffocation as in the gold brocade of their pretended majesties and their conciliatory graces, stood smirking on its passage with the last cynicism of hypocrisy. The exhibition is wonderful for that, for the suggested sense of a promiscuity which manages to be at the same time an inordinate untempered monotony; manages to be so, on such ground as this, by an extraordinary trick of its own, wherever one finds it. The combination forms, I think, largely, the very interest, such as it is, of these phases of the human scene in the United States—if only for the pleasant puzzle of our wondering how, when types, aspects, conditions, have so much in common, they should seem at all to make up a conscious miscellany. That question, however, the question of the play and range, the practical elasticity, of the social sameness, in America, will meet us elsewhere on our path, and I confess that all questions gave way, in my mind, to a single irresistible obsession. This was just the ache of envy of

the spirit of a society which had found there, in its
prodigious public setting, so exactly what it wanted.
One was in presence, as never before, of a realized ideal
and of that childlike rush of surrender to it and clutch at
it which one was so repeatedly to recognize, in America, as the note of the supremely gregarious state. It
made the whole vision unforgettable, and I am now
carried back to it, I confess, in musing hours, as to one
of my few glimpses of perfect human felicity. It had the
admirable sign that it was, precisely, so comprehen-
sively collective—that it made so vividly, in the old
phrase, for the greatest happiness of the greatest
number. Its rare beauty, one felt with instant clarity of
perception, was that it was, for a "mixed" social mani-
festation, blissfully exempt from any principle or possibility of disaccord with itself. It was absolutely a fit to
its conditions, those conditions which were both its
earth and its heaven, and every part of the picture, every
item of the immense sum, every wheel of the wondrous
complexity, was on the best terms with all the rest.

The sense of these things became for the hour as the
golden glow in which one's envy burned, and through
which, while the sleet and the slosh, and the clangorous
charge of cars, and the hustling, hustled crowds held
the outer world, one carried one's charmed attention
from one chamber of the temple to another. For that is
how the place speaks, as great constructed and achieved
harmonies mostly speak—as a temple builded, with
clustering chapels and shrines, to an idea. The hundreds and hundreds of people in circulation, the innumerable huge-hatted ladies in especial, with their air of
finding in the gilded and storied labyrinth the very
firesides and pathways of home, became thus the serene
faithful, whose rites one would no more have scepti-
cally brushed than one would doff one's disguise in a
Mohammedan mosque. The question of who they all
might be, seated under palms and by fountains, or
communing, to some inimitable New York tune, with
the shade of Marie Antoinette in the queer recaptured
actuality of an easy Versailles or an intimate Trianon—
such questions as that, interesting in other societies and
at other times, insisted on yielding here to the mere elo-

quence of the general truth. Here was a social order in positively stable equilibrium. Here was a world whose relation to its form and medium was practically imperturbable; here was a conception of publicity *as* the vital medium organized with the authority with which the American genius for organization, put on its mettle, alone could organize it. The whole thing remains for me, however, I repeat, a gorgeous golden blur, a paradise peopled with unmistakable American shapes, yet in which, the general and the particular, the organized and the extemporized, the element of ingenuous joy below and of consummate management above, melted together and left one uncertain which of them one was, at a given turn of the maze, most admiring. When I reflect indeed that without my clue I should not have even known the maze—should not have known, at the given turn, whether I was engulfed, for instance, in the *vente de charité* of the theatrical profession and the onset of persuasive peddling actresses, or in the annual tea-party of German lady-patronesses (of I know not what) filling with their Oriental opulence and their strange idiom a playhouse of the richest rococo, where some other expensive anniversary, the ball of a guild or a carouse of a club, was to tread on their heels and instantly mobilize away their paraphernalia—when I so reflect I see the sharpest dazzle of the eyes as precisely the play of the genius for organization.

There are a thousand forms of this ubiquitous American force, the most ubiquitous of all, that I was in no position to measure; but there was often no resisting a vivid view of the form it may take, on occasion, under pressure of the native conception of the hotel. Encountered embodiments of the gift, in this connection, master-spirits of management whose influence was as the very air, the very expensive air, one breathed, abide with me as the intensest examples of American character; indeed as the very interesting supreme examples of a type which has even on the American ground, doubtless, not said its last word, but which has at least treated itself there to a luxury of development. It gives the impression, when at all directly met, of having at its service something of that fine flame that makes up personal greatness; so that, again and again, as I found, one would have liked to see it more intimately at work. Such failures of opportunity and of penetration, however, are but the daily bread of the visionary tourist. Whenever I dip back, in fond memory, none the less, into the vision I have here attempted once more to call up, I see the whole thing overswept as by the colossal extended arms, waving the magical bâton, of some high-stationed orchestral leader, the absolute presiding power, conscious of every note of every instrument, controlling and commanding the whole volume of sound, keeping the whole effect together and making it what it is. What may one say of such a spirit if not that he understands, so to speak, the forces he sways, understands his boundless American material and plays with it like a master indeed? One sees it thus, in its crude plasticity, almost in the likeness of an army of puppets whose strings the wealth of his technical imagination teaches him innumerable ways of pulling, and yet whose innocent, whose always ingenuous agitation of their members he has found means to make them think of themselves as delightfully free and easy. Such was my impression of the perfection of the concert that, for fear of its being spoiled by some chance false note, I never went into the place again.

It might meanwhile seem no great adventure merely to walk the streets; but (beside the fact that there is, in general, never a better way of taking in life), this pursuit irresistibly solicited, on the least pretext, the observer whose impressions I note—accustomed as he had ever been conscientiously to yield to it: more particularly with the relenting year, when the breath of spring, mildness being really installed, appeared the one vague and disinterested presence in the place, the one presence not vociferous and clamorous. Any definite presence that doesn't bellow and bang takes on in New York by that simple fact a distinction practically exquisite; so that one goes forth to meet it as a guest of honour, and that, for my own experience, I remember certain aimless strolls as snatches of intimate communion with the spirit of May and June—as abounding, almost to enchantment, in the comparatively *still* condition. Two secrets, at this time, seemed to profit by that influence to tremble out; one of these to the effect that New York would really have been "meant" to be charming, and the other to the effect that the restless analyst, willing at the lightest persuasion to let so much of its ugliness edge away unscathed from his analysis, must have had for it, from far back, one of those loyalties that are beyond any reason.

"It's all very well," the voice of the air seemed to say, if I may so take it up; "it's all very well to 'criticize,' but you distinctly take an interest and are the victim of your interest, be the grounds of your perversity what they will. You can't escape from it, and don't you see that this, precisely, is what *makes* an adventure for you (an adventure, I admit, as with some strident, battered, questionable beauty, truly some 'bold bad' charmer), of almost any odd stroll, or waste half-hour, or other promiscuous passage, that results for you in an impression? There is always your bad habit of receiving through almost any accident of vision more impressions than you know what to do with; but that, for common convenience, is your eternal handicap and may not be allowed to plead here against your special responsibility. You *care* for the terrible town, yea even for the 'horrible,' as I have overheard you call it, or at least think it, when you supposed no one would know; and you see now how, if you fly such fancies as that it was conceivably meant to be charming, you are tangled by that weakness in some underhand imagination of its possibly, one of these days, as a riper fruit of time, becoming so. To do that, you indeed sneakingly provide, it must get away from itself; but you are ready to follow its hypothetic dance even to the mainland and to the very end of its tether. What makes the general relation of your adventure with it is that, at bottom, you are all the while wondering, in presence of the aspects of its genius and its shame, what elements or parts, if any, would be worth its saving, worth carrying off for the fresh embodiment and the better life, and which of them would have, on the other hand, to face the notoriety of going *first* by the board. I have literally heard you qualify the monster as 'shameless'—though that was wrung from you, I admit, by the worst of the winter conditions, when circulation, in any fashion consistent with personal decency or dignity, was merely mocked at, when the stony-hearted 'trolleys,' cars of Juggernaut in their power to squash, triumphed all along the line, when the February blasts became as cyclones in the darkened gorges of masonry (which down-town, in particular, put on, at their mouths, the semblance of black rat-holes, holes of gigantic rats, inhabited by whirlwinds;) when all the pretences and impunities and infirmities, in fine, had massed themselves to be hurled at you in the fury of the elements, in the character of the traffic, in the unadapted state of the place to almost *any* dense movement, and, beyond everything, in that pitch of all the noises which acted on your nerves as so much wanton provocation, so much conscious cynicism. The fury of sound took the form of derision of the rest of your woe, and thus it *might*, I admit, have struck you as brazen that the horrible place should, in such confessed collapse, still be swaggering and shouting. It might have struck you that great cities, with the eyes of the world on them, as the phrase is, should be capable either of a proper form or (failing this) of a proper compunction; which tributes to propriety were, on the part of New York, equally wanting. This made you remark, precisely, that nothing was wanting, on the other hand, to that analogy with the character of the bad bold beauty, the creature the most blatant of whose pretensions is that she is one of those to whom everything is always forgiven. On what ground 'forgiven'? of course you ask; but note that you ask it while you're in the very act of forgiving. Oh yes, you are; you've as much as said so yourself. So there it all is; arrange it as you can. Poor dear bad bold beauty; there must indeed be something about her—!"

Let me grant then, to get on, that there *was* doubtless, in the better time, something about her; there was enough about her, at all events, to conduce to that distinct cultivation of her company for which the contemplative stroll, when there was time for it, was but another name. The analogy was in truth complete; since the repetition of such walks, and the admission of the beguiled state contained in them, resembled nothing so much as the visits so often still incorrigibly made to compromised charmers. I defy even a master of morbid observation to perambulate New York unless he be interested; so that in a case of memories so gathered the interest must be taken as a final fact. Let me figure it, to this end, as lively in every connection—and so indeed no more lively at one mild crisis than at another. The crisis—even of observation at the morbid pitch—is inevitably mild in cities intensely new; and it was with the quite peculiarly insistent newness of the upper reaches of the town that the spirit of romantic inquiry had always, at the best, to reckon. There are new cities enough about the world, goodness knows, and there are new parts enough of old cities—for examples of which we need go no farther than London, Paris and Rome, all of late so mercilessly renovated. But the newness of New York—unlike even that of Boston, I seemed to discern—had this mark of its very own, that it affects one, in every case, as having treated itself as still more provisional, if possible, than any poor dear little interest of antiquity it may have annihilated. The very sign of its energy is that it doesn't believe in itself; it fails to succeed, even at a cost of millions, in persuading you that it does. Its mission would appear to be, exactly, to guild the temporary, with its gold, as many inches thick as may be, and then, with a fresh shrug, a shrug of its splendid cynicism for its freshly detected inability to convince, give up its actual work, however exorbitant, as the merest of stop-gaps. The difficulty with the compromised charmer is just this constant inability to convince; to convince ever, I mean, that she is serious, serious about any form whatever, or about anything but that perpetual passionate pecuniary purpose which plays with all forms, which derides and devours them, though it may pile up the cost of them in order to rest a while, spent and haggard, in the illusion of their finality.

The perception of this truth grows for you by your simply walking up Fifth Avenue and pausing a little in presence of certain forms, certain exorbitant structures, in other words, the elegant domiciliary, as to which the

illusion of finality was within one's memory magnificent and complete, but as to which one feels to-day
that their life wouldn't be, as against any whisper of a
higher interest, worth an hour's purchase. They sit
there in the florid majesty of the taste of their time—a
light now, alas, generally clouded; and I pretend of
course to speak, in alluding to them, of no individual
case of danger or doom. It is only a question of that
unintending and unconvincing expression of New York
everywhere, as yet, on the matter of the *maintenance* of
a given effect—which comes back to the general insincerity of effects, and truly even (as I have already noted)
to the insincerity of the effect of the sky-scrapers themselves. There results from all this—and as much where
the place most smells of its millions as elsewhere—that
unmistakable New York admission of unattempted,
impossible maturity. The new Paris and the new Rome
do at least propose, I think, to be old—one of these
days; the new London even, erect as she is on lease-
holds destitute of dignity, yet does, for the period,
appear to believe in herself. The vice I glance at is, however, when showing, in our flagrant example, on the
forehead of its victim, much more a cause for pitying
than for decrying them. Again and again, in the upper
reaches, you pause with that pity; you learn, on the
occasion of a kindly glance up and down a quiet cross-
street (there being objects and aspects in many of them
appealing to kindness), that such and such a house, or a
row, is "coming down"; and you gasp, in presence of
the elements involved, at the strangeness of the moral
so pointed. It rings out like the crack of that lash in the
sky, the play of some mighty teamster's whip, which
ends by affecting you as the poor New Yorker's one
association with the idea of "powers above." "No"—
this is the tune to which the whip seems flourished—
"there's no step at which you shall rest, no form, as I'm
constantly showing you, to which, consistently with
my interests, you *can*. I build you up but to tear you
down, for if I were to let sentiment and sincerity once
take root, were to let any tenderness of association once
accumulate, or any 'love of the old' once passed
unsnubbed, what would become of *us*, who have our

hands on the whipstock, please? Fortunately we've
learned the secret for keeping association at bay. We've
learned that the great thing is not to suffer it to so much
as begin. Wherever it does begin we find we're lost; but
as that takes some time we get in ahead. It's the reason,
if you must know, why you shall 'run,' all, without
exception, to the fifty floors. We defy you even to aspire
to venerate shapes so grossly constructed as the
arrangement in fifty floors. You may have a feeling for
keeping on with an old staircase, consecrated by the
tread of generations—especially when it's 'good,' and
old staircases are often so lovely; but how can you have
a feeling for keeping on with an old elevator, how can
you have it anymore than for keeping on with an old
omnibus? You'd be ashamed to venerate the arrangement in fifty floors, accordingly, even if you could;
whereby, saving you any moral trouble or struggle,
they are conceived and constructed—and you must do
us the justice of this care for your sensibility—in a manner to put the thing out of the question. In such a manner, moreover, as that there shall be immeasurably
more of them, in quantity, to tear down than of the
actual past that we are now sweeping away. Wherefore
we shall be kept in precious practice. The word will perhaps be then—who knows?—for building from the
earth-surface downwards; in which case it will be a
question of tearing, so to speak, 'up.' It little matters, so
long as we blight the superstition of rest."

Yet even in the midst of this vision of eternal waste,
of conscious, sentient-looking houses and rows, full
sections of streets, to which the rich taste of history is
forbidden even while their fresh young lips are just
touching the cup, something charmingly done, here
and there, some bid for the ampler permanence, seems
to say to you that the particular place only asks, as a
human home, to lead the life it has begun, only asks to
enfold generations and gather in traditions, to show
itself capable of growing up to character and authority.
Houses of the best taste are like clothes of the best tai-
lors—it takes their age to show us how good they are;
and I frequently recognized, in the region of the upper
reaches, this direct appeal of the individual case of

happy construction. Construction at large abounds in
the upper reaches, construction indescribably precipi-
tate and elaborate—the latter fact about it always so
oddly hand in hand with the former; and we should
exceed in saying that felicity is always its mark. But
some highly liberal, some extravagant intention almost
always is, and we meet here even that happy accident,
already encountered and acclaimed, in its few examples, down-town, of the object shining almost absurdly
in the light of its merely comparative distinction. All
but lost in the welter of instances of sham refinement,
the shy little case of real refinement detaches itself
ridiculously, as being (like the saved City Hall, or like
the pleasant old garden-walled house on the north-west
corner of Washington Square and Fifth Avenue) of so
beneficent an admonition as to show, relatively speaking, for priceless. These things, which I may not take
time to pick out, are the salt that saves, and it is enough
to say for their delicacy that they are the direct counterpart of those other dreadful presences, looming round
them, which embody the imagination of new kinds and
new clustered, emphasized quantities of vulgarity. To
recall these fine notes and these loud ones, the whole
play of wealth and energy and untutored liberty, of the
movement of a breathless civilization reflected, as brick
and stone and marble may reflect, through all the con-
trasts of prodigious flight and portentous stumble, is to
acknowledge, positively, that one's rambles were
delightful, and that the district abutting on the east side
of the Park, in particular, never engaged my attention
without, by the same stroke, making the social question dance before it in a hundred interesting forms.

The social question quite fills the air, in New York,
for any spectator whose impressions at all follow themselves up; it wears, at any rate, in what I have called the
upper reaches, the perpetual strange appearance as of
Property perched high aloft and yet itself looking
about, all ruefully, in the wonder of what it is exactly
doing there. We see it perched, assuredly, in other and
older cities, other and older social orders; but it strikes
us in those situations as knowing a little more where it
is. It strikes us as knowing how it has got up and why it

must, infallibly, stay up; it has not the frightened look, measuring the spaces around, of a small child set on a mantel-shelf and about to cry out. If old societies are interesting, however, I am far from thinking that young ones may not be more so—with their collective countenance so much more presented, precisely, to observation, as by their artless need to get themselves explained. The American world produces almost everywhere the impression of appealing to any attested interest for the word, the *fin mot,* of what it may mean; but I somehow see those parts of it most at a loss that are already explained not a little by the ample possession of money. This is the amiable side there of the large developments of private ease in general—the amiable side of those numerous groups that are rich enough and, in the happy vulgar phrase, bloated enough, to be candidates for the classic imputation of haughtiness. The amiability proceeds from an essential vagueness; whereas real haughtiness is never vague about itself—it is only vague about others. That is the human note in the huge American rattle of gold—so far as the "social" field is the scene of the rattle. The "business" field is a different matter—as to which the determination of the audibility in it of the human note (so interesting to try for if one had but the warrant) is a line of research closed to me, alas, by my fatally uninitiated state. My point is, at all events, that you cannot be "hard," really, with any society that affects you as ready to learn from you, and from this resource for it of your detachment combining with your proximity, what in the name of all its possessions and all its destitutions it would honestly be "at."

HENRY JAMES *(1843-1916), novelist, short-story writer, essayist, playwright, and critic, was born in New York City. His earliest works appeared in the* North American Review *and the* Atlantic Monthly.

After extended trips to Europe from 1869 to 1876, he settled in London and lived there until 1896, writing, among other works, his novels Roderick Hudson, The American, The Europeans, Daisy Miller, Washington

Square, The Portrait of a Lady *(after a visit to Florence),* The Bostonians, The Princess Cassamassima, *and the* Aspern Papers. The Turn of the Screw *(1899, his tale of the uncanny), was followed by novels* The Awkward Age, The Sacred Fount, The Wings of the Dove, The Ambassadors, The Golden Bowl, *and* Outcry *(his last completed novel, 1911), as well as more short stories, and three volumes of autobiography.*

He returned to the United States in 1904, traveled again to Italy and France in 1907-1908, went back to England and became a British citizen in 1915.

The preceding excerpts are from The American Scene *(1907), chronicling a year-long lecture and sightseeing tour of the United States.*

F. Scott Fitzgerald

My Lost City

July, 1932

There was first the ferry boat moving softly from the Jersey shore at dawn—the moment crystallized into my first symbol of New York. Five years later when I was fifteen I went into the city from school to see Ina Claire in *The Quaker Girl* and Gertrude Bryan in *Little Boy Blue*. Confused by my hopeless and melancholy love for them both, I was unable to choose between them—so they blurred into one lovely entity, the girl. She was my second symbol of New York. The ferry boat stood for triumph, the girl for romance. In time I was to achieve some of both, but there was a third symbol that I have lost somewhere, and lost forever.

I found it on a dark April afternoon after five more years.

"Oh, Bunny," I yelled. "*Bunny!*"

He did not hear me—my taxi lost him, picked him up again half a block down the street. There were black spots of rain on the sidewalk and I saw him walking briskly through the crowd wearing a tan raincoat over his inevitable brown get-up; I noted with a shock that he was carrying a light cane.

"Bunny!" I called again, and stopped. I was still an undergraduate at Princeton while he had become a New Yorker. This was his afternoon walk, this hurry along with his stick through the gathering rain, and as I was not to meet him for an hour it seemed an intrusion to happen upon him engrossed in his private life. But the taxi kept pace with him and as I continued to watch I was impressed: he was no longer the shy little scholar of Holder Court—he walked with confidence, wrapped in his thoughts and looking straight ahead, and it was obvious that his new background was entirely sufficient to him. I knew that he had an apartment where he lived with three other men, released now from all undergraduate taboos, but there was something else that was nourishing him and I got my first impression of that new thing—the Metropolitan spirit.

Up to this time I had seen only the New York that offered itself for inspection—I was Dick Whittington up from the country gaping at the trained bears, or a youth of the Midi dazzled by the boulevards of Paris. I had come only to stare at the show, though the designers of the Woolworth Building and the Chariot Race Sign, the producers of musical comedies and problem plays, could ask for no more appreciative spectator, for I took the style and glitter of New York even above its own valuation. But I had never accepted any of the practically anonymous invitations to debutante balls that turned up in an undergraduate's mail, perhaps because I felt that no actuality could live up to my conception of New York's splendor. Moreover, she to whom I fatuously referred as "my girl" was a Middle Westerner, a fact which kept the warm center of the world out there, so I thought of New York as essentially cynical and heartless—save for one night when she made luminous the Ritz Roof on a brief passage through.

Lately, however, I had definitely lost her and I wanted a man's world, and this sight of Bunny made me see New York as just that. A week before, Monsignor Fay had taken me to the Lafayette where there was spread before us a brilliant flag of food, called an *hors d'oeuvre*, and with it we drank claret that was as brave as Bunny's confident cane—but after all it was a restaurant and afterwards we would drive back over a bridge into the hinterland. The New York of undergraduate dissipation, of Bustanoby's, Shanley's, Jack's, had become a horror and though I returned to it, alas, through many an alcoholic mist, I felt each time a betrayal of a persistent idealism. My participation was prurient rather than licentious and scarcely one pleasant memory of it remains from those days; as Ernest

Hemingway once remarked, the sole purpose of the cabaret is for unattached men to find complaisant women. All the rest is a wasting of time in bad air.

But that night, in Bunny's apartment, life was mellow and safe, a finer distillation of all that I had come to love at Princeton. The gentle playing of an oboe mingled with city noises from the street outside, which penetrated into the room with difficulty through great barricades of books; only the crisp tearing open of invitations by one man was a discordant note. I had found a third symbol of New York and I began wondering about the rent of such apartments and casting about for the appropriate friends to share one with me.

Fat chance—for the next two years I had as much control over my own destiny as a convict over the cut of his clothes. When I got back to New York in 1919 I was so entangled in life that a period of mellow monasticism in Washington Square was not to be dreamed of. The thing was to make enough money in the advertising business to rent a stuffy apartment for two in the Bronx. The girl concerned had never seen New York but she was wise enough to be rather reluctant. And in a haze of anxiety and unhappiness I passed the four most impressionable months of my life.

New York had all the iridescence of the beginning of the world. The returning troops marched up Fifth Avenue and girls were instinctively drawn East and North toward them—this was the greatest nation and there was gala in the air. As I hovered ghost-like in the Plaza Red Room of a Saturday afternoon, or went to lush and liquid garden parties in the East Sixties or tippled with Princetonians in the Biltmore Bar I was haunted always by my other life—my drab room in the Bronx, my square foot of the subway, my fixation upon the day's letter from Alabama—would it come and what would it say?—my shabby suits, my poverty, and love. While my friends were launching decently into life I had muscled my inadequate bark into midstream. The gilded youth circling around young Constance Bennett in the Club de Vingt, the classmates in the Yale-Princeton Club whooping up our first after-the-war reunion, the atmosphere of the millionaires' houses that I sometimes frequented—these things were empty for me, though I recognized them as impressive scenery and regretted that I was committed to other romance. The most hilarious luncheon table or the most moony cabaret—it was all the same; from them I returned eagerly to my home on Claremont Avenue—home because there might be a letter waiting outside the door. One by one my great dreams of New York became tainted. The remembered charm of Bunny's apartment faded with the rest when I interviewed a blowsy landlady in Greenwich Village. She told me I could bring girls to the room, and the idea filled me with dismay—why should I want to bring girls to my room?—I had a girl. I wandered through the town of 127th Street, resenting its vibrant life; or else I bought cheap theatre seats at Gray's drugstore and tried to lose myself for a few hours in my old passion for Broadway. I was a failure—mediocre at advertising work and unable to get started as a writer. Hating the city, I got roaring, weeping drunk on my last penny and went home. . . .

. . . Incalculable city. What ensued was only one of a thousand success stories of those gaudy days, but it plays a part in my own movie of New York. When I returned six months later the offices of editors and publishers were open to me, impresarios begged plays, the movies panted for screen material. To my bewilderment, I was adopted, not as a Middle Westerner, not even as a detached observer, but as the arch type of what New York wanted. This statement requires some account of the metropolis in 1920.

There was already the tall white city of today, already the feverish activity of the boom, but there was a general inarticulateness. As much as anyone the columnist F. P. A. guessed the pulse of the individual and the crowd, but shyly, as one watching from a window. Society and the native arts had not mingled—Ellen Mackay was not yet married to Irving Berlin. Many of Peter Arno's people would have been meaningless to the citizen of 1920, and save for F. P. A.'s column there was no forum for metropolitan urbanity.

Then, for just a moment, the "younger generation" idea became a fusion of many elements in New York life. People of fifty might pretend there was still a four hundred or Maxwell Bodenheim might pretend there was a Bohemia worth its paint and pencils—but the blending of the bright, gay, vigorous elements began then and for the first time there appeared a society a little livelier than the solid mahogany dinner parties of Emily Price Post. If this society produced the cocktail party, it also evolved Park Avenue wit and for the first time an educated European could envisage a trip to New York as something more amusing than a gold-trek into a formalized Australian Bush.

For just a moment, before it was demonstrated that I was unable to play the role, I, who knew less of New York than any reporter of six months standing and less of its society than any hall-room boy in a Ritz stag line, was pushed into the position not only of spokesman for the time but of the typical product of that same moment. I, or rather it was "we" now, did not know exactly what New York expected of us and found it rather confusing. Within a few months after our embarkation on the Metropolitan venture we scarcely knew any more who we were and we hadn't a notion what we were. A dive into a civic fountain, a casual brush with the law, was enough to get us into the gossip columns, and we were quoted on a variety of subjects we knew nothing about. Actually our "contacts" included half a dozen unmarried college friends and a few new literary acquaintances—I remember a lonesome Christmas when we had not one friend in the city, nor one house we could go to. Finding no nucleus to which we could cling, we became a small nucleus ourselves and gradually we fitted our disruptive personalities into the contemporary scene of New York. Or rather New York forgot us and let us stay.

This is not an account of the city's changes but of the changes in this writer's feeling for the city. From the confusion of the year 1920 I remember riding on top of a taxi-cab along deserted Fifth Avenue on a hot Sunday night, and a luncheon in the cool Japanese gardens at the Ritz with the wistful Kay Laurel and George Jean Nathan, and writing all night again and again, and paying too much for minute apartments, and buying magnificent but broken-down cars. The first speakeasies

had arrived, the toddle was *passé,* the Montmartre was
the smart place to dance and Lillian Tashman's fair hair
weaved around the floor among the enliquored college
boys. The plays were *Declasée* and *Sacred and Profane
Love,* and at the Midnight Frolic you danced elbow to
elbow with Marion Davies and perhaps picked out the
vivacious Mary Hay in the pony chorus. We thought
we were apart from all that; perhaps everyone thinks
they are apart from their milieu. We felt like small children in a great bright unexplored barn. Summoned out
to Griffith's studio on Long Island, we trembled in the
presence of the familiar faces of the *Birth of a Nation;*
later I realized that behind much of the entertainment
that the city poured forth into the nation there were
only a lot of rather lost and lonely people. The world of
the picture actors was like our own in that it was in
New York and not of it. It had little sense of itself and
no center: when I first met Dorothy Gish I had the feeling that we were both standing on the North Pole and
it was snowing. Since then they have found home but it
was not destined to be New York.

When bored we took our city with a Huysmans-like
perversity. An afternoon alone in our "apartment" eating olive sandwiches and drinking a quart of Bushmill's
whiskey presented by Zoë Atkins, then out into the
freshly bewitched city, through strange doors into
strange apartments with intermittent swings along in
taxis through the soft nights. At last we were one with
New York, pulling it after us through every portal.
Even now I go into many flats with the sense that I
have been there before or in the one above or below—
was it the night I tried to disrobe in the *Scandals,* or the
night when (as I read with astonishment in the paper
next morning) "Fitzgerald Knocks Officer This Side of
Paradise"? Successful scrapping not being among my
accomplishments, I tried in vain to reconstruct the
sequence of events which led up to this dénouement in
Webster Hall. And lastly from that period I remember
riding in a taxi one afternoon between very tall buildings under a mauve and rosy sky. I began to bawl
because I had everything I wanted and knew I would
never be so happy again.

It was typical of our precarious position in New York that when our child was to be born we played safe and went home to St. Paul—it seemed inappropriate to bring a baby into all that glamor and loneliness. But in a year we were back and we began doing the same things over again and not liking them so much. We had run through a lot, though we had retained an almost theatrical innocence by preferring the role of the observed to that of the observer. But innocence is no end in itself and as our minds unwillingly matured we began to see New York whole and try to save some of it for the selves we would inevitably become.

It was too late—or too soon. For us the city was inevitably linked up with Bacchic diversions, mild or fantastic. We could organize ourselves only on our return to Long Island and not always there. We had no incentive to meet the city half way. My first symbol was now a memory, for I knew that triumph is in oneself; my second one had grown commonplace—two of the actresses whom I had worshipped from afar in 1913 had dined in our house. But it filled me with a certain fear that even the third symbol had grown dim—the tranquillity of Bunny's apartment was not to be found in the ever-quickening city. Bunny himself was married, and about to become a father, other friends had gone to Europe, and the bachelors had become cadets of houses larger and more social than ours. By this time we "knew everybody"—which is to say most of those whom Ralph Barton would draw as in the orchestra on an opening night.

But we were no longer important. The flapper, upon whose activities the popularity of my first books was based, had become *passé* by 1923—anyhow in the East. I decided to crash Broadway with a play, but Broadway sent its scouts to Atlantic City and quashed the idea in advance, so I felt that, for the moment, the city and I had little to offer each other. I would take the Long Island atmosphere that I had familiarly breathed and materialize it beneath unfamiliar skies.

It was three years before we saw New York again. As the ship glided up the river, the city burst thunderously upon us in the early dusk—the white glacier of lower

New York swooping down like a strand of a bridge to rise into uptown New York, a miracle of foamy light suspended by the stars. A band started to play on deck, but the majesty of the city made the march trivial and tinkling. From that moment I knew that New York, however often I might leave it, was home.

The tempo of the city had changed sharply. The uncertainties of 1920 were drowned in a steady golden roar and many of our friends had grown wealthy. But the restlessness of New York in 1927 approached hysteria. The parties were bigger—those of Condé Nast, for example, rivaled in their way the fabled balls of the nineties; the pace was faster—the catering to dissipation set an example to Paris; the shows were broader, the buildings were higher, the morals were looser and the liquor was cheaper; but all these benefits did not really minister to much delight. Young people wore out early—they were hard and languid at twenty-one and save for Peter Arno none of them contributed anything new; perhaps Peter Arno and his collaborators said everything there was to say about the boom days in New York that couldn't be said by a jazz band. Many people who were not alcoholics were lit up four days out of seven, and frayed nerves were strewn everywhere; groups were held together by a generic nervousness and the hangover became a part of the day as well allowed-for as the Spanish siesta. Most of my friends drank too much—the more they were in tune to the times the more they drank. And as effort *per se* had no dignity against the mere bounty of those days in New York, a depreciatory word was found for it: a successful programme became a racket—I was in the literary racket.

We settled a few hours from New York and I found that every time I came to the city I was caught up into a complication of events that deposited me a few days later in a somewhat exhausted state on the train for Delaware. Whole sections of the city had grown rather poisonous, but invariably I found a moment of utter peace in riding south through Central Park at dark toward where the façade of 59th Street thrusts its lights through the trees. There again was my lost city, wrapped cool in its mystery and promise. But that detachment never lasted long—as the toiler must live in the city's belly, so I was compelled to live in its disordered mind.

Instead there were the speakeasies—the moving from luxurious bars, which advertised in the campus publications of Yale and Princeton, to the beer gardens where the snarling face of the underworld peered through the German good nature of the entertainment, then on to strange and even more sinister localities where one was eyed by granite-faced boys and there was nothing left of joviality but only a brutishness that corrupted the new day into which one presently went out. Back in 1920 I shocked a rising young business man by suggesting a cocktail before lunch. In 1929 there was liquor in half the downtown offices, and a speakeasy in half the large buildings.

One was increasingly conscious of the speakeasy and of Park Avenue. In the past decade Greenwich Village, Washington Square, Murray Hill, the châteaux of Fifth Avenue had somehow disappeared, or become unexpressive of anything. The city was bloated, glutted, stupid with cake and circuses, and a new expression "Oh yeah?" summed up all the enthusiasm evoked by the announcement of the last super-skyscrapers. My barber retired on a half million bet in the market and I was conscious that the head waiters who bowed me, or failed to bow me, to my table were far, far wealthier than I. This was no fun—once again I had enough of New York and it was good to be safe on shipboard where the ceaseless revelry remained in the bar in transport to the fleecing rooms of France.

"What news from New York?"

"Stocks go up. A baby murdered a gangster."

"Nothing more?"

"Nothing. Radios blare in the street."

I once thought that there were no second acts in American lives, but there was certainly to be a second act to New York's boom days. We were somewhere in North Africa when we heard a dull distant crash which echoed to the farthest wastes of the desert.

"What was that?"

"Did you hear it?"

"It was nothing."

"Do you think we ought to go home and see?"

"No—it was nothing."

In the dark autumn of two years later we saw New York again. We passed through curiously polite customs agents, and then with bowed head and hat in hand I walked reverently through the echoing tomb. Among the ruins a few childish wraiths still played to keep up the pretense that they were alive, betraying by their feverish voices and hectic cheeks the thinness of the masquerade. Cocktail parties, a last hollow survival from the days of carnival, echoed to the plaints of the wounded: "Shoot me, for the love of God, someone shoot me!", and the groans and wails of the dying: "Did you see that United States Steel is down three more points?" My barber was back at work in his shop; again the head waiters bowed people to their tables, if there were people to be bowed. From the ruins, lonely and inexplicable as the sphinx, rose the Empire State Building and, just as it had been a tradition of mine to climb to the Plaza Roof to take leave of the beautiful city, extending as far as eyes could reach, so now I went to the roof of the last and most magnificent of towers. Then I understood—everything was explained: I had discovered the crowning error of the city, its Pandora's box. Full of vaunting pride the New Yorker had climbed here and seen with dismay what he had never suspected, that the city was not the endless succession of canyons that he had supposed but that *it had limits*— from the tallest structure he saw for the first time that it faded out into the country on all sides, into an expanse of green and blue that alone was limitless. And with the awful realization that New York was a city after all and not a universe, the whole shining edifice that he had reared in his imagination came crashing to the ground. That was the rash gift of Alfred E. Smith to the citizens of New York.

Thus I take leave of my lost city. Seen from the ferry boat in the early morning, it no longer whispers of fantastic success and eternal youth. The whoopee mamas who prance before its empty parquets do not suggest to me the ineffable beauty of my dream girls of 1914. And

Bunny, swinging along confidently with his cane toward his cloister in a carnival, had gone over to Communism and frets about the wrongs of southern mill workers and western farmers whose voices, fifteen years ago, would not have penetrated his study walls.

All is lost save memory, yet sometimes I imagine myself reading, with curious interest, a *Daily News* of the issue of 1945:

MAN OF FIFTY RUNS AMUCK IN NEW YORK
Fitzgerald Feathered Many Love Nests Cutie Avers
Bumped Off By Outraged Gunman

So perhaps I am destined to return some day and find in the city new experiences that so far I have only read about. For the moment I can only cry out that I have lost my splendid mirage. Come back, come back, O glittering and white!

———————

F. SCOTT FITZGERALD *(1896-1940), novelist, short-story writer, and embodiment of what he himself dubbed the Jazz Age, grew up in St. Paul, Minnesota. In 1919 he moved to Manhattan to write copy for an advertising agency. He returned to St. Paul to live with his parents and rewrite his novel, published in 1920 as* This Side of Paradise. *That same year he and Zelda were married.*

Fitzgerald's second novel, The Beautiful and Damned, *was published in 1922, along with a collection of stories,* Tales of the Jazz Age. *His early success enabled the Fitzgeralds to move to the affluent Long Island community of Great Neck, which became background for* The Great Gatsby, *published in 1925.*

Between 1924 and 1930—when Zelda had the first of the mental breakdowns that would hospitalize her periodically until her death in 1948—the Fitzgeralds moved back and forth between Europe and the United States. The novel Tender Is the Night *was published in 1934.*

"My Lost City" (1936) is from The Crack-Up, *a 1945 collection of essays edited by Edmund Wilson.*

A. J. Liebling

Apology for Breathing

People I know in New York are incessantly on the point of going back where they came from to write a book, or of staying on and writing a book about back where they came from. Back where they came from, I gather, is the American scene (New York, of course, just isn't America). It is all pretty hard on me because I have no place to go back to. I was born in an apartment house at Ninety-third Street and Lexington Avenue, about three miles from where I now live. Friends often tell me of their excitement when the train on which they are riding passes from Indiana into Illinois, or back again. I am ashamed to admit that when the Jerome Avenue express rolls into Eighty-sixth Street station I have absolutely no reaction.

I always think of back where my friends came from as one place, possessing a homogeneous quality of not being New York. The thought has been well expressed by my literary adviser, Whitey Bimstein, who also trains prizefighters. I once asked him how he liked the country. He said, "It is a nice spot." I have been to the country myself. I went to a college in New Hampshire. But I seldom mention this, because I would like to be considered quaint and regional, like Jesse Stuart or Kenneth Roberts.

The finest thing about New York City, I think, is that it is like one of those complicated Renaissance clocks where on one level an allegorical marionette pops out to mark the day of the week, on another a skeleton death bangs the quarter hour with his scythe, and on a third the Twelve Apostles do a cakewalk. The variety of the sideshows distracts one's attention from the advance of the hour hand. I know people who say that, as in the clock, all the exhibits depend upon the same movement. This they insist is economic. But they are the sort of people who look at a fine woman and remind you that the human body is composed of one dollar and sixty-two cents worth of chemicals.*

I like to think of all the city microcosms so nicely synchronized though unaware of one another: the worlds of the weight-lifters, yodelers, tugboat captains and sideshow barkers, of the book-dutchers, sparring partners, song pluggers, sporting girls and religious painters, of the dealers in rhesus monkeys and the bishops of churches that they establish themselves under the religious corporations law. It strengthens my hold on reality to know when I awake with a brandy headache in my house which is nine blocks due south of the Chrysler Building and four blocks due east of the Empire State, that Eddie Arcaro, the jockey, is galloping a horse around the track at Belmont while Ollie Thomas, a colored clocker of my acquaintance, is holding a watch on him. I can be sure that Kit Coates, at the Aquarium, is worrying over the liverish deportment of a new tropical fish, that presently Whitey will be laying out the gloves and headguards for the fighters he trains at Stillman's gymnasium, while Miss Ira, the Harlem modiste, will be trying to talk a dark-complexioned girl out of buying herself an orange turban and Hymie the Tummler ruminates a plan for opening a new night club. It would be easier to predicate the existence of God on such recurrences than on the cracking of ice in ponds, the peeping of spring peepers in their peeperies and the shy green sprigs of poison ivy so well advertised by writers like Thoreau.

There are New Yorkers so completely submerged in one environment, like the Garment Centre or Jack and Charlie's, that they live and die oblivious of the other worlds around them. Others are instinctively aware of the wonders of New York natural history, but think them hardly worthy of mention. My father was a New

---

* The author has not checked on this figure. — *The Editor*

Yorker of the latter sort. In separate phases of his business life, he had occasion to retain Monk Eastman, a leading pre-war gangster, and the Rev. Charles Parkhurst, a notorious crusader against vice. This seemed to him no more paradoxical than going to Coward's for his shoes while he bought his hats of Knox. When Father was President of an association of furriers during a strike he hired Eastman to break up a strikers' mass meeting. His employment of Dr. Parkhurst was more subtle. In about 1910 Father bought some real estate in West Twenty-sixth Street on which he purposed to put several loft buildings. He believed that the fur industry was going to move up in that direction from below Twenty-third. But Twenty-sixth Street between Sixth and Seventh Avenues was full of brothels, and there was no hope of getting tenants for the new buildings until the block was made more respectable. First Father dispossessed the hock shops from the houses which he had acquired with his building lots. But the watchmen rented the empty rooms to the drabs for fifty cents a night. Then Father made a substantial gift to Dr. Parkhurst's society, enclosing with his check a letter that called attention to the sinful conditions on West Twenty-sixth Street. Dr. Parkhurst raised Hell with the police, who made the girls move on to another block, and then Father put up his buildings. Father always said Monk and Dr. Parkhurst gave him his money's worth, but he never liked either of them. He became labor conscious after he retired from business, and toward the end of his life often said that unions were a fine thing, but that they had doubtless changed a lot since the time he hired Eastman. He died a staunch Roosevelt man.

Even though he made his home during the second part of his life among middle-class enterprisers with horizons slimmer than a gnat's waist, Father lived in other milieus in retrospect. He liked to talk of the lower East Side in the eighties, when the carters left their wagons in the streets of nights and the small boys would roll the wains away and burn them on election day, and of how he, a workingman at ten, boxed with the other furriers' apprentices using beaver muffs for mitts. He would even tell of the gay life of London and Paris and Leipzig in the late nineties when he was a bachelor buyer, although, he always protested, he had finished with that sort of thing when he got married. And he early introduced me to those worlds into which one may escape temporarily for the payment of a fee, the race course and the baseball park. These have their own conflicts that do not follow scenarios pre-determined in Hollywood.

Since this is a regional book about people I met back where I came from, I should like to say something here about the local language. This is a regional tongue imported from the British Isles, as is the dialect spoken by the retarded inhabitants of the Great Smoky Mountains back where *they* come from. Being spoken by several million people, it has not been considered of any philological importance. Basically, New Yorkese is the common speech of early nineteenth century Cork, transplanted during the mass immigration of the South Irish a hundred years ago. Of this Cork dialect Thomas Crofton Croker in 1839 wrote: "The vernacular of this region may be regarded as the ancient cockneyism of the mixed race who held the old city—Danes, English and Irish. It is a jargon, whose principal characteristic appears in the pronunciation of *th*, as exemplified in *dis*, *dat*, *den*, *dey*—this, that, then, they; and in the dovetailing of words as, 'kum our rish' for 'come of this.'" New York example, "gerradahere" for "get out of here." The neo-Corkonian proved particularly suited to the later immigrants who came here from continental Europe— the *th* sound is equally impossible for French, Germans and Italians. Moreover, it was impressed upon the latecomers because it was the talk of the police and the elementary school teachers, the only Americans who would talk to them at all. Father, who was born in Austria but came here when he was seven years old, spoke New Yorkese perfectly.

It is true that since the diaspora the modern dialects of Cork and New York have diverged slightly like Italian and Provençal, both of which stem from vulgar Latin. Yet Sean O'Faolain's modern story of Cork, "A Born Genius," contains dialogue that might have come out of Eleventh Avenue: "He's after painting two swans on deh kitchen windes. Wan is facin' wan way and d'oder is facin' d'oder way.—So dat so help me God dis day you'd tink deh swans was floatin' in a garden! And deh garden was floatin' in trough deh winda! And dere was no winda!"

There are interesting things about New York besides the language. It is one of the oldest places in the United States, but doesn't live in retrospect like the professionally picturesque provinces. Any city may have one period of magnificence, like Boston or New Orleans or San Francisco, but it takes a real one to keep renewing itself until the past is perennially forgotten. There were plenty of clipper ships out of New York in the old days and privateers before them, but there are better ships out of here today. The Revolution was fought all over town, from Harlem to Red Hook and back again, but that isn't the revolution you will hear New Yorkers discussing now.

Native New Yorkers are the best mannered people in America; they never speak out of turn in saloons, because they have experience in group etiquette. Whenever you hear a drinker let a blat out of him you can be sure he is a recent immigrant from the south or middle west. New Yorkers are modest. It is a distinction for a child in New York to be the brightest on one block; he acquires no exaggerated idea of his own relative intelligence. Prairie geniuses are raced in cheap company when young. They are intoxicated by the feel of being boy wonders in Amarillo, and when they bounce off New York's skin as adults they resent it.

New York women are the most beautiful in the world. They have their teeth straightened in early youth. They get their notions of chic from S. Klein's windows instead of the movies. Really loud and funny New Yorkers, like Bruce Barton, are invariably carpetbaggers. The climate is extremely healthy. The death rate is lower in Queens and the Bronx than in any other large city in the United States, and the average life expectancy is so high that one of our morning newspapers specializes in interviewing people a hundred years old and upward. The average is slightly lowered, however, by the inlanders who come here and insist on eating in Little Southern Tea Roomes on side streets.

The natives put up with a lot back here where I came from. If the inhabitants of Kentucky are distrustful of strangers, that is duly noted as an entertaining local trait. But if a New Yorker says that he doesn't like Kentuckians he is marked a cold churl. It is perennially difficult for the New Yorker who subscribes to a circulating library to understand how the city survived destruction during the Civil War. When he reads about those regional demigods haunted by ancestral daemons and festooned in magnolia blossoms and ghosts who composed practically the whole Confederate Army, he wonders what happened to them en route. I asked Whitey Bimstein what he thought of that one. He said: "Our guys must have slapped their ears down." Whitey does not know that we have been paying a war indemnity ever since in the form of royalties.

━━━━━━━━

A. J. (ABBOTT JOSEPH) LIEBLING (1904-1963), *journalist, critic, and gourmet, spent his life in New York and Europe. He was born in Lawrence, New York, a suburb of Long Island, and graduated from Columbia University's School of Journalism. He wrote for the* New York World-Telegram *before going to work in 1935 for Harold Ross at* The New Yorker, *originally as a "Talk of the Town" reporter and eventually as a feature writer.*

In 1939 he left New York to cover World War II for The New Yorker, *a move that not only transformed him from a reporter to a foreign correspondent, but also helped to establish* The New Yorker *as a magazine of national interest.*

After the liberation of Paris, he returned to New York, where, for a decade, he worked as a press critic.

In the 1950s he returned to Europe to cover British affairs. There he penned Normandy Revisited *and* Between Meals *(1962), an unapologetic account of a life committed to serious appetite.*

"Apology for Breathing" is Liebling's ode to his home town, written in 1938 and published in a collection titled Back Where I Came From.

Tom Wolfe

Stalking the Billion-Footed Beast

May I be forgiven if I take as my text the sixth page of the fourth chapter of *The Bonfire of the Vanities*? The novel's main character, Sherman McCoy, is driving over the Triborough Bridge in New York City in his Mercedes roadster with his twenty-six-year-old girl-friend, not his forty-year-old wife, in the tan leather bucket seat beside him, and he glances triumphantly off to his left toward the island of Manhattan. "The towers were jammed together so tightly, he could feel the mass and stupendous weight. Just think of the millions, from all over the globe, who yearned to be on that island, in those towers, in those narrow streets! There it was, the Rome, the Paris, the London of the twentieth century, the city of ambition, the dense magnetic rock, the irresistible destination of all those who insist on being *where things are happening —*"

To me the idea of writing a novel about this astonish-ing metropolis, a big novel, cramming as much of New York City between covers as you could, was the most tempting, the most challenging, and the most obvious idea an American writer could possibly have. I had first vowed to try it in 1968, except that what I had in mind then was a nonfiction novel, to use a much-discussed term from the period. I had just written one, *The Electric Kool-Aid Acid Test,* about the psychedelic, or hippie, movement, and I had begun to indulge in some brave speculations about nonfiction as an art form. These were eventually recorded in a book called *The New Jour-nalism.* Off the record, however, alone in my little apart-ment on East Fifty-eighth Street, I was worried that somebody out there was writing a big realistic fictional novel about the hippie experience that would blow *The Electric Kool-Aid Acid Test* out of the water. Somebody? There might be droves of them. After all, among the hippies were many well-educated and presumably, not to mention avowedly, creative people. But one, two, three, four years went by, and to my relief, and then my bafflement, those novels never appeared. (And to this day they remain unwritten.)

Meantime, I turned to the proposed nonfiction novel about New York. As I saw it, such a book should be a novel *of the city*, in the sense that Balzac and Zola had written novels *of Paris* and Dickens and Thackeray had written novels *of London*, with the city always in the foreground, exerting its relentless pressure on the souls of its inhabitants. My immediate model was Thackeray's *Vanity Fair*. Thackeray and Dickens had lived in the first great era of the metropolis. Now, a century later, in the 1960s, certain powerful forces had converged to create a second one. The economic boom that had begun in the middle of the Second World War surged through the decade of the sixties without even a mild recession. The flush times created a sense of immunity, and standards that had been in place for millennia were swept aside with a merry, rut-boar abandon. One result was the so-called sexual revolution, which I always thought was a rather prim term for the lurid carnival that actually took place.

Indirectly, the boom also triggered something else: overt racial conflict. Bad feelings had been rumbling on low boil in the cities ever since the great migrations from the rural South had begun in the 1920s. But in 1965 a series of race riots erupted, starting with the Harlem riot in 1964 and the Watts riot in Los Angeles in 1965, moving to Detroit in 1967, and peaking in Washington and Chicago in 1968. These were riots that only the sixties could have produced. In the sixties, the federal government had created the War on Poverty, at the heart of which were not alms for the poor but setups called CAPs, Community Action Programs. CAPs were something new in the history of political science. They were official invitations from the govern-

ment to people in the slums to improve their lot by rising up and rebelling against the establishment, including the government itself. The government would
provide the money, the headquarters, and the advisers.
So people in the slums obliged. The riots were merely
the most sensational form the strategy took, however.
The more customary form was the confrontation.
"Confrontation" was a sixties term. It was not by mere
coincidence that the most violent of the sixties' confrontational groups, the Black Panther Party of America, drew up its ten-point program in the North
Oakland poverty center. That was what the poverty
center was there for.

Such was the backdrop one day in January of 1970
when I decided to attend a party that Leonard Bernstein and his wife, Felicia, were giving for the Black
Panthers in their apartment at Park Avenue and Seventy-ninth Street. I figured that here might be some
material for a chapter in my nonfiction *Vanity Fair*
about New York. I didn't know the half of it. It was at
this party that a Black Panther field marshal rose up
beside the north piano—there was also a south
piano—in Leonard Bernstein's living room and out-
lined the Panthers' ten-point program to a roomful of
socialites and celebrities, who, giddy with *nostalgie de
la boue,* entertained a vision of the future in which,
after the revolution, there would no longer be any
such thing as a two-story, thirteen-room apartment on
Park Avenue, with twin grand pianos in the living
room, for one family.

All I was after was material for a chapter in a nonfiction novel, as I say. But the party was such a perfect
set piece that I couldn't hold back. I wrote an account
of the evening for *New York* magazine entitled "Radical
Chic" and, as a companion piece, an article about the
confrontations the War on Poverty had spawned in San
Francisco, "Mau-mauing the Flak Catchers." The two
were published as a book in the fall of 1970. Once again
I braced and waited for the big realistic novels that were
sure to be written about this phenomenon that had
played such a major part in American life in the late
1960s and early 1970s: racial strife in the cities. Once

again the years began to roll by, and these novels never appeared.

This time, however, my relief was not very profound. I still had not written my would-be big book about New York. I had merely put off the attempt. In 1972 I put it off a little further. I went to Cape Canaveral to cover the launch of *Apollo 17,* the last mission to the moon, for *Rolling Stone*. I ended up writing a four-part series on the astronauts, then decided to spend the next five or six months expanding the material into a book. The five or six months stretched into a year, eighteen months, two years, and I began to look over my shoulder. Truman Capote, for one, had let it be known that he was working on a big novel about New York entitled *Answered Prayers*. No doubt there were others as well. The material was rich beyond belief and getting richer every day.

Another year slipped by . . . and, miraculously, no such book appeared.

Now I paused and looked about and tried to figure out what was, in fact, going on in the world of American fiction. I wasn't alone, as it turned out. Half the publishers along Madison Avenue—at that time, publishing houses could still afford Madison Avenue—had their noses pressed against their Thermopane glass walls, scanning the billion-footed city for the approach of the young novelists who, surely, would bring them the big novels of the racial clashes, the hippie movement, the New Left, the Wall Street boom, the sexual revolution, the war in Vietnam. But such creatures, it seemed, no longer existed.

The strange fact of the matter was that young people with serious literary ambitions were no longer interested in the metropolis or any other big, rich slices of contemporary life. Over the preceding fifteen years, while I had been immersed in journalism, one of the most curious chapters in American literary history had begun. (And it is not over yet.) The story is by turns bizarre and hilarious, and one day some lucky doctoral candidate with the perseverance of a Huizinga or a Hauser will do it justice. I can offer no more than the broadest outline.

After the Second World War, in the late 1940s, American intellectuals began to revive a dream that had glowed briefly in the 1920s. They set out to create a native intelligentsia on the French or English model, an intellectual aristocracy—socially unaffiliated, beyond class distinctions—active in politics and the arts. In the arts, their audience would be the inevitably small minority of truly cultivated people as opposed to the mob, who wished only to be entertained or to be assured they were "cultured." By now, if one need edit, the mob was better known as the middle class.

Among the fashionable European ideas that began to circulate was that of "the death of the novel," by which was meant the realistic novel. Writing in 1948, Lionel Trilling gave this notion a late-Marxist twist that George Steiner and others would elaborate on. The realistic novel, in their gloss, was the literary child of the nineteenth-century industrial bourgeoisie. It was a slice of life, a cross section, that provided a true and powerful picture of individuals and society—as long as the bourgeois order and the old class system were firmly in place. But now that the bourgeoisie was in a state of "crisis and partial rout" (Steiner's phrase) and the old class system was crumbling, the realistic novel was pointless. What could be more futile than a cross section of disintegrating fragments?

The truth was, as Arnold Hauser had gone to great pains to demonstrate in *The Social History of Art,* the intelligentsia have always had contempt for the realistic novel—a form that wallows so enthusiastically in the dirt of everyday life and the dirty secrets of class envy and that, still worse, is so easily understood and obviously relished by the mob, that is, the middle class. In Victorian England, the intelligentsia regarded Dickens as "the author of the uneducated, undiscriminating public." It required a chasm of time—eighty years, in fact—to separate his work from its vulgar milieu so that Dickens might be canonized in British literary circles. The intelligentsia have always preferred more refined forms of fiction, such as that long-time French intellectual favorite, the psychological novel.

By the early 1960s, the notion of the death of the

realistic novel had caught on among young American writers with the force of revelation. This was an extra-ordinary turnabout. It had been only yesterday, in the 1930s, that the big realistic novel, with its broad social sweep, had put American literature up on the world stage for the first time. In 1930 Sinclair Lewis, a realistic novelist who used reporting techniques as thorough as Zola's, became the first American writer to win the Nobel Prize. In his acceptance speech, he called on his fellow writers to give America "a literature worthy of her vastness," and, indeed, four of the next five Ameri-cans to win the Nobel Prize in literature—Pearl Buck, William Faulkner, Ernest Hemingway, and John Stein-beck—were realistic novelists. (The fifth was Eugene O'Neill.) For that matter, the most highly regarded new novelists of the immediate postwar period—James Jones, Norman Mailer, Irwin Shaw, William Styron, Calder Willingham—were all realists.

Yet by 1962, when Steinbeck won the Noble Prize, young writers, and intellectuals generally, regarded him and his approach to the novel as an embarrassment. Pearl Buck was even worse, and Lewis wasn't much bet-ter. Faulkner and Hemingway still commanded respect, but it was the respect you give to old boys who did the best they could with what they knew in their day. They were "squares" (John Gardner's term) who actually thought you could take real life and spread it across the pages of a book. They never comprehended the fact that a novel is a sublime literary game.

All serious young writers—"serious" meaning those who aimed for literary prestige—understood such things, and they were dismantling the realistic novel just as fast as they could think of ways to do it. The dividing line was the year 1960. Writers who went to college after 1960 . . . *understood*. For a serious young writer to stick with realism after 1960 required contrari-ness and courage.

Writers who had gone to college before 1960, such as Saul Bellow, Robert Stone, and John Updike, found it hard to give up realism, but many others were caught betwixt and between. They didn't know which way to turn. For example, Philip Roth, a 1954 graduate of

Bucknell, won the National Book Award in 1960 at the age of twenty-seven for a collection entitled *Goodbye, Columbus*. The title piece was a brilliant novella of manners—brilliant . . . but, alas, highly realistic. By 1961 Roth was having second thoughts. He made a statement that had a terrific impact on other young writers. We now live in an age, he said, in which the imagination of the novelist lies helpless before what he knows he will read in tomorrow morning's newspaper. "The actuality is continually outdoing our talents, and the culture tosses up figures daily that are the envy of any novelist."

Even today—perhaps especially today—anyone, writer or not, can sympathize. What novelist would dare concoct a plot in which, say, a southern television evangelist has a tryst in a motel with a church secretary from Babylon, New York—did you have to make it *Babylon?*—and is ruined to the point where he has to sell all his worldly goods at auction, including his air-conditioned doghouse—*air-conditioned doghouse?*—whereupon he is termed a "decadent pompadour boy" by a second television evangelist, who, we soon learn, has been combing his own rather well-teased blond hair forward over his forehead and wearing headbands in order to disguise himself as he goes into Louisiana waterbed motels with combat-zone prostitutes—oh, *come on*—prompting a third television evangelist, who is under serious consideration for the Republican presidential nomination, to charge that the damning evidence has been leaked to the press by the vice president of the United States . . . while, meantime, the aforesaid church secretary has now bared her chest to the photographers and has thereby become an international celebrity and has gone to live happily ever after in a castle known as the Playboy Mansion . . . and her erstwhile tryst mate, evangelist number one, was last seen hiding in the fetal position under his lawyer's couch in Charlotte, North Carolina . . .

What novelist would dare dream up such crazy stuff and then ask you to suspend your disbelief?

The lesson that a generation of serious young writers learned from Roth's lament was that it was time to avert their eyes. To attempt a realistic novel with the scope of Balzac, Zola, or Lewis was absurd. By the mid-1960s the conviction was not merely that the realistic novel was no longer possible but that American life itself no longer deserved the term "real." American life was chaotic, fragmented, random, discontinuous; in a word, absurd. Writers in the university creative writing programs had long, phenomenological discussions in which they decided that the act of writing words on a page was the real thing and the so-called real world of America was the fiction, requiring the suspension of disbelief. "The so-called real world" became a favorite phrase.

New types of novels came in waves, each trying to establish an avant-garde position out beyond realism. There were Absurdist novels, Magical Realist novels, and novels of Radical Disjunction (the novelist and critic Robert Towers's phrase) in which plausible events and plausible characters were combined in fantastic or outlandish ways, often resulting in dreadful catastrophes that were played for laughs in the ironic mode. Irony was the attitude supreme, and nowhere more so than in the Puppet Master novels, a category that often overlapped with the others. The Puppet Masters were in love with the theory that the novel was, first and foremost, a literary game, words on a page being manipulated by an author. Ronald Sukenick, author of a highly praised 1968 novel called *Up,* would tell you what he looked like while he was writing the words you were at that moment reading. At one point you are informed that he is stark naked. Sometimes he tells you he's crossing out what you've just read and changing it. Then he gives you the new version. In a story called "The Death of the Novel," he keeps saying, à la Samuel Beckett, "I can't go on." Then he exhorts himself, "Go on," and on he goes. At the end of *Up* he tells you that none of the characters was real: "I just make it up as I go along."

The Puppet Masters took to calling their stories *fictions,* after the manner of Jorge Luis Borges, who spoke of his *ficciones*. Borges, an Argentinian, was one of the gods of the new breed. In keeping with the cosmopolitan yearnings of the native intelligentsia, all gods now came from abroad: Borges, Nabokov, Beckett, Pinter, Kundera, Calvino, García Márquez, and, above all, Kafka; there was a whole rash of stories with characters named H or V or T or P (but, for some reason, none named A, B, D, or E). It soon reached the point where a creative writing teacher at Johns Hopkins held up Tolstoy as a master of the novel—and was looked upon by his young charges as rather touchingly old-fashioned. As one of them, Frederick Barthelme, later put it, "He talked Leo Tolstoy when we were up to here with Laurence Sterne, Franz Kafka, Italo Calvino, and Gabriel García Márquez. In fact, Gabriel García Márquez was already *over* by then."

By the 1970s there was a headlong rush to get rid of not only realism but everything associated with it. One of the most highly praised of the new breed, John Hawkes, said, "I began to write fiction on the assumption that the true enemies of the novel were plot, character, setting, and theme." The most radical group, the Neo-Fabulists, decided to go back to the primal origins of fiction, back to a happier time, before realism and all its contaminations, back to myth, fable, and legend. John Gardner and John Irving both started out in this vein, but the peerless leader was John Barth, who wrote a collection of three novellas called *Chimera,* recounting the further adventures of Perseus and Andromeda and other characters from Greek mythology. *Chimera* won the 1972 National Book Award for fiction.

Other Neo-Fabulists wrote modern fables, à la Kafka, in which the action, if any, took place at no specific location. You couldn't even tell what hemisphere it was. It was some nameless, elemental terrain—the desert, the woods, the open sea, the snowy wastes. The characters had no backgrounds. They came from nowhere. They didn't use realistic speech. Nothing they said, did, or possessed indicated any class or ethnic origin. Above all, the Neo-Fabulists avoided all big, obvious sentiments and emotions, which the realistic novel, with its dreadful Little Nell scenes, specialized in. Perfect anesthesia; that was the ticket, even in the death scenes. Anesthetic solitude became one of the great motifs of serious fiction in the 1970s. The Minimalists, also known as the K Mart Realists, wrote about real situations, but very tiny ones, tiny domestic ones, for the most part, usually in lonely Rustic Septic Tank Rural settings, in a deadpan prose composed of disingenuously short, simple sentences—with the emotions anesthetized, given a shot of novocaine. My favorite Minimalist opening comes from a short story by Robert Coover: "In order to get started, he went to live alone on an island and shot himself."

Many of these writers were brilliant. They were virtuosos. They could do things within the narrow limits they had set for themselves that were more clever and amusing than anyone could have ever imagined. But what was this lonely island they had moved to? After all, they, like me, happened to be alive in what was, for better or for worse, the American century, the century in which we had become the mightiest military power in all history, capable of blowing up the world by turning two cylindrical keys in a missile silo but also capable, once it blew, of escaping to the stars in space ships. We were alive in the first moment since the dawn of time in which man was able at last to break the bonds of Earth's gravity and explore the rest of the universe. And, on top of that, we had created an affluence that reached clear down to the level of mechanics and tradesmen on a scale that would have made the Sun King blink, so that on any given evening even a Neo-Fabulist's or a Minimalist's electrician or air-conditioner mechanic or burglar-alarm repairman might very well be in St. Kitts or Barbados or Puerto Vallarta wearing a Harry Belafonte cane-cutter shirt, open to the sternum, the better to reveal the gold chains twinkling in his chest hair, while he and his third wife sit on the terrace and have a little designer water before dinner . . .

What a feast was spread out before every writer in America! How could any writer resist plunging into it? I couldn't.

In 1979, after I had finally completed my book about the astronauts, *The Right Stuff,* I returned at last to the idea of a novel about New York. I now decided the book would not be a nonfiction novel but a fictional one. Part of it, I suppose, was curiosity or, better said, the question that rebuked every writer who had made a point of experimenting with nonfiction over the preceding ten or fifteen years: Are you merely ducking the big challenge—The Novel? Consciously, I wanted to prove a point. I wanted to fulfill a prediction I had made in the introduction to *The New Journalism* in 1973; namely, that the future of the fictional novel would be in a highly detailed realism based on reporting, a realism more thorough than any currently being attempted, a realism that would portray the individual in intimate and inextricable relation to the society around him.

One of the axioms of literary theory in the seventies was that realism was "just another formal device, not a permanent method for dealing with experience" (in the words of the editor of *Partisan Review,* William Phillips). I was convinced then—and I am even more strongly convinced now—that precisely the opposite is true. The introduction of realism into literature in the eighteenth century by Richardson, Fielding, and Smollett was like the introduction of electricity into engineering. It was not just another device. The effect on the emotions of an everyday realism such as Richardson's was something that had never been conceived of before. It was realism that created the "absorbing" or "gripping" quality that is peculiar to the novel, the quality that makes the reader feel that he has been pulled not only into the setting of the story but also into the minds and central nervous systems of the characters. No one was ever moved to tears by reading about the unhappy fates of heroes and heroines in Homer, Sophocles, Molière, Racine, Sydney, Spenser, or Shakespeare. Yet even the impeccable Lord Jeffrey, editor of *Edinburgh Review,* confessed to having cried— blubbered, boohooed, snuffled, and sighed—over the death of Little Nell in *The Old Curiosity Shop.* For writers to give up this power in the quest for a more up-to-date kind of fiction—it is as if an engineer were to set out to develop a more sophisticated machine technology by first of all discarding the principle of electricity, on the grounds that it has been used ad nauseam for a hundred years.

One of the specialties of the realistic novel, from Richardson on, was the demonstration of the influence of society on even the most personal aspects of the life of the individual. Lionel Trilling was right when he said, in 1948, that what produced great characters in the nineteenth-century European novel was the portrayal of "class traits modified by personality." But he went on to argue that the old class structure by now had disintegrated, particularly in the United States, rendering the technique useless. Again, I would say that precisely the opposite is the case. If we substitute for "class," in Trilling's formulation, the broader term "status," that technique has never been more essential in portraying the innermost life of the individual. This is above all true when the subject is the modern city. It strikes me as folly to believe that you can portray the individual in the city today without also portraying the city itself.

Asked once what three novels he would most recommend to a creative writing student, Faulkner said (or is said to have said), "*Anna Karenina, Anna Karenina,* and *Anna Karenina.*" And what is at the core of not only the private dramas but also the very psychology of *Anna Karenina?* It is Tolstoy's concept of the heart at war with the structure of society. The dramas of Anna, Vronsky, Karenin, Levin, and Kitty would be nothing but slow-moving romances without the panorama of Russian society against which Tolstoy places them. The characters' electrifying irrational acts are the acts of the heart brought to a desperate edge by the pressure of society.

If Trilling were here, he would no doubt say, But of course: "class traits modified by personality." These are substantial characters ("substantial" was one of Trilling's favorite terms) precisely because Russian society in Tolstoy's day was so clearly defined by social classes, each with its own distinctive culture and traditions. Today, in New York, Trilling could argue, Anna would just move in with Vronsky, and people in their social set would duly note the change in their Scully &

Scully address books; and the arrival of the baby, if they chose to have it, would occasion no more than a grinning snigger in the gossip columns. To which I would say, Quite so. The status structure of society has changed, but it has not disappeared for a moment. It provides an infinite number of new agonies for the Annas and Vronskys of the Upper East Side, and, as far as that goes, of Leningrad. Anyone who doubts that need only get to know them.

American society today is no more or less chaotic, random, discontinuous, or absurd than Russian society or French society or British society a hundred years ago, no matter how convenient it might be for a writer to think so. It is merely more varied and complicated and harder to define. In the prologue to *The Bonfire of the Vanities,* the mayor of New York delivers a soliloquy in a stream of consciousness as he is being routed from a stage in Harlem by a group of demonstrators. He thinks of all the rich white New Yorkers who will be watching this on television from within the insulation of their cooperative apartments. "Do you really think this is *your* city any longer? Open your eyes! The greatest city of the twentieth century! Do you think *money* will keep it yours? Come down from you swell co-ops, you general partners and merger lawyers! It's the Third World down there! Puerto Ricans, West Indians, Haitians, Dominicans, Cubans, Colombians, Hondurans, Koreans, Chinese, Thais, Vietnamese, Ecuadorians, Panamanians, Filipinos, Albanians, Senegalese, and Afro-Americans! Go visit the frontiers, you gutless wonders! Morningside Heights, St. Nicholas Park, Washington Heights, Fort Tryon—*por qué pagar más!* The Bronx—the Bronx is finished for you!"—and on he goes. New York and practically every large city in the United States are undergoing a profound change. The fourth great wave of immigrants—this one from Asia, North Africa, Latin America, and the Caribbean—is now pouring in. Within ten years political power in most major American cities will have passed to the nonwhite majorities. Does that render these cities incomprehensible, fragmented beyond the grasp of all logic, absurd, meaningless to gaze upon in a literary sense?

Not in my opinion. It merely makes the task of the writer more difficult if he wants to know what truly presses upon the heart of the individual, white or non-white, living in the metropolis in the last decade of the twentieth century.

That task, as I see it, inevitably involves reporting, which I regard as the most valuable and least under-stood resource available to any writer with exalted ambitions, whether the medium is print, film, tape, or the stage. Young writers are constantly told, "Write about what you know." There is nothing wrong with that rule as a starting point, but it seems to get quickly magnified into an unspoken maxim: The only valid experience is personal experience.

Emerson said that every person has a great autobiog-raphy to write, if only he understands what is truly his own unique experience. But he didn't say every person had *two* great autobiographies to write. Dickens, Dosto-evski, Balzac, Zola, and Sinclair Lewis *assumed* that the novelist had to go beyond his personal experience and head out into society as a reporter. Zola called it docu-mentation, and his documenting expeditions to the slums, the coal mines, the races, the *folies*, department stores, wholesale food markets, newspaper offices, barnyards, railroad yards, and engine decks, notebook and pen in hand, became legendary. To write *Elmer Gantry,* the great portrait of not only a corrupt evange-list but also the entire Protestant clergy at a time when they still set the moral tone of America, Lewis left his home in New England and moved to Kansas City. He organized Bible study groups for clergymen, delivered sermons from the pulpits of preachers on summer vaca-tion, attended tent meetings and Chautauqua lectures and church conferences and classes at the seminaries, all the while doggedly taking notes on five-by-eight cards.

It was through this process, documentation, that Lewis happened to scoop the Jim Bakker story by sixty years—and to render it totally plausible, historically and psychologically, in fiction. I refer to the last two chapters of *Elmer Gantry*. We see Elmer, the great evan-gelist, get caught in a tryst with . . . the church secretary

(Hettie Dowler is her name) . . . who turns out to be in league with a very foxy lawyer . . . and the two of them present Elmer with a hefty hush-money demand, which he is only too eager to pay. With the help of friends, however, Elmer manages to turn the tables, and is absolved and vindicated in the eyes of humanity and the press. On the final page, we see Elmer on his knees beside the pulpit on Sunday morning before a packed house, with his gaze lifted heavenward and his hands pressed together in Albrecht Dürer mode, tears running down his face, loudly thanking the Lord for delivering him from the vipers. As the book ends, he looks toward the choir and catches a glimpse of a new addition, "a girl with charming ankles and lively eyes."

Was it reporting that made Lewis the most highly regarded American novelist of the 1920s? Certainly not by itself. But it was the material he found through reporting that enabled Lewis to exercise with such rich variety his insights, many of them exceptionally subtle, into the psyches of men and women and into the status structure of society. Having said that, I will now reveal something that practically every writer has experienced—and none, as far as I know, has ever talked about. The young person who decides to become a writer because he has a subject or an issue in mind, because he has "something to say," is a rare bird. Most make that decision because they realize they have a certain musical facility with words. Since poetry is the music of language, outstanding young poets are by no means rare. As he grows older, however, our young genius keeps running into this damnable problem of *material,* of what to write about, since by now he realizes that literature's main arena is prose, whether in fiction or the essay. Even so, he keeps things in proportion. He tells himself that 95 percent of literary genius is the unique talent that is secure inside some sort of crucible in his skull and 5 percent is the material, the clay his talent will mold.

I can remember going through this stage myself. In college, at Washington and Lee, I decided I would write crystalline prose. That was the word: crystalline. It would be a prose as ageless, timeless, exquisite, soaring, and transparently dazzling as Scarlatti at his most sublime. It would speak to the twenty-fifth century as lucidly as to my own. (I was, naturally, interested to hear, years later, that Iris Murdoch had dreamed of the same quality and chosen the same word, crystalline, at a similar point in her life.) In graduate school at Yale, I came upon the Elizabethan books of rhetoric, which isolated, by my count, 444 figures of speech, covering every conceivable form of word play. By analyzing the prose of writers I admired—De Quincey, I remember, was one of them—I tried to come up with the perfect sequences of figures and make notations for them, like musical notes. I would flesh out this perfect skeleton with some material when the time came.

Such experiments don't last very long, of course. The damnable beast, material, keeps getting bigger and more obnoxious. Finally, you realize you have a choice. Either hide from it, wish it away, or wrestle with it. I doubt that there is a writer over forty who does not realize in his heart of hearts that literary genius, in prose, consists of proportions more on the order of 65 percent material and 35 percent talent in the sacred crucible.

I never doubted for a moment that to write a long piece of fiction about New York City I would have to do the same sort of reporting I had done for *The Right Stuff* or *Radical Chic & Mau-mauing the Flak Catchers,* even though by now I had lived in New York for almost twenty years. By 1981, when I started work in earnest, I could see that Thackeray's *Vanity Fair* would not be an adequate model. *Vanity Fair* deals chiefly with the upper orders of British society. A book about New York in the 1980s would have to deal with New York high and low. So I chose Wall Street as the high end of the scale and the South Bronx as the low. I knew a few more people on Wall Street than in the South Bronx, but both were terrae incognitae as far as my own experience was concerned. I headed forth into I knew not exactly what. Any big book about New York, I figured, should have at least one subway scene. I started riding the subways in the Bronx. One evening I looked across the car and saw someone I knew sitting there in a strange rig. He was a Wall Street broker I hadn't seen for nine or ten years. He was dressed in a business suit, but his pant legs were rolled up three or four hitches, revealing a pair of olive-green army surplus socks, two bony lengths of shin, and some decomposing striped orthotic running shoes. On the floor between his feet was an A&P shopping bag made of slippery white polyethylene. He had on a dirty raincoat and a greasy rain hat, and his eyes were darting from one end of the car to the other. I went over, said hello, and learned the following. He and his family lived in the far North Bronx, where there are to this day some lively, leafy Westchester-style neighborhoods, and he worked on Wall Street. The subways provided fine service, except that lately there had been a problem. Packs of young toughs had taken to roaming the cars. They would pick out a likely prey, close in on his seat, hem him in, and ask for money. They kept their hands in their pockets and never produced weapons, but their leering, menacing looks were usually enough. When this fellow's turn came, he had capitulated, given them all he had—and he'd been a nervous wreck on the subway ever since. He had taken to traveling to and from Wall Street in this pathetic disguise in order to avoid looking worth robbing. In the A&P shopping bag he carried his Wall Street shoes and socks.

I decided I would use such a situation in my book. It was here that I began to run into not Roth's Lament but Muggeridge's Law. While Malcolm Muggeridge was editor of *Punch,* it was announced that Khrushchev and Bulganin were coming to England. Muggeridge hit upon the idea of a mock itinerary, a lineup of the most ludicrous places the two paunchy, pear-shaped little Soviet leaders could possibly be paraded through during the solemn business of a state visit. Shortly before press time, half the feature had to be scrapped. It coincided exactly with the official itinerary, just released, prompting Muggeridge to observe: We live in an age in which it is no longer possible to be funny. There is nothing you can imagine, no matter how ludicrous, that will not promptly be enacted before your very eyes, probably by someone well known.

This immediately became my problem. I first wrote *The Bonfire of the Vanities* serially for *Rolling Stone,* producing a chapter every two weeks with a gun at my temple. In the third chapter, I introduced one of my main characters, a thirty-two-year-old Bronx assistant district attorney named Larry Kramer, sitting in a subway car dressed as my friend had been dressed, his eyes jumping about in a bughouse manner. This was supposed to create unbearable suspense in the readers. What on earth had reduced this otherwise healthy young man to such a pathetic state? This chapter appeared in July of 1984. In an installment scheduled for April of 1985, the readers would learn of his humiliation by a wolf pack, who had taken all his money plus his little district attorney's badge. But it so happened that in December of 1984 a young man named Bernhard Goetz found himself in an identical situation on a subway in New York, hemmed in by four youths who were, in fact, from the South Bronx. Far from caving in, he pulled out a .38-caliber revolver and shot all four of them and became one of the most notorious figures in America. Now, how could I, four months later, in April of 1985, proceed with my plan? People would say, This poor fellow Wolfe, he has no imagination. He reads the newspapers, gets these obvious ideas, and then gives us this wimp Kramer, who caves in. So I abandoned the plan, dropped it altogether. The *Rolling Stone* readers' burning thirst, if any, to know what accounted for Assistant D.A. Kramer's pitiful costume and alarming facial tics was never slaked.

In one area, however, I was well ahead of the news, and this lent the book a curious kind of after-life. The plot turns on a severe injury to a black youth in an incident involving a white couple in an automobile. While the youth lies in a coma, various forces close in on the case—the press, politicians, prosecutors, real estate brokers, black activists—each eager, for private reasons, to turn the matter into a racial Armageddon. Supreme among them is Reverend Bacon, a Harlem minister, a genius at handling the press who soon has the entire city throbbing to the young man's outrageous fate. In the book, the incident casts its shadow across the upcoming elections and threatens to cost the white mayor City Hall.

The Bonfire of the Vanities reached bookstores in October of 1987, a week before the Wall Street crash. From the start, in the press, there was a certain amount of grumbling, some of it not very nice, about my depiction of Reverend Bacon. He was a grotesque caricature of a black activist, grotesque or worse. Then, barely three months later, the Tawana Brawley case broke. At the forefront of the Brawley case appeared an activist black minister, the Reverend Al Sharpton, who was indeed a genius at handling the press, even when he was in the tightest corners. At one point the *New York Post* got a tip that Sharpton was having his long Byronic hair coiffed at a beauty parlor in Brooklyn. A reporter and photographer waited until he was socketed in under the dryer, then burst in. Far from throwing up his hands and crying out about invasion of privacy, Sharpton nonchalantly beckoned his stalkers. "Come on in, boys, and bring your cameras. I want you to see how . . . a real man . . . gets his hair done." Just like that!—another Sharpton media triumph, under the heading of "Masculinity to Burn." In fact, Sharpton was so flamboyant, the grumbling about Reverend Bacon swung around 180 degrees. Now I heard people complain, This poor fellow Wolfe, he has no imagination. Here, on the front page of every newspaper, are the real goods—and he gives us this little divinity student, Reverend Bacon.

But I also began to hear and read with increasing frequency that *The Bonfire of the Vanities* was "prophetic." The Brawley case turned out to be only one in a series of racial incidents in which young black people were, or were seen as, the victims of white brutality. And these incidents did, indeed, cast their shadow across the race for mayor in New York City. As in the prologue to the book, the mayor, in real life, was heckled, harassed, and shouted down by demonstrators in Harlem, although he was never forced to flee the podium. And perhaps these incidents were among the factors that cost the white mayor City Hall. But not for a moment did I ever think of *The Bonfire of the Vanities* as prophetic. The book only showed what was obvious to anyone who had done what I did, even as far back as the early eighties, when I began; anyone who had gone out and looked frankly at the new face of the city and paid attention not only to what the voices said but also to the roar.

This brings me to one last point. It is not merely that reporting is useful in gathering the *petits faits vrais* that create verisimilitude and make a novel gripping or absorbing, although that side of the enterprise is worth paying attention to. My contention is that, especially in an age like this, they are essential for the very greatest effects literature can achieve. In 1884 Zola went down into the mines at Anzin to do the documentation for what was to become the novel *Germinal*. Posing as a secretary for a member of the French Chamber of Deputies, he descended into the pits wearing his city clothes, his frock coat, high stiff collar, and high stiff hat (this appeals to me for reasons I won't delay you with), and carrying a notebook and pen. One day Zola and the miners who were serving as his guides were 150 feet below the ground when Zola noticed an enormous workhorse, a Percheron, pulling a sled piled with coal through a tunnel. Zola asked, "How do you get that animal in and out of the mine every day?" At first the miners thought he was joking. Then they realized he was serious, and one of them said, "Mr. Zola, don't you understand? That horse comes down here *once*, when he's a colt, barely more than a foal, and still able to fit into the buckets that bring *us* down here. That horse grows up down here. He grows blind down here after a year or two, from the lack of light. He hauls coal down here until he can't haul it anymore, and then he dies down here, and his bones are buried down here." When Zola transfers this revelation from the pages of his documentation notebook to the pages of *Germinal*, it makes the hair on your arms stand on end. You realize, without the need of amplification, that the horse is the miners themselves, who descend below the face of the earth as children and dig coal down in the pit until they can dig no more and then are buried, often literally, down there.

The moment of The Horse in *Germinal* is one of the supreme moments in French literature—and it would have been impossible without that peculiar drudgery that Zola called documentation. At this weak, pale, tabescent moment in the history of American literature, we need a battalion, a brigade, of Zolas to head out into this wild, bizarre, unpredictable, Hog-stomping Baroque country of ours and reclaim it as literary property. Philip Roth was absolutely right. The imagination of the novelist is powerless before what he knows he's going to read in tomorrow morning's newspaper. But a generation of American writers has drawn precisely the wrong conclusion from that perfectly valid observation. The answer is not to leave the rude beast, the material, also known as the life around us, to the journalists but to do what journalists do, or are supposed to do, which is to wrestle the beast and bring it to terms.

Of one thing I am sure. If fiction writers do not start facing the obvious, the literary history of the second half of the twentieth century will record that journalists not only took over the richness of American life as their domain but also seized the high ground of literature itself. Any literary person who is willing to look back over the American literary terrain of the past twenty-five years—look back candidly, in the solitude of the study—will admit that in at least four years out of five the best nonfiction books have been *better literature* than the most highly praised books of fiction. Any truly candid observer will go still further. In many years, the most highly praised books of fiction have been over-shadowed *in literary terms* by writers whom literary people customarily dismiss as "writers of popular fiction" (a curious epithet) or as genre novelists. I am thinking of novelists such as John le Carré and Joseph Wambaugh. Leaving the question of talent aside, le Carré and Wambaugh have one enormous advantage over their more literary confreres. They are not only willing to wrestle the beast; they actually love the battle.

In 1973, in *The New Journalism,* I wrote that nonfiction had displaced the novel as American literature's "main event." That was not quite the same as saying that nonfiction had dethroned the novel, but it was close enough. At the time, it was a rash statement, but *como Fidel lo ha dijo,* history will absolve me. Unless some movement occurs in American fiction over the next ten years that is more remarkable than any detectable right now, the pioneering in nonfiction will be recorded as the most important experiment in American literature in the second half of the twentieth century.

I speak as a journalist, with some enthusiasm, as you can detect, a journalist who has tried to capture the beast in long narratives of both nonfiction and fiction. I started writing *The Bonfire of the Vanities* with the supreme confidence available only to a writer who doesn't know quite what he is getting into. I was soon plunged into despair. One very obvious matter I had not reckoned with: in nonfiction you are very conveniently provided with the setting and the characters and the plot. You now have the task—and it is a huge one— of bringing it all alive as convincingly as the best of realistic fiction. But you don't have to concoct the story. Indeed, you can't. I found the sudden freedom of fiction intimidating. It was at least a year before I felt comfortable enough to use that freedom's advantages, which are formidable. The past three decades have been decades of tremendous and at times convulsive social change, especially in large cities, and the tide of the fourth great wave of immigration has made the picture seem all the more chaotic, random, and discontinuous, to use the literary clichés of the recent past. The economy with which realistic fiction can bring the many currents of a city together in a single, fairly simply story was something that I eventually found exhilarating. It is a facility that is not available to the journalist, and it seems more useful with each passing month. Despite all the current talk of "coming together," I see the fast-multiplying factions of the modern cities trying to insulate themselves more diligently than ever before. However brilliant and ambitious, a nonfiction novel about, say, the Tawana Brawley case could not get all of New York in 1989 between two covers. It could illuminate many things, most especially the press and the workings of the justice system, but it would not reach into Wall Street or Park Avenue, precincts even the resourceful Al Sharpton does not frequent. In 1970 the Black Panthers *did* turn up in Leonard Bernstein's living room. Today, there is no chic, radical or otherwise, in mixing colors in the grand salons.

So the doors close and the walls go up! It is merely another open invitation to literature, especially in the form of the novel. And how can any writer, in fiction or nonfiction, resist going to the beano, to the rout! At the end of *Dead Souls,* Gogol asks, "Whither art thou soaring away to, then, Russia? Give me an answer!" Russia gives none but only goes faster, and "the air, rent to shreds, thunders and turns to wind," and Gogol hangs on, breathless, his eyes filled with wonder. America today, in a headlong rush of her own, may or may not truly need a literature worthy of her vastness. But American novelists, without any doubt, truly need, in their neurasthenic hour, the spirit to go along for that wild ride.

———————

Tom Wolfe *was born in 1931 in Richmond, Virginia, where his father edited a magazine called* Southern Planter. *Wolfe's first aspiration to go to New York was as a pitcher. He made it as far as the Giants tryout camp. In 1962 he finally moved to New York as a writer for the* Herald-Tribune. *In 1963 Wolfe's first book,* The Kandy-Kolored Tangerine-Flake Streamline Baby, *a compilation of his articles written since moving to New York, rocketed him to fame. In the late sixties, while living in Richmond and caring for his ailing father, he wrote* The Electric Kool-Aid Acid Test, *achieving superstar status for himself and the New Journalism.* The Bonfire of the Vanities, *a novel—his first—about New York City, was published in 1987.* "Stalking the Billion-Footed Beast" *is an essay which he wrote about* Bonfire *for* Harper's *Magazine in 1989. Though he summers in Southampton, Wolfe still lives in New York City.*

Harold Brodkey

The Return of the Native

Imagine a couch reporter travelling. A flying couch, a miniature R.V. that allowed you to take your own life with you wherever you went, would be fine, but reality is cruel, Consider, I ask you, the postures and detailed discomfort of a tall couch potato on a medium-sized jet or even a jumbo, that flying slum. Then the return to New York after three months abroad, trying to relocate the walls of your apartment and to remember and set in place the intricate system of assertions and responses, the mental and physical aggressions, that are necessary in this city, that you don't use as a tourist passing through a place.

Each place my wife and I went to—Berlin, Venice, Rome—has its own inner systems interlocking aggressions and violences, its famous culture of them. I became attuned to the gladiatorial spirit at Rome's Fiumicino airport and to the grim, order-giving xenophobia at Tegel, in Berlin. New York systems don't work in those towns—you get out of practice with New York systems, unless you stay in hotels that specialize in your class and nationality. Mostly, nationalities ghettoize themselves by choice when they travel. But if you've been a tourist immersed in other places for three months the return to Manhattan, the home ghetto of choice—bitter cabdrivers, high-pressure face-lifted old ladies, mad landlords, and hard-edged homeless—it's like being dipped in Hell, especially when you're jet-lagged.

The Nietzschean self-assertion of the locals is part of the mystic wonder of New York. And this begins in the overwhelmingly strange experience of using a New York airport. What do you suppose makes the customs guards and the guides who indicate which window you go to with your passport so sad? The aggressions of ethnic groups begin at Kennedy. This time, a flying squad of Wasp heroines pushed into the line of people waiting for taxis and had to be chased off by a Russian-speaker in golfing hat and Day-Glo wheelchair with a phenomenally militant sense of justice. Earlier, Italians were taking over the best places along the conveyor belt for luggage, elbowing you, looking at you piteously. Or taking over vast sections of the airport for greeting, and warmheartedly blocking all the exits from the luggage area into the daylight. And the silently angry French people in really good clothes were cutting across your path with their luggage carts.

If your taxi-driver is not aggressive you will never get out of Kennedy Airport, since people shamelessly block the crosswalks and ignore the lights. No one coöperates. Kind liberals in cars who refuse to edge forward into the shameless mass cause gridlock at the intersections.

The visual blight along the roads has behind it the great secret that a glimpse of the incredible Manhattan skyline is coming, the towers under a large sky, airplane-dotted, and with wheeling seabirds, and bustling with clouds and light, including a glowing pale-yellow corona of pollution around the towers themselves.

In narrow side streets and at the lights occur traffic confrontations, negotiations, bluster, and jockeying. Surely treeless Manhattan is the home of the bald ego, the American national bird.

Different styles of aggression seem to be basic to gender. The virility syndrome is different from the exoticism of the being-not-male-and-to-be-looked-at syndrome that women labor under. New York women either deny or exaggerate the exoticism element. Denial and exaggeration, and male and female distrust of them, underlie much of New York's psychoanalytic culture. But what is most striking on a return here after a long absence is the extreme obviousness of male assertion, beginning with the size and shape of the skyscrapers, the behavior of truck drivers, the partly sly, half-mad swagger of some of the male homeless, and the often unconvincing humility of others.

A crisis of the virility thing is apparent everywhere in the world. For instance, the reunification of Germany means for the more or less unemployable men of the East a loss of their women to—let's say—capitalist practices. If the men then establish a style of violent virility, it is as comprehensible as is their fear of the rape of their women and contamination of them by foreigners, by Jews, when there are no Jews around—the term "Jew" in Austria and Germany and Italy, in France and England and Spain being taken by the right-wing movements to mean a new style of *successful* masculinity, unviolent, modern, and sophisticated and moneyed and sympathetic to women. The actual war between the old and the new specifically involves the standards for virility and relations—or, in a primitive sense, for access—to women. Italian television is lunatic about the escape of women from the old social controls.

In New York, male pretensions and female ones—women having their own exotic visual compromises and degrees of rebellion against being visual symbols—suffer particularly. It is almost impossible in New York to be rich enough for comfort in regard to your own gender. You have to be so rich—as in having your own plane or chauffeur, the lucky ones being whisked off by a retainer—that you are part of the general scene only in a small way, glancingly.

But those of us who are not that rich do not exactly return to New York. We return to a fortress segment of it, a willfully isolated, specialized part of it. And our exposure to the city's violence of spirit is determined by our style.

Drenched in momentary inadequacy and adrenaline, I arrived at my apartment house. The doorman on duty was the Hindu guy. The Guatemalan doorman of the earlier shift was just leaving, dressed in his helmet and quilted Tyvek jacket; he has a BMW motorcycle. The Romanian doorman, who has our mailbox key, wasn't there. The boiler was "half broken." Polish workmen were pounding on the roof. The Sunday *Times* when I bought it was missing the book-review and style sections, which I took as advice on what not to bother reading. The local macrobiotic restaurant was crowded with people dealing macrobiotically with the virility and exoticism factors. The wind was cold and aggressive. The lassitude, the listlessness of Manhattan mark the era as one of waiting for a style, waiting for an economic direction to declare itself.

Anton, the Romanian doorman, is a genuinely competitive human being. He has about as much sense of social class as an elephant does. But he has an exceptionally alert sense of power, and he is very aware of menace. When I am jet-lagged, I can read my condition in how he acts—whether he is maternal or dodgy, amused or respectful.

He said when I saw him, "Well, are you ready for the madness here?"

HAROLD BRODKEY, *an O. Henry prizewinner and a regular contributor to* The New Yorker *since 1950, is the author of two novels (*The Runaway Soul *and* Profane Friendship*) and two collections of stories (*First Love *and* Other Stories *and* Stories in an Almost Classical Mode*).*

Harold Brodkey has taught writing and literature at Cornell University and City College of New York. He has twice received the O. Henry Prize and has been granted fellowships from the National Endowment for the Arts and the American Academy in Rome. He lives in New York City.

"The Return of the Native" appeared in The New Yorker *in 1990.*

6

City of Burned Voices

Rita Dove

Canary

for Michael S. Harper

Billie Holiday's burned voice
had as many shadows as lights,
a mournful candelabra against a sleek piano,
the gardenia her signature under that ruined face.

(Now you're cooking, drummer to bass,
magic spoon, magic needle.
Take all day if you have to
with your mirror and your bracelet of song.)

Fact is, the invention of women under siege
has been to sharpen love in the service of myth.

It you can't be free, be a mystery.

RITA DOVE *has published several collections of poetry,
including* Thomas and Beulah, *for which she won a
Pulitzer Prize, as well as a collection of stories, a novel
(*Through the Ivory Gate*) and a play (*The Darker the
Face of the Earth*). In 1993 she was appointed Poet
Laureate of the United States.*

*She was born in 1952 in Akron, Ohio. Her work has been
recognized by Guggenheim and Fulbright fellowships, as
well as grants from the National Endowment for the Arts
and the Mellon Foundation.*

*Rita Dove is the Commonwealth Professor of English at
the University of Virginia. The poem "Canary" is reprinted
from her collection* Grace Notes *(1989).*

Vernon Duke

Autumn in New York

It's time to end my lonely holiday
and bid the country a hasty farewell.
So on this gray and melancholy day
I'll move to a Manhattan hotel.

I'll dispose of my rose-colored chattels
and prepare for my share of adventures and battles.
Here on my twenty-seventh floor,
looking down on the city I hate and adore!

Autumn in New York, why does it seem so inviting?
Autumn in New York, it spells the thrill of first nighting
Glittering crowds and shimmering clouds in canyons of
    steel,
they're making me feel I'm home.

It's autumn in New York that brings the promise of new
    love;
Autumn in New York is often mingled with pain.
Dreamers with empty hands may sigh for exotic lands;
It's Autumn in New York, it's good to live it again.

Autumn in New York, the gleaming rooftops at sun
    down.
Autumn in New York, it lifts you up when you're run
    down.
Jaded roués and gay divorcees who lunch at the Ritz,
will tell you that "it's divine!"

This autumn in New York transforms the slums into
  Mayfair;
Autumn in New York, you'll need no castles in Spain.
Lovers that bless the dark on benches in Central Park
  greet
Autumn in New York; it's good to live it again.

———————

VERNON DUKE *(1903-1969) was born Vladimir Dukelsky
in Parfianovka, Russia. A child prodigy, he studied at the
Kiev Conservatory. In the 1920s he began composing in the
fashion of popular songwriters George Gershwin and Irving
Berlin, writing under pen names. In 1920 he emigrated to
the U.S. Dukelsky spent much of the 1920s in Paris and
London composing for the piano, ballet, and stage. He
continued composing both classical music and pop standards
throughout his life. "Autumn in New York," for which he
wrote his own lyrics, was composed for the 1934 show*
Thumbs Up, *and Billie Holiday made the song famous.*

Chris Offutt

excerpt from The Same River Twice

Where I'm from, the foothills of southern Appalachia are humped like a kicked rug, full of steep furrows. Families live scattered among the ridges and hollows in tiny communities containing no formal elements save a post office. My hometown is a zip code with a creek. We used to have a store but the man who ran it died. Long before my birth, a union invalidated the company scrip, shut the mines, and left a few men dead. Two hundred people live there now.

Our hills are the most isolated area of America, the subject of countless doctoral theses. It's an odd sensation to read about yourself as counterpart to the aborigine or Eskimo. If VISTA wasn't bothering us, some clown was running around the hills with a tape recorder. Strangers told us we spoke Elizabethan English, that we were contemporary ancestors to everyone else. They told us the correct way to pronounce "Appalachia," as if we didn't know where we'd been living for the past three hundred years.

One social scientist proclaimed us criminal Scotch-Irish clansmen deemed unfit to live in Britain — our hills as precursor to Australia's penal colony. Another book called us the heirs to errant Phoenicians shipwrecked long before Columbus seduced Isabella for tub fare. My favorite legend made us Melungeons, a mysterious batch of folk possessing ungodly woodskills. We can spot fleas hopping from dog to dog at a hundred yards; we can track a week-old snake trail across bare rock. If you don't believe it, just ask the sociologist who spent a season like a fungus in the hills.

The popular view of Appalachia is a land where every man is willing, at the drop of a proverbial overall strap, to shoot, fight, or fuck anything on hind legs. We're men who buy half-pints of bootlegged liquor and throw the lids away in order to finish the whiskey in one laughing, brawling night, not caring where we wake or how far from home. Men alleged to eat spiders off the floor to display our strength, a downright ornery bunch.

The dirt truth is a hair different. The men of my generation live in the remnants of a world that still maintains a frontier mentality. Women accept and endure, holding the families tight. Mountain culture expects its males to undergo various rites of manhood, but genuine tribulation under fire no longer exists. We've had to create our own.

Once a week, Mom drove fifteen miles to town for groceries, accompanied by her children. We visited the interstate, which was creeping closer in tiny increments, bisecting hills and property, rerouting creeks. We called it the four-laner. It slithered in our direction like a giant snake. Mom said I-64 ran clear to California, a meaningless distance since none of us had ever crossed the county line. The completed road linked the world to the hills, but failed to connect us to the world.

I never intended to quit high school, but like many of my peers, I simply lost the habit. Education was for fools. Girls went to college seeking a husband; boys went to work. The pool hall's grimy floor, stained block walls, and furtive tension suited me well. The only requirement was adherence to an unspoken code of ethics, a complex paradigm that I still carry today. A rack of balls cost a dime, cheeseburgers a quarter. I ran the table three times in a row one day, and afterwards could not find a willing player. Inadvertently I had alienated myself from the only society that had ever tolerated me, a pattern that would continue for years.

After a week of shooting pool alone, I was ripe for an army recruiter who culled the pool hall like a pimp at Port Authority. I was under age but my parents gleefully signed the induction papers. The recruiter ferried me a hundred miles to Lexington, where I failed the physical examination.

"Albumin in the urine," the doctor said. "No branch will take you."

I felt weak. Tears cut lines down my face. My own body had trapped me in the hills, spirit pinioned by the flesh. I didn't know which was worse, the shame of physical betrayal or the humiliation of having cried in front of a hundred eager men-to-be. They moved away from me to hide their own embarrassment. I was subsequently denied admittance to the Peace Corps, park rangers, the ranks of firemen and police. I'd never know camaraderie, or test myself in sanctioned ways against other men.

That summer I began to steal and smoke dope, and in the fall I had no choice but to attend college. The only school within the mountains had recently become a university. After two years, I quit and announced my plans to become an actor in New York. Jennipher, the one girl I'd had the courage to love, had married a quarterback and moved far away. My sisters considered me a hopeless redneck. My brother refused to live with me, and my father and I hadn't spoken civilly in upwards of thirty-eight months.

Mom fixed me a sack lunch the morning I left. We sat quietly at the completed highway, staring at the fresh, clean blacktop. Mom was trying not to cry. I felt bad for being the first to erode the family, though I'd already been at it for a while. The road stretched to the horizon like a wide creek and I thought of Daniel Boone questing for space. The road in had become a way out.

Mom pressed a ten-dollar bill in my hand and dropped her head.

"Write when you get work," she mumbled.

Birdsong spilled from the wooded hills. I began walking, the pack on my back angled like a cockeyed turtle shell. A pickup stopped and hauled me out of Kentucky. The hills relaxed their taut furls, billowing gently like sheets on a clothesline. I had a fresh haircut, two hundred dollars, and a grade school photograph of Jennipher. I was already homesick.

When I told drivers that I was heading for New York to be an actor, they grinned and shook their heads. A trucker pointed to the radio and told me to act like I was turning it on. I slept under a tree in Ohio and camped the next night behind a truck stop in Pennsylvania. On the third day, I entered the Holland Tunnel.

The world on the other side was so alien that my chief advantage was the ability to speak and read English. My accent's raucous twang betrayed me. I vowed to eliminate the guttural tones, swallowed endings, and stretching of single-syllable words. Until then, I remained silent. Manhattan was filthy and loud but similar to the hills: packed with illiterate men, unattainable women, and threat of injury. I regarded avenues as ridges, and the cross streets as hollows. Alleys were creeks that trickled into the river of Broadway. New York wasn't that big, just tall.

Like most groups of immigrants, Kentuckians abroad form a tight community that helps newcomers. Having left family and land, we could not quite rid ourselves of the clannish impulse dating back to the Celts. We still roved the civilized world, but no longer painted ourselves blue before the attack. I moved into an apartment on the Upper West Side with three natives of Kentucky. They were graduates of the college I'd quit, older students I vaguely knew, struggling actors. They let me sleep on the couch. The halls between apartments were so narrow that if two people met, both had to turn sideways for passage. More people lived in my building than on my home hill.

The city seemed predicated upon one's innate ability to wait, a learned craft, routine as tying a shoe. You had to wait for a buzzer to enter a building, wait for the subway, wait for an elevator. I stood for two hours in a movie line only to learn that it was sold out and the line was for the next showing, two more hours away. Groups of people rushed down subway steps, then stood perfectly still. They rushed onto the train, and again became immobile until their stop, whereupon they'd rush out. The waiting was more exhausting than motion. People hurried, I decided, not because they were late but because they were sick of standing still.

The simple act of walking became a problem for me. I kept bumping into people, often tripping them or myself. I'd never had this problem before, possessing if not grace, at least a certain agility and physical awareness. It seemed as if people rushed into my path. One Saturday I sat on a bench at midtown and watched pedestrians, seeking insight. My error was a long, steady stride, necessary to cover the open ground of home. I simply set myself in motion and put my legs to work. New Yorkers took quick, short steps. They darted and danced, stopped short and sidestepped, constantly twisting their torsos and dipping their shoulders to dodge people. Since everyone was likewise engaged, the whole comedic street dance worked. I took a bus home and practiced in my room. As long as I concentrated, everything was jake, but the minute my attention wavered, my gait lengthened and someone's legs entangled with mine.

I spent another two hours observing foot traffic and noticed that most New Yorkers possessed a morbid fear of automobiles. They assiduously avoided the curb, which left a narrow open lane at the edge of the sidewalk. I began walking as close to the gutter as possible.

My roommates were seldom home. To show appreciation for having been taken in, I decided to wash everyone's laundry. The laundromat was a narrow chamber, very hot. I was the only white person and the only male. Conversation around me was incomprehensible. I'd read about black dialects of the inner city and was pleased in an odd way that I couldn't understand what was being said. English had been melted and recast into their own tongue. It reminded me of being home. I wanted to tell the women that my native language was equally enigmatic to outsiders.

Folding laundry was a skill I lacked, and I started with the sheets, believing them to be easier. My arms weren't long enough to span the sheet and it dragged the floor. I tried to fold it like a flag, draping one end over the table and working forward. The table didn't provide enough tension and again the sheet slipped to the floor. I sorted a few socks while considering the problem.

Controlling the four corners of the sheet was essential, which led to a plan of theoretic elegance. I doubled the sheet and held two of its corners. I spread my legs, mentally counted to three, and threw the sheet into the air, snapping my wrists. The sheet unfurled and arced back. I caught one corner but missed the other. Encouraged, I took a deep breath and concentrated, knowing that I needed a slight correction in toss and grab. As I threw the sheet, someone entered the laundromat, producing a strong draft. The sheet blew over my head and shoulders. I dropped one corner. Unable to see, I stepped forward, placed my foot on the sheet and not so much fell as actually pulled myself to my knees. I jerked the sheet off my head. Above the cacophony of washers and dryers came the pearly sound of women laughing.

They walked past me and started folding my laundry. Perfect columns of T-shirts began to rise on the table. With an unerring sense of size, the women sorted the pants into stacks corresponding to my roommates and me. They refused my assistance and talked among themselves. I listened carefully, trying to isolate a word or phrase, but they spoke too fast for me to follow. They moved to their own chores without looking at me, as if embarrassed by their benevolence. I approached the nearest woman and thanked her. She nodded.

"I'm from Kentucky," I said. "It's not like New York."

"Nothing is."

"How did you learn to fold clothes so well?"

"My mother taught me."

"In Harlem?"

Her eyes widened and her lips drew tight across her teeth. I realized the stupidity of assuming that all blacks grew up in Harlem, like thinking all Kentuckians came from Lexington or Louisville. She bent to her work, her face furious.

"I'm sorry," I said. "Maybe not Harlem."

"No! Not Harlem."

"Where, then?"

"Puerto Rico. I am Puerto Rico!" She lifted her arms

to include everyone in the laundromat. "Puerto Rico!"

"Puerto Rico," I said.

"*Sí.*"

I leaned against the table, absolutely clobbered by an awareness that they'd been speaking Spanish. During the next few days, I wandered the blocks near my building. It was not a black neighborhood as I'd previously thought. Everyone was of Hispanic descent, but I felt more comfortable here than among the white people. My culture had much in common with the Latin—loyalty to a family that was often large, respect for the elderly and for children, a sharp delineation between genders. The men were governed by a sense of machismo similar to that which ruled in the hills. There was one quite obvious drawback—to them I was just another white man.

The random progress of a nose-down dog dropped me into a job on the Lower East Side of Manhattan. Belched from the subway each morning, I strolled the Bowery past dozens of men dirty as miners. Many could not speak. Each payday, I gave away two packs' worth of cigarettes, one at a time.

For six months I worked at a warehouse in the neighborhood, the first full-time job of my life. I collected clothing orders for a professional shipping clerk with forty years' experience. His passive numbness frightened me. I was gatherer of shirts and slacks; he was a hunter of numbers. The day's highlight was staring at a Polaroid of a nude woman I'd found on the street. Ancient priests of South America used fake knives and animal blood to save the sacrificial virgins for themselves. Up north I just wanted a goddess to worship.

After work, I saw a tall woman with a huge jaw being harassed by a junkie. I chased the junkie away. The woman smiled and led me to an abandoned subway station with a boarded entrance. A pink dress hung loose on her lanky frame. She pried three planks free and slipped in, motioning down the steps to a bare mattress. She wasn't attractive, but no one else had shown me the least bit of attention. I followed her. A musty breeze from the bowels of the earth fluttered trash along the floor. I felt snug and primal in the dank urban temple. I would become an albino, a blind white harlot in service to Ishtar.

She asked for a match. When I lit her cigarette, she caressed my face and grabbed my crotch, lashing my tongue with hers. I slid my hand down her stomach and between her legs. My fingers hit something hard tucked low against her abdomen. I was accustomed to people carrying guns and it seemed natural for a woman alone in the city to be armed. The only feasible option was to gain control of the pistol.

I ran my hand up her dress, wrapped my fingers around the barrel, and gave a quick tug. She moaned low and very deep. I pulled again and suddenly realized the gun was made of flesh. My entire body trembled in a fury of incomprehension. I stood, unable to speak. She threw her purse at me and laughed a taunting crackle that echoed in the tunnel. I ran up the stairs, plunged through the opening, and fell on the sidewalk. Two men holding hands stepped off the curb to avoid me.

The following day, I called in sick to the warehouse and stayed in the tub all day. When the water cooled, I refilled it, still hearing that laughter throbbing in my head. I was sure I'd found a circus freak, a hermaphrodite, the only one in the city and perhaps the entire country. At nineteen, it was beyond my understanding that a grown man would impersonate a female. Not all transvestites are gay, I later learned, but mine was. This seemed a crucial difference between the city and the hills—Appalachian men could acceptably fornicate with daughters, sisters, and livestock, but carnal knowledge of a man was a hanging offense.

I ate lunch daily at a diner on Great Jones Street. The joint was a showcase of deformity—goiters swelled throats, and tumors jutted from bodies, stretching gray skin. Hair sprouted in odd places. The owner kept a sawed-off shotgun close at hand. One day a stray woman appeared in a booth. She was short and dark, wearing tight pants which I studied closely for a telltale bulge. She notice my observation and I quickly looked away. She moved near.

"Are you a mechanic?" she said. "My car needs work."

"No. I'm an actor. Are you a girl?"

"Everybody I know is bisexual now."

"Not me," I said. "Want to go to the museum on Saturday?"

"Can't."

"Why not?"

"Just can't. Why don't you visit me in Brooklyn on Sunday."

"Where's Brooklyn?"

She laughed and spoke loudly to all. "He wants to know where Brooklyn is!"

The simple purity of Jahi's directions enthralled me: Take the Flatbush train to the end and get out. Walk down the street and go left. Ring the second bell. Finding a place at home involved landmarks such as the creek, the big tree, or the third hollow past the wide place in the road. After the quantum mechanics of lower Manhattan, Brooklyn sounded like simple geometry. I bought a new shirt for the date. That she was black didn't matter—she was female and I was lonely. We were both at the bottom of our republic's fabled melting pot.

Noisy people thronged the streets of Flatbush Avenue. Tattoos covered the men like subway graffiti. Women wore neon skirts drawn so tight that their thighs brushed audibly at every step. The stores were barred by padlocked gates that reminded me of ramparts under siege.

Jahi's apartment was absolutely bare save for a couch, a table, two chairs, and a bed. We drank wine and passed a joint. After four hours she seduced me because, she later told me, I had not pounced on her all afternoon. She considered me a southern gentleman. I didn't mention the white trash truth—every country boy knew city women would breed quicker than a striking snake. Expecting sex as urban custom, I was in no hurry. Plus I didn't know much about it.

When the time came, I pounded into her, spurted, and rolled away. She raised her eyebrows and blinked several times.

"Are you a virgin?" she said.

"How could I be?"

"You don't have to use your whole body. Just your hips."

"I know," I said quickly.

"Look, nobody knows until they learn."

"I've read about it plenty."

"I'm not saying anything against you, Chris. Everybody's different and you may as well learn about me."

She stood on the bed and told me to look at her body very carefully. I'd never seen a woman fully nude before. Jahi had a peculiar frame—strongly muscled dancer's legs, a delightful bottom, and the dark torso of a young girl. Her small breasts sported enormous nipples, ebon pegs an inch long, hard as clay. A few black hairs surrounded them, reminding me of crippled spiders.

She lay beside me and invited me to touch her everywhere, methodic as a surveyor, covering every square inch. Next she explained the complex labyrinth of her plumbing. From its nook she retrieved her clitoris and demonstrated the proper action for maximum pleasure. She counseled me on the rising barometer of orgasm and cued me to a steady drilling until the dam broke. I received a cursory lecture on the soft crest where buttock met leg, the inner thigh, and lastly the anus. I balked, believing this too advanced. With time, she assured me, even that arena would be old hat.

Two hours later I was a sweaty scholar eager to matriculate. Jahi rolled on her back and aimed her heels at the ceiling while I wriggled down the graduation aisle. Propping my weight on knees and elbows allowed her some maneuvering room. The prescribed circular motion reminded me of sharpening a knife on an oily whetstone: apply pressure on the upstroke and ease away, alternating sides for a balanced edge.

To forestall ejaculation, she had suggested I concentrate on baseball. I thought about Cincinnati's Big Red Machine, squirmed my hips correctly, and remembered how the manager always hopped over the sprinkled white baseline to avoid bad luck. The summer I turned twelve, VISTA bused a load of hill boys to Crosley Field for a game. In the parking lot I was astounded to see a black kid, the first I'd ever seen. He was my size and wore clothes identical to mine—jeans and T-shirt. I stared at him so hard that I walked into a streetlight, which didn't exist in the hills either. The VISTA man made me sit beside him the whole game.

Suddenly Jahi was squirming like an epileptic, thrashing her legs and ripping my back. Convinced I'd made a mistake, I slowed the rhythm to a bullpen warm-up. The manager's hand signals blurred to gibberish and she began screaming.

"Fuck me, you white motherfucker!"

Appalled, I pistoned my hips until the dugout began moving across the floor. I went to my fastball right down the old piperino. Hum, baby, hum. I fiddled and diddled, kicked and delivered.

"Give it to me," she grunted.

"I am, I am!"

"Talk dirty."

"What!"

"Talk dirty!"

"Well, hell," I said. "You're a horse's ass."

She clicked into automatic pilot, writhing and moaning, cursing and shrieking. "You like this!" she bellowed. "You like fucking me!"

I loosened my tongue for locker room talk. "Batter up, batter down, who's that monkey on the mound?"

"I'm coming!"

"She's coming around third. Here's the throw. It's in the dirt, safe at home!"

My body twitched, heat surging from my feet and skull to join at the crotch and erupt. The fans shrieked my name. They were leaping from the stands, peeling the artificial turf, ripping bases out of the ground. Pooled sweat like celebration champagne swirled down my side as I rolled over.

"That was great, Jahi!"

"Yeah, you're a natural."

She gave me a postgame pep talk on how to talk dirty in bed. I nodded and thanked her and she sent me out for pizza, her scent covering me like infield dust. I relived the game in my mind, conjuring instant replays of the best parts.

During the next few weeks, Jahi commandeered my urban safari to Coney Island, Times Square, Radio City, and a hundred bars in between. On the Staten Island Ferry she climbed over the railing to dangle by her arms. The murky water whirlpooled below, filled with plastic tampon tubes and toxic fish. Jahi grinned at me and kicked the side of the boat.

"Don't jump," she yelled. "Hang on, Chris. Hang on!"

After the crew hauled her up, she began hurling life preservers overboard. "I can't swim," she explained. "I have to save myself."

The angry captain assigned us a guard, whom Jahi charmed through subtle exposure of her chest. He leaned to the port for a glimpse down her shirt. The boat rocked in the wake of a tug and he stumbled, face red, and banned her from the ferry.

"Starting when?" she said.

"Now."

"Stop the boat!" she yelled. "Take me back." She slapped him across the face. "That nutball grabbed my ass. Help, help!"

Passengers turned away in a slack-eyed city manner, but a couple of burly men advanced. Jahi grabbed them by their belt buckles, on in each tiny hand.

"He's the one," she said, her voice sliding into the plaintive tone of a child. "He's the one who touched me down there."

One of her saviors had two tears tattooed below his right eye. At the base of his hairline were the letters H.A.N.Y.C. The taller one had a subway token embedded in his ear hole, the flesh grown around it like a board nailed to a tree.

"Which one," the tall guy said.

"Don't know," Jahi said. "Can't remember."

"Stomp both," said the other one.

"It was him." The boat guard pointed at me. "He's the freak."

"Rat knows its own hole," the tall one said.

"Yeah," I said. "Smeller's the feller."

The hard guys looked at me and I realized that I'd pulled their focus from the uniform.

"You two are big bullies," Jahi said.

She spread her legs and arched her back, tipping her head to look up at them. Her voice came hard and mean.

"Nervous without your hogs. I'd half-and-half you on the spot if you took a shower. Don't dime me on this fucking tub, boys. Here's the front. The citizen's with me but he's cherry for a mule. The boat heat's a cowboy looking for a notch. You clippers cross the wise and it's a hard down, with no help from your brothers. They took their taste last night in the Alphabet."

The bikers stiffened beneath her onslaught, eyes turning reptile-flat. The tall one eased backwards, disappearing among the passengers, his friend following. The boat guard tracked them at a coward's distance. Jahi wiped a sheen of sweat from each temple.

"What was all that?" I asked. "I didn't understand a word you said."

"They did." She brushed her knuckles against my crotch. "You understand this, right?"

I nodded and when the ferry docked across the bay, we crawled into one of the emergency rowboats lashed to the side and frolicked in the bow.

The following Saturday she took me to the nude area of Rockaway Beach, where fat voyeurs trailed ugly women. Men with perfect hair trooped naked in pairs. I remembered my grandmother's opinion of a *Playgirl* magazine my sister showed her one Christmas. "They're just like on the farm," Grandmaw had said. "All those old-fashioned pumps with the handles hanging down."

Jahi chose a few square yards of dirty sand amid condoms and cigarette butts. I've always hated the beach except in winter. The sun's too hot, the sea's too cold, and the presence of humanity spoils any natural beauty still lurking in the sand. Jahi refused to disrobe on the grounds that she was brown enough. We'd never discussed her heritage and I didn't want to embarrass myself with the stupidity of asking if she tanned. She insisted that I undress. Since I would not lie on my stomach and proffer myself to the steady parade of men, I lay on my back. The sun scorched my testicles within five minutes.

Jahi teased me for days. In the subway she cocked her head, voice loud to draw attention.

"Are your balls still sunburnt, Chris? They must itch like fire." She addressed the nearest stranger. "Burnt to cinders at the beach. If he's not bragging, he's complaining."

Our public time was a constant duel designed to make me angry, jealous, or embarrassed. As she ran low on ammo against my nonchalance, her improvisations became more outrageous. While waiting for a train, she asked a stranger's opinion of my eyes. Soon she had him leaning close to inspect my face. He agreed that my eyes were slightly crossed, especially the left one. "Yes," she said. "That one has got to go. Do you have a knife? You take it out. You, you, you!"

We rode the subway for hours per day, Jahi's method of rehearsing for her stage career with myriad strangers as her audience. She considered her antics a necessary corrective to my rural background. In the middle of mischief, she'd grin my way, eager for approval. She once stole a ream of paper and opened the bundle on a windy sidewalk. "Oh my God!" she shrieked. "My manuscript!" We watched twelve samaritans chase blank pages down the avenue. At a topless bar she removed her shirt to bus tables, piling empty glasses on the lap of a drunk who'd been pawing the dancers. A bouncer with shoulders like a picnic table came our way. I stayed in my chair, aware that standing would get my head thumped, trusting Jahi to avert trouble.

"Hey, sugar," the bouncer said to her. "You need a job? We could use your kind of spunk."

"I got a job," she said, pointing to me. "I watch out for him. He's a famous actor."

The bouncer helped Jahi with her coat, then turned to me. "You're a lucky man, my friend."

That evening we lounged in her apartment while twilight pollution streaked orange across the sky. Construction noise had ceased at the nearby condo site where future dwellers would pay extra for the fetid river breeze. Jahi had spent the day trying unsuccessfully to make me jealous on the street. Angry at herself, she told me my acting career was a joke. I spent too much time merely watching, writing in my journal.

I'd never told her about my single audition, crammed into a hot room with sixty guys, each of whom clutched a satchel of résumés. Everyone seemed to know each other, like members of a club. They sparred and parried in dirty verbal fighting until a slow response brought on a death jab. The winner smiled and wished the loser luck.

When my name was called, I stepped through a door and crossed the dark stage to an oval swatch of light. Someone thrust a typed page into my hand. A nasal voice whined from the darkness: "Start at the red arrow."

Twenty seconds later the same voice interrupted to thank me. Confused, I nodded and continued reading.

"I said thank you," the voice said. "Can someone please . . ."

A hand took my arm while another retrieved the script. They led me away like an entry at the county fair, a recalcitrant steer who'd balked before the judging stand. I decided to become a movie actor, and skip fooling around with the legitimate theater.

Jahi had surreptitiously removed her underwear from beneath her dress. The thin cloth dangled from her foot. She kicked and her panties arched neatly onto my head.

"Do you write about me?" she said.

"Maybe."

"You should."

"Why?"

"Because I'm alive."

"So am I, Jahi."

"Without me, you weren't. You were young, dumb, and full of come. Now you're just young."

"I'm glad you don't think I'm dumb anymore."

"Oh you are, Chris. I made you smart enough to know you are, that's all. Write that in your little notebook."

The journal was my combat arena, the final refuge of privacy in a city of eight million. Each day I saw perhaps two thousand different faces, an enjoyable fact until I realized that my face was one of the two thousand each of them saw too. My math collapsed from the exponential strain. Jahi wasn't in my journal. Those pages were filled with me. Some of the pages held my full name and place of birth on every line to remind me that I lived.

"Write down everything I say," she said. "Make me live forever."

"Come on, Jahi. I don't even write good letters."

"You don't know it but you will. You'll reach a point where you have no choice."

"Yeah, and I can be president too."

"You can do anything you want. You're a white American man."

"Right."

"And I'm a nigger bitch who sleeps with Whitey."

"Goddamn it, Jahi!"

"See," she muttered through a smile. "I knew I could get to you."

I stomped the floor. "I don't care what you pull on the street. Go naked! Start trouble! You're the only friend I've got, remember. There's maybe fifty people who know me at home. Everybody in Brooklyn knows you, and half of Manhattan. I'm the nobody, not you!"

"Not forever." Her voice dulled to a monotone, "I traveled your dreams."

She stiffened to catatonia, eyes glazed, her fingers twined in her lap. She tensed her jaw to stop the chattering of her teeth.

"You will make gold from lead, flowers from ash. Cut the scabs and stab them. Cut the scabs—"

"Stop it, Jahi."

I considered slapping her, but had never hit a female and wasn't sure if it was different from hitting a man. Her droning halted before I found out. Jahi slid from the coach to the floor, limbs pliant as rope. The pulse in her neck throbbed very fast. She opened her eyes and rubbed her face with the back of her fists, looking around as if lost.

"Has that happened before?" I said.

"Many times," she said. "You never asked about my family."

"So what. You didn't ask about mine."

She moved across the floor to my feet, gently stroking my leg. Her eyes were very old. I noticed gray in her hair.

"I didn't know my father," she said. "My mother was an Obeah woman from the mountains. She died before I learned to control what she taught. I went to Kingston and hustled money. I came to Brooklyn when I was sixteen, too old for work down there. I can't help what I am."

"What?"

"They said I was a witch bastard whore in Jamaica. Here they just say I'm crazy."

She sighed and tipped her face to mine.

"I feel the new gray hair," she said. "Pluck it."

I obeyed. She flicked it with her fingers and the hair whipped, taut as wire.

"Strong," she muttered. "I see strong tonight."

She leaned against my legs and closed her eyes. Through the window and over the tenement roofs, the full moon gleamed like the top of a skull. No doubt she was a tad nutty, but I hadn't met anyone in the city who wasn't. New York appeared to be a voluntary asylum where all the cranks and sociopaths escaped from their small towns; nobody I knew had been born and raised there. Half the population was crazy and the rest were therapists.

The moon disappeared into the neon glare. Jahi faded into sleep. I moved to the couch and opened my journal. It had begun as proof of my identity, but under Jahi's onslaught, it began a transformation as I tentatively set my goal to be an actual writer. The standard rule was to write what you know, but I did not believe I knew anything worthwhile. The only thing I could write with any confidence was a considered record of daily events.

Jahi found me on the couch, fully clothed. She was giddy with a plan to ride horses the following Saturday. When the unicorn came for her she wanted to be ready. I bragged outrageously at my ability to ride. After two months of tagging behind her in the city, I was eager for a familiar undertaking.

We rode the train to Prospect Park. Jahi wore a pair of brand-new jodhpurs given to her by her sugar daddy, a phrase I didn't understand. We found a bunch of kids on ancient mares with cracked saddles. The guy in charge was a weight lifter named Tony, dressed in boots, Stetson, and fringed shirt. When I asked where he was from, he said, "Roun' de co'nuh."

Tony led his motley posse along a dirt path through the park. The horses walked a lazy single file. Half an hour later they still strolled with heads down, performing their function like machines. I was embarrassed for the animals, domesticated to disgrace.

Tony left the path for a wide paved road that curved around a pond. The horses began a brief trot. Following instinct, I snapped the reins across the horse's neck and hunkered down. A gallop was much easier to ride. The old mare lifted her head and, for the first time since retiring to Brooklyn, heaved into a run. Her hooves sounded odd pounding the tar. I guided her to the outside and around the others. Jahi whooped behind me.

Tony shouted for me to stop, his face red and snarling, finally looking as if he was from the neighborhood instead of Montana. I floated above the pavement, well seated and moving with the mare's rhythm. I looked for Jahi and saw a horse following at full speed. Someone screamed. I reined in and a horse shot past me, its rider slowly tilting sideways like a centaur splitting at the seam. The horse swerved toward the edge of the road. The rider slid from the saddle. His head slammed against a streetlight, spinning his body in a pinwheel, slinging blood that spattered the street.

A few hundred people formed a tight circle around the kid. Teenage boys dared each other to step in the blood. An ambulance arrived. Tony was mad and wanted to fight but Jahi pulled me away, screaming that she'd sue. She held very tightly to my arm, pushing her groin against my leg. Her palms were hot.

We took a cab to her apartment. She hurried upstairs and when I walked in, she was waiting, bent over the back of the couch with the jodhpurs at her ankles.

"Please, Chris," begged her disembodied voice.

Mechanically I unbuckled my pants. As I lowered

them, I heard again the sound of the boy's head hitting the steel pole, like a boot dropped into a fifty-gallon drum. Swallowing bile, I turned and ran down the steps. The public sacrifice had been too great, too unexpected. I was unable to merge with the priestess for recovery of life.

I wandered Flatbush in a muddled stupor. The day's event unfurled in my head at varying speeds. I watched the scene from above in slow motion, seeing myself on a tiny horse. I became the kid sliding for miles from the saddle, waiting for impact. I became Tony, drop-jawed and aghast, primed for a fight. I was the horse; I was Jahi; I was the bored medic. I was anyone but myself.

I missed work for a week, staying in bed like a hog wrapped in the warm, wet mud of misery. When I finally went to the warehouse, Jahi called, petulant and forgiving. I hung up on her laugher and never saw her again.

A week later, on my twentieth birthday, I joined some guys playing football in Riverside Park. Quick and lean with good hands, I made a spectacular catch on a thirty-yard pass. The ball was spiraling high, thrown too hard and over my head. I leaped, twisting in the air to snag it from the sky, seeing at my zenith the New Jersey smokestacks reflected in the river's glare. My left foot landed one way while my momentum carried me the other. A tackler smashed me a third direction altogether.

The next day I limped to a hospital and emerged with my left leg encased in plaster. The knee ligaments were destroyed but I was happy. The cast gave me a legitimate reason for going home. I rode an airplane for the first time and my mother picked me up in Lexington. She drove me two hours into the eastern hills, where the community accepted my return as a wounded hero. My family's attitude was one of justice having been done; the cosmos had exacted its price for the sheer audacity of leaving the land. Dad and I drank beer together, a rite we'd never performed before. He repeated again and again, "They shoot horses in your shape."

The cast was due for removal in eight weeks but took ten because the local doctor had to import a special cutting tool. He was so impressed with the New York cast that he asked to keep it. My leg revealed itself pale, withered, and hairless. Every evening, I filled a purse with rocks, fastened it to my ankle, and lifted it from a sitting position. Between repetitions I plucked ticks from the dogs, watching night arrive. The black air seeped down the hills to fuse land and sky in a darkness absent from the city.

My acting career had failed but I had been to all the museums, and many galleries. The paintings overpowered me. I often sat for hours before a single canvas, studying each nuance of brushstroke, seeking to understand not the painting, but the painter. Galleries had the effect of a swift cold shower. Museums left me exhausted. Limping in the womb of the hills, I decided to become a painter without ever having applied brush to canvas. First, I needed a job to finance the supplies. Second, I needed unusual clothes. Third and most important, I needed inspiration.

I thought of Jahi offering herself as reward for violence. I had shunned the ritual as a petrifact. Becoming a grownup had to mean more than sex, needed to be independent of women. The traditional arena of sports had left me with a leg unable to tolerate the required pivots. I could stay at home and cut trees, dig the earth, and kill animals, but using nature as my testing ground would prove nothing. The woods were full of damaged men. Nature always won.

———————

CHRIS OFFUTT, *author of* Kentucky Straight *and* The Same River Twice, *grew up in the Appalachian Mountains of eastern Kentucky and now lives in the Rocky Mountains of western Montana.*

His writing has earned many honors for him, including an award from the American Academy of Arts and Letters and a fellowship from the National Endowment for the Arts. His short stories have appeared in such magazines as Esquire *and* Gentlemen's Quarterly *and have been anthologized in* Best American Short Stories 1994 *and* The Picador Book of American Stories.

The preceding excerpt is from his memoir The Same River Twice *(1993).*

Bob Dylan

Talking New York

Ramblin' outa the wild West,
Leavin' the towns I love the best.
Thought I'd seen some ups and downs,
'Til I come into New York town.
People goin' down to the ground,
Buildings goin' up to the sky.

Wintertime in New York town,
The wind blowin' snow around.
Walk around with nowhere to go,
Somebody could freeze right to the bone.
I froze right to the bone.
New York Times said it was the coldest winter
    in seventeen years;
I didn't feel so cold then.

I swung on to my old guitar,
Grabbed hold of a subway car,
And after a rocking, reeling, rolling ride,
I landed up on the downtown side;
Greenwich Village.

I walked down there and ended up
In one of them coffee-houses on the block.
Got on the stage to sing and play,
Man there said, "Come back some other day,
You sound like a hillbilly;
We want folk singers here."

Well, I got a harmonica job, begun to play,
Blowin' my lungs out for a dollar a day.
I blowed inside out and upside down.
The man there said he loved m' sound.
He was ravin' about how he loved m' sound;
Dollar a day's worth.

And after weeks and weeks of hangin' around,
I finally got a job in New York town,
In a bigger place, bigger money too.
Even joined the union and paid m' dues.

Now, a very great man once said
That some people rob you with a fountain pen.
It didn't take too long to find out
Just what he was talkin' about.
A lot of people don't have much food on their table,
But they got a lot of forks 'n' knives,
And they gotta cut somethin'.

So one mornin' when the sun was warm,
I rambled out of New York town.
Pulled my cap down over my eyes
And headed out for the western skies.
So long, New York.
Howdy, East Orange.

Hard Times in New York Town

Come you ladies and you gentlemen, a-listen
    to my song.
Sing it to you right, but you might think it's wrong.
Just a little glimpse of a story I'll tell
'Bout an East Coast city that you all know well.
It's hard times in the city,
Livin' down in New York town.

Old New York City is a friendly old town,
From Washington Heights to Harlem on down.
There's a-mighty many people all millin' all around,
They'll kick you when you're up and knock you when
    you're down.
It's hard times in the city,
Livin' down in New York town.

It's a mighty long ways from the Golden Gate
To Rockefeller Plaza 'n' the Empire State.
Mister Rockefeller sets up as high as a bird,
Old Mister Empire never says a word.
It's hard times from the country,
Livin' down in New York town.

Well, it's up in the mornin' tryin' to find a job of work.
Stand in one place till your feet begin to hurt.
If you got a lot o' money you can make yourself merry,
If you only got a nickel, it's the Staten Island Ferry.
And it's hard times in the city,
Livin' down in New York town.

Mister Hudson come a-sailin' down the stream
And old Mister Minuet paid for his dream.
Bought your city on a one-way track,
'F I had my way I'd sell it right back.
And it's hard times in the city,
Livin' down in New York town.

I'll take all the smog in Cal-i-for-ne-ay,
'N' every bit of dust in the Oklahoma plains,
'N' the dirt in the caves of the Rocky Mountain mines.
It's all much cleaner than the New York kind.
And it's hard times in the city,
Livin' down in New York town.

So all you newsy people, spread the news around,
You c'n listen to m' story, listen to m' song.
You c'n step on my name, you c'n try 'n' get me beat.
When I leave New York, I'll be standin' on my feet.
And it's hard times in the city,
Livin' down in New York town.

———————

Songwriter-poet and singer-guitarist BOB DYLAN, *whose impact on the music scene of the 1960s and beyond is uncontestable, was born Robert Zimmerman in 1941 in Duluth, Minnesota. After dropping out of the University of Minnesota, he moved to New York in 1961 and began playing at coffee houses in Greenwich Village. There, producer John Hammond signed him to Columbia Records, which released his debut album in 1962.*

Dylan produced records prolifically, including The Freewheelin' Bob Dylan, Bringing It All Back Home, Highway 61 Revisited, *and* Blonde on Blonde, *until a 1966 motorcycle crash prompted a two-year hiatus from touring and the public eye. During that time he recorded at home the songs released in 1975 as* The Basement Tapes. *He has continued to record and perform, exploring diverse styles and messages, until he now has over thirty albums to his credit, recorded over the past three decades.*

The lyrics from "Talkin' New York" and "Hard Times in New York Town" are from his first album, Bob Dylan.

Joan Didion

Goodbye to All That

> How many miles to Babylon?
> Three score miles and ten—
> Can I get there by candlelight?
> Yes, and back again—
> If your feet are nimble and light
> You can get there by candlelight.

It is easy to see the beginnings of things, and harder to see the ends. I can remember now, with a clarity that makes the nerves in the back of my neck constrict, when New York began for me, but I cannot lay my finger upon the moment it ended, can never cut through the ambiguities and second starts and broken resolves to the exact place on the page where the heroine is no longer as optimistic as she once was. When I first saw New York I was twenty, and it was summertime, and I got off a DC-7 at the old Idlewild temporary terminal in a new dress, which had seemed very smart in Sacramento but seemed less smart already, even in the old Idlewild temporary terminal, and the warm air smelled of mildew and some instinct, programmed by all the movies I had ever seen and all the songs I had ever heard sung and all the stories I had ever read about New York, informed me that it would never be quite the same again. In fact it never was. Some time later there was a song on all the jukeboxes on the upper East Side that went "but where is the schoolgirl who used to be me," and if it was late enough at night I used to wonder that. I know now that almost everyone wonders something like that, sooner or later and no matter what he or she is doing, but one of the mixed blessing of being twenty and twenty-one and even twenty-three is the conviction that nothing like this, all evidence to the contrary notwithstanding, has ever happened to anyone before.

Of course it might have been some other city, had circumstances been different and the time been different and had I been different, might have been Paris or Chicago or even San Francisco, but because I am talking about myself I am talking here about New York. That first night I opened my window on the bus into town and watched for the skyline, but all I could see were the wastes of Queens and the big signs that said MIDTOWN TUNNEL THIS LANE and then a flood of summer rain (even that seemed remarkable and exotic, for I had come out of the West where there was no summer rain), and for the next three days I sat wrapped in blankets in a hotel room air-conditioned to 35° and tried to get over a bad cold and a high fever. It did not occur to me to call a doctor, because I knew none, and although it did occur to me to call the desk and ask that the air conditioner be turned off, I never called, because I did not know how much to tip whoever might come—was anyone ever so young? I am here to tell you that someone was. All I could do during those three days was talk long-distance to the boy I already knew I would never marry in the spring. I would stay in New York, I told him, just six months, and I could see the Brooklyn Bridge from my window. As it turned out the bridge was the Triborough, and I stayed eight years.

In retrospect it seems to me that those days before I knew the names of all the bridges were happier than the ones that came later, but perhaps you will see that as we go along. Part of what I want to tell you is what it is like to be young in New York, how six months can become eight years with the deceptive ease of a film dissolve, for that is how those years appear to me now, in a long sequence of sentimental dissolves and old-fashioned trick shots—the Seagram Building fountains dissolve into snowflakes, I enter a revolving door at twenty and come out a good deal older, and on a different street.

But most particularly I want to explain to you, and in the process perhaps to myself, why I no longer live in New York. It is often said that New York is a city for only the very rich and the very poor. It is less often said that New York is also, at least for those of us who came there from somewhere else, a city for only the very young.

I remember once, one cold bright December evening in New York, suggesting to a friend who complained of having been around too long that he come with me to a party where there would be, I assured him with the bright resourcefulness of twenty-three, "new faces." He laughed literally until he choked, and I had to roll down the taxi window and hit him on the back. "New faces," he said finally, "don't tell me about *new faces.*" It seemed that the last time he had gone to a party where he had been promised "new faces," there had been fifteen people in the room, and he had already slept with five of the women and owed money to all but two of the men. I laughed with him, but the first snow had just begun to fall and the big Christmas trees glittered yellow and white as far as I could see up Park Avenue and I had a new dress and it would be a long while before I would come to understand the particular moral of the story.

It would be a long while because, quite simply, I was in love with New York. I do not mean "love" in any colloquial way, I mean that I was in love with the city, the way you love the first person who ever touches you and never love anyone quite that way again. I remember walking across Sixty-second Street one twilight that first spring, or the second spring, they were all alike for a while. I was late to meet someone but I stopped at Lexington Avenue and bought a peach and stood on the corner eating it and knew that I had come out of the West and reached the mirage. I could taste the peach and feel the soft air blowing from a subway grating on my legs and I could smell lilac and garbage and expensive perfume and I knew that it would cost something sooner or later—because I did not belong there, did not come from there—but when you are twenty-two or twenty-three, you figure that later you will have a high emotional balance, and be able to pay whatever it costs.

I still believed in possibilities then, still had the sense, so peculiar to New York, that something extraordinary would happen any minute, any day, any month. I was making only $65 or $70 a week then ("Put yourself in Hattie Carnegie's hands," I was advised without the slightest trace of irony by an editor of the magazine for which I worked), so little money that some weeks I had to charge food at Bloomingdale's gourmet shop in order to eat, a fact which went unmentioned in the letters I wrote to California. I never told my father that I needed money because then he would have sent it, and I would never know if I could do it by myself. At that time making a living seemed a game to me, with arbitrary but quite inflexible rules. And except on a certain kind of winter evening—six-thirty in the Seventies, say, already dark and bitter with a wind off the river, when I would be walking very fast toward a bus and would look in the bright windows of brownstones and see cooks working in clean kitchens and imagine women lighting candles on the floor above and beautiful children being bathed on the floor above that—except on nights like those, I never felt poor; I had the feeling that if I needed money I could always get it. I could write a syndicated column for teenagers under the name "Debbi Lynn" or I could smuggle gold into India or I could become a $100 call girl, and none of it would matter.

Nothing was irrevocable; everything was within reach. Just around every corner lay something curious and interesting, something I had never before seen or done or known about. I could go to a party and meet someone who called himself Mr. Emotional Appeal and ran The Emotional Appeal Institute for Tina Onassis Blandford or a Florida cracker who was then a regular on what he called "the Big C," the Southampton-El Morocco circuit ("I'm well-connected on the Big C, honey," he would tell me over collard greens on his vast borrowed terrace), or the widow of the celery king of the Harlem market, or a piano salesman from Bonne Terre, Missouri, or someone who had already made and lost two fortunes in Midland, Texas. I could make promises to myself and to other people and there would be all the time in the world to keep them. I could stay up all night and make mistakes, and none of it would count.

You see I was in a curious position in New York: it never occurred to me that I was living a real life there. In my imagination I was always there for just another few months, just until Christmas or Easter or the first warm day in May. For that reason I was most comfortable in the company of Southerners. They seemed to be in New York as I was, on some indefinitely extended leave from wherever they belonged, disinclined to consider the future, temporary exiles who always knew when the flights left for New Orleans or Memphis or Richmond or, in my case, California. Someone who lives always with a plane schedule in the drawer lives on a slightly different calendar. Christmas, for example, was a difficult season. Other people could take it in stride, going to Stowe or going abroad or going for the day to their mothers' places in Connecticut; those of us who believed that we lived somewhere else would spend it making and cancelling airline reservations, waiting for weatherbound flights as if for the last plane out of Lisbon in 1940, and finally comforting one another, those of us who were left, with the oranges and mementos and smoked-oyster stuffings of childhood, gathering close, colonials in a far country.

Which is precisely what we were. I am not sure that it is possible for anyone brought up in the East to appreciate entirely what New York, the idea of New York, means to those of us who came out of the West and the South. To an Eastern child, particularly a child who has always had an uncle on Wall Street and who has spent several hundred Saturdays first at F. A. O. Schwarz and being fitted for shoes at Best's and then waiting under the Biltmore clock and dancing to Lester Lanin, New York is just a city, albeit *the* city, a plausible place for people to live. But to those of us who came from places where no one had heard of Lester Lanin and Grand Central Station was a Saturday radio program, where Wall Street and Fifth Avenue and Madison Avenue were not places at all but abstractions ("Money," and "High Fashion," and "The Hucksters"),

New York was no mere city. It was instead an infinitely romantic notion, the mysterious nexus of all love and money and power, the shining and perishable dream itself. To think of "living" there was to reduce the miraculous to the mundane; one does not "live" at Xanadu.

In fact it was difficult in the extreme for me to understand those young women for whom New York was not simply an ephemeral Estoril but a real place, girls who bought toasters and installed new cabinets in their apartments and committed themselves to some reasonable future. I never bought any furniture in New York. For a year or so I lived in other people's apartments; after that I lived in the Nineties in an apartment furnished entirely with things taken from storage by a friend whose wife had moved away. And when I left the apartment in the Nineties (that was when I was leaving everything, when it was all breaking up) I left everything in it, even my winter clothes and the map of Sacramento County I had hung on the bedroom wall to remind me who I was, and I moved into a monastic four-room floor-through on Seventy-fifth Street. "Monastic" is perhaps misleading here, implying some chic severity; until after I was married and my husband moved some furniture in, there was nothing at all in those four rooms except a cheap double mattress and box springs, ordered by telephone the day I decided to move, and two French garden chairs lent me by a friend who imported them. (It strikes me now that the people I knew in New York all had curious and self-defeating sidelines. They imported garden chairs which did not sell very well at Hammacher Schlemmer or they tried to market hair straighteners in Harlem or they ghosted exposés of Murder Incorporated for Sunday supplements. I think that perhaps none of us was very serious, *engagé* only about our most private lives.)

All I ever did to that apartment was hang fifty yards of yellow theatrical silk across the bedroom windows, because I had some idea that the gold light would make me feel better, but I did not bother to weight the curtains correctly and all that summer the long panels of transparent golden silk would blow out the windows and get tangled and drenched in the afternoon thunderstorms. That was the year, my twenty-eighth, when I was discovering that not all of the promises would be kept, that some things are in fact irrevocable and that it had counted after all, every evasion and every procrastination, every mistake, every word, all of it.

That is what it was all about, wasn't it? Promises? Now when New York comes back to me it comes in hallucinatory flashes, so clinically detailed that I sometimes wish that memory would effect the distortion with which it is commonly credited. For a lot of the time I was in New York I used a perfume called *Fleurs de Rocaille,* and then *L'Air du Temps,* and now the slightest trace of either can short-circuit my connections for the rest of the day. Nor can I smell Henri Bendel jasmine soap without falling back into the past, or the particular mixture of spices used for boiling crabs. There were barrels of crab boil in a Czech place in the Eighties where I once shopped. Smells, of course, are notorious memory stimuli, but there are others things which affect me the same way. Blue-and-white striped sheets. Vermouth cassis. Some faded nightgowns which were new in 1959 or 1960, and some chiffon scarves I bought about the same time.

I suppose that a lot of us who have been young in New York have the same scenes on our home screens. I remember sitting in a lot of apartments with a slight headache about five o'clock in the morning. I had a friend who could not sleep, and he knew a few other people who had the same trouble, and we would watch the sky lighten and have a last drink with no ice and then go home in the early morning light, when the streets were clean and wet (had it rained in the night? we never knew) and the few cruising taxis still had their headlights on and the only color was the red and green of traffic signals. The White Rose bars opened very early in the morning; I recall waiting in one of them to watch an astronaut go into space, waiting so long that at the moment it actually happened I had my eyes not on the television screen but on a cockroach on the tile floor. I liked the bleak branches above Washington

Square at dawn, and the monochromatic flatness of Second Avenue, the fire escapes and the grilled storefronts peculiar and empty in their perspective.

It is relatively hard to fight at six-thirty or seven in the morning without any sleep, which was perhaps one reason we stayed up all night, and it seemed to me a pleasant time of day. The windows were shuttered in that apartment in the Nineties and I could sleep a few hours and then go to work. I could work then on two or three hours' sleep and a container of coffee from Chock Full O' Nuts. I liked going to work, liked the soothing and satisfactory rhythm of getting out a magazine, liked the orderly progression of four-color closings and two-color closings and black-and-white closings and then The Product, no abstraction but something which looked effortlessly glossy and could be picked up on a newsstand and weighed in the hand. I liked all the minutiae of proofs and layouts, liked working late on the nights the magazine went to press, sitting and reading *Variety* and waiting for the copy desk to call. From my office I could look across town to the weather signal on the Mutual of New York Building and the lights that alternately spelled out TIME and LIFE above Rockefeller Plaza; that pleased me obscurely, and so did walking uptown in the mauve eight o'clocks of early summer evenings and looking at things, Lowestoft tureens in Fifty-seventh Street windows, people in evening clothes trying to get taxis, the trees just coming into full leaf, the lambent air, all the sweet promises of money and summer.

Some years passed, but I still did not lose that sense of wonder about New York. I began to cherish the loneliness of it, the sense that at any given time no one need know where I was or what I was doing. I liked walking, from the East River over to the Hudson and back on brisk days, down around the Village on warm days. A friend would leave me the key to her apartment in the West Village when she was out of town, and sometimes I would just move down there, because by that time the telephone was beginning to bother me (the canker, you see, was already in the rose) and not many people had that number. I remember one day when someone who did have the West Village number came to pick me up for lunch there, and we both had hangovers, and I cut my finger opening him a beer and burst into tears, and we walked to a Spanish restaurant and drank Bloody Marys and *gazpacho* until we felt better. I was not then guilt-ridden about spending afternoons that way, because I still had all the afternoons in the world.

And even late in the game I still liked going to parties, all parties, bad parties, Saturday-afternoon parties given by recently married couples who lived in Stuyvesant Town, West Side parties given by unpublished or failed writers who served cheap red wine and talked about going to Guadalajara, Village parties where all the guests worked for advertising agencies and voted for Reform Democrats, press parties at Sardi's, the worst kinds of parties. You will have perceived by now that I was not one to profit by the experience of others, that it was a very long time indeed before I stopped believing in new faces and began to understand the lesson in that story, which was that it is distinctly possible to stay too long at the Fair.

I could not tell you when I began to understand that. All I know is that it was very bad when I was twenty-eight. Everything that was said to me I seemed to have heard before, and I could no longer listen. I could no longer sit in little bars near Grand Central and listen to someone complaining of his wife's inability to cope with the help while he missed another train to Connecticut. I no longer had any interest in hearing about the advances other people had received from their publishers, about plays which were having second-act trouble in Philadelphia, or about people I would like very much if only I would come out and meet them. I had already met them, always. There were certain parts of the city which I had to avoid. I could not bear upper Madison Avenue on weekday mornings (this was a particularly inconvenient aversion, since I then lived just fifty or sixty feet east of Madison), because I would see women walking Yorkshire terriers and shopping at Gristede's, and some Veblenesque gorge would rise in my throat. I could not go to Times Square in the afternoon, or to the New York Public Library for any reason whatsoever. One day I could not go into a Schrafft's; the next day it would be Bonwit Teller.

I hurt the people I cared about, and insulted those I did not. I cut myself off from the one person who was closer to me than any other. I cried until I was not even aware when I was crying and when I was not, cried in elevators and in taxis and in Chinese laundries, and when I went to the doctor he said only that I seemed to be depressed, and should see a "specialist." He wrote down a psychiatrist's name and address for me, but I did not go.

Instead I got married, which as it turned out was a very good thing to do but badly timed, since I still could not walk on upper Madison Avenue in the mornings and still could not talk to people and still cried in Chinese laundries. I had never before understood what "despair" meant, and I am not sure that I understand now, but I understood that year. Of course I could not work. I could not even get dinner with any degree of certainty, and I would sit in the apartment on Seventy-fifth Street paralyzed until my husband would call from his office and say gently that I did not have to get dinner, that I could meet him at Michael's Pub or at Toots Shor's or at Sardi's East. And then one morning in April (we had been married in January) he called and told me that he wanted to get out of New York for a while, that he would take a six-month leave of absence, that we would go somewhere.

It was three years ago that he told me that, and we have lived in Los Angeles since. Many of the people we knew in New York think this a curious aberration, and in fact tell us so. There is no possible, no adequate answer to that, and so we give certain stock answers, the answers everyone gives. I talk about how difficult it would be for us to "afford" to live in New York right now, about how much "space" we need. All I mean is that I was very young in New York, and that at some point the golden rhythm was broken, and I am not that young any more. The last time I was in New York was in a cold January, and everyone was ill and tired. Many of the people I used to know there had moved to Dallas or had gone on Antabuse or had bought a farm in New Hampshire. We stayed ten days, and then we took an afternoon flight back to Los Angeles, and on the way home from the airport that night I could see the moon on the Pacific and smell jasmine all around and we both knew that there was no longer any point in keeping the apartment we still kept in New York. There were years when I called Los Angeles "the Coast," but they seem a long time ago.

———————

Novelist and essayist JOAN DIDION *was born in 1934 in Sacramento, a sixth-generation Californian. In her senior year at the University of California at Berkeley, she won* Vogue *magazine's Prix de Paris. The award was either a trip to Paris or a job at* Vogue. *She chose the job and, after graduating in 1956, moved to New York. She worked as a staff writer for* Vogue *until 1963, then continued writing film criticism for the magazine as she devoted more time to writing fiction. Her first novel,* Rum River, *was published that same year.*

In 1964 she and her husband, John Gregory Dunne, then a writer for Time, *took leaves of absence from their respective magazines and moved to Los Angeles.*

Joan Didion is perhaps best known for her 1970 novel Play It as It Lays. *"Goodbye to All That" is her account of leaving New York. It was published as part of* Slouching Towards Bethlehem, *her first collection of essays, in 1968.*

David Frishberg

Do You Miss New York?

Since I took a left and moved out to the Coast,
from time to time I find myself engrossed
with other erstwhile denizens of the Apple—
While we sit around and take L.A. to task,
there's a question someone's bound to ask
And with this complex question we must grapple.

Do you miss New York?
The anger, the action?
Does this laid-back lifestyle lack a certain satisfaction?
Do you ever burn to pack up and return to the thick of it?
Or are you really sick of it?
As you always say?

Do you miss the strain?
The traffic, the tension?
Do you view your new terrain with a touch of condescension?
On this quiet street, is it really as sweet as it seems out here?
Do you dream your dreams out here?
Or is that passé?

Do you miss the pace?
The rat race, the racket?

And if you had to face it now, do you still think you could hack it?
When you're back in town for a quick look around, how is it?
Does it seem like home or just another nice place to visit?
And were those halcyon days just a youthful phase you outgrew?
Tell me, do you miss New York?
Do you miss New York?

Do you miss the scene?
The frenzy, the faces?
And did you trade the whole parade for a pair of parking places?
If you had the choice would you still choose to do it all again?
Do you find yourself standing in line to see Annie Hall again?
And do you ever run into that guy who used to be you?
Tell me,
Do you miss New York?
Me too.
Me too.

Pianist, singer, and songwriter DAVID FRISHBERG *was born in 1933 in St. Paul, Minnesota. In 1957 he moved to New York City, where he performed first as a piano soloist and then with Carmen McRae. He played with Gene Krupa's band in the early 1960s and later with Al Cohn and the Zoot Sims Quintet. He was also the resident pianist at the Half Note in New York.*

In 1971 he moved to Los Angeles where, during the early seventies, he played with Jack Sheldon and Joe Pass. He still lives in Los Angeles and misses New York. "Do You Miss New York?" was written in 1980. His score for the song, which appears here, was handwritten especially for this book.

7

Strange Forests

Bill McKibben

Elsewhere in the Empire

A month or so after I graduated from college in 1982, I moved to the city. My parents drove me to Manhattan on the 4th of July; we were supposed to arrive in mid-afternoon, but Dad crimped the fuel line on a gas station curb in Stamford and we spent most of the day getting it fixed. We finally reached the edge of the Bronx at dusk, and just as we passed the sign, fireworks began to erupt: small blooms from backyard parties, bigger bursts from neighborhood parks. We got lost, of course, and toured the Brooklyn-Queens Express-way—the whole time we were driving, light explosives kept raining down. We finally reached the 71st Street sublet I was to share with a friend just as the mighty howitzers on the Hudson let loose and the gaudy chains of light stretched across the entire city sky.

It seemed an auspicious omen—to be welcomed to the city like a conquering hero when all I'd conquered was a gas-line problem on the interstate. And it fit my image of New York perfectly—a place so energized and vital it gave off sparks! The only other time my parents had taken me to Manhattan I'd been in sixth grade. I'm sure we visited the Statue of Liberty and Central Park, but all I can remember is sitting up all night in a hotel room off Times Square and staring out the window at some dingy side street. There was a custard stand on the corner, and my suburban soul was thrilled by the idea that *all night long* people were going in and out of this establishment. There was an anonymous *hecticity* that delighted me.

It delighted me as long as I lived there. I used to

stand on Fifth Avenue at lunchtime, a block from my
office, and just stare down the street at the throng that
filled the sidewalks. The subways thrilled me—they still
do, so many people on so many errands. So many
stops—I tried to get to most of them, but some are still
on my list. New Lots Avenue, Ditmars Boulevard. It
seemed unknowably vast, magnificent not because it
was a unity but because it was a collection so enormous
as to defy knowing, a human Louvre with so many
rooms no one could even compile a map. I remember
reading somewhere that you could eat every meal every
day in a different restaurant and never catch up with the
number of eateries in the city: they opened too fast.
Everything seemed magically that way to me: millions
upon millions of stories.

I tried to tell some of those stories. My job when I
came to the city was as a "Talk of the Town" writer at
The New Yorker, The New Yorker run in those days by
William Shawn, much as it had been run for decades.
In the hall by the elevator on the 18th floor, there were
file cabinets filled with tens of thousands of old pro-
posals for Talk stories, and as I waited for the elevator
to arrive I would read them: descriptions of air raid
wardens from the Second World War, or the myriad
inventors (runless nylons, noiseless dog whistles), or
the jingle writers or the crossword-puzzle solvers or
the bunco square lieutenants or the people with the
leopard in their apartment. Before long I had added a
few hundred to the list myself. My first story was about
a man in the South Bronx who wrote thousands of
terse letters to the editor of prominent newspapers
demanding that subways carry freight, that railroads
be built with concrete crossties, that skyscrapers be
covered with ivy to soak up carbon dioxide. From
there I chronicled charisma teachers, furniture sales-
men who used the signs of the zodiac to plan our
decor, a man who invented an electric device that stim-
ulated your stomach muscles to perform the equiva-
lent of a thousand sit-ups while you rested comfortably
on a couch. I folded paper with the elderly woman at
the Museum of Natural History who made thousands
of origami ornaments each year for their Christmas

tree, and reported on the new Aroma Disc machine which could make any room smell like stale hot buttered popcorn, and climbed through the ceiling of the Holland Tunnel with repair crews fixing the ventilators. It was me and me alone who found the first person making earrings out of the plastic sushi that Japanese restaurants use for window decorations; I went to the heron sanctuary in the oily channel between Staten Island and New Jersey, and chatted with the Brooklyn dentist, a native of Grenada, who was appointed that country's United Nations ambassador following the American invasion. ("No other dentist has represented an English-speaking country, I think. Perhaps one of the Latin countries. But there is a lot of diplomacy in dentistry. You have to have a lot of diplomacy to be able to inflict pain and get paid for it. But the pain is for the greater good, of course, for the greater good.") I toured a community garden in Greenpoint where they grew peaches, and talked to Tamilee Webb who had invented a new aerobic workout employing giant rubber bands—Tamilee encouraged her adherents to point their rubber bands away from their own faces or the faces of others. I collected the messages that people left on department store typewriters when they tried them out: "Sometimes I wonder why I spend these lonely nights dreaming a dream an haunting melody in myn in my reverie," or

> Allison and Nanette where here
> but now they're gone
> they left their names to carry on
> those who knew them knew them well
> those who didn't GO TO HELL!!!!!!!!!!!!!

I had, I think, the best job on earth. Free to wander the city, talking to a man who wanted to open a bowling museum with a full-size recreation of Martin Luther bowling—the first Protestant was also, after all, an ardent kegler. As time went on, though, I began to have a strange sense for a 25-year-old: a strong feeling that I was living in the past, that I was as out-of-date as a typewriter in a department store. That is, I was describing a New York that was increasingly marginal, a New York of characters still hanging on but not being created anew. I was gleeful when I found them: the world's greatest spoons player, newly arrived from the Great Plains and demonstrating his art in front of the public library, or the world's strongest man, a Romanian exile living (and breaking roofing tiles with his mighty hands) in Long Island City. But they seemed like living relics, rule-proving exceptions. The city seemed to me to be growing more boring. I am aware that this must seem a trivial reason to grow dissatisfied, and I wish I could say that the misery of the homeless, say, drove me to leave the city. I noticed it: I wrote about it, and I helped start a small shelter in my church basement, but it didn't depress me as much as it should have. Frankly, there was at least something *interesting* about despair, and I was a trained voyeur. It was the lack of other fascinating windows to peek in that began to worry me.

I conjured up a number of possible explanations. For instance: as the number of daily newspapers declined, so did the possible ink—and in my experience ink was as important as food or water in maintaining many of these characters. When Joe Mitchell compiled some of his stories from the *Herald Tribune* in the years before the war, he was able to fill a whole chapter with interviews with strippers, including one girl who came out naked and then slowly clothed herself: even the tabloids now are so thin they can barely keep up with the freshest murders.

Money probably explained more, however. For one thing, living in New York had become absurdly expensive, at least for the class of those who had arrived too late to scoop up a rent-controlled eight-room apartment over the park. I lived in six sublets in five years, and I was luckier than most: the young actors and painters and necessary misfits arriving in Manhattan had to work so hard waiting tables to pay their share of the rent on a crowded apartment that they had no time left to recite their new lyrics over beers at the White Horse, where beer was three bucks a glass in any event.

But the lack of cash in certain sectors of the city was only half the story, and not the most important half.

These were the early 1980s, the years before "yuppie" had become a tired cliché, and Manhattan was younger and more professional than any urban enclave on the planet. Most of the people I'd gone to school with had come straight to Wall Street (although some had detoured through law school on their way) and almost immediately they earned large sums of money. They worked long hours, too, and between overwork and overpay they were largely oblivious to the charms of the city. They added little: perhaps it was a failure of the imagination, but I found fewer and fewer Talk stories about young people. A kind of emptiness was spreading.

And in that emptiness, people's definition of what was appealing began to change. More and more, readers (and their advocates, editors) seemed to value as interesting that which was successful. Famous for their fame, celebrities appeared time and again on magazine covers. As a reporter it held no appeal for me—I liked stories no one had ever heard of—and I rebelled in small ways. I wrote an endless piece on the physical reality of Manhattan, for instance, following every pipe and wire in my apartment to its ultimate source. And I sought out the characters on the furthest edges of this media culture: the man who sat outside Zabars selling sections of the Sunday *Times* for a quarter apiece, for instance.

Eventually the new reality caught up with me. *The New Yorker* was the last holdout against this fascination with the timely and the topical: when people talked about how "out of touch" the magazine was, or how "old-fashioned," or how "exasperating," they meant precisely the 20,000 word pieces on sewer tunnels, the Talk stories about people building hovercraft in the basements of their apartment buildings. *I* was out of touch. I left the magazine when Mr. Shawn did, knowing that it was still a fine magazine staffed by the finest people, but sensing that as time went on its notion of what was magical would diverge from mine. At 27 I felt both too old and too innocent for the city.

Where to go? Joining some other magazine would have felt anti-climactic; so too moving to some other city, at best a reminder of the diversity and energy that I had adored in New York. So I went to the woods—to a house seven miles from a town of 200, on the edge of millions of acres of trackless wilderness. At the time I thought I was escaping, retreating; as the years have gone by, though, I realize that instead I had come almost by accident to a spot as *sui generis* as Manhattan. And I had done it without leaving the Empire State.

Along with the city—the greatest collection of human talent and energy and angst the world has ever seen—New York State can boast one other world-class achievement: the restoration of the mighty Adirondack Mountains. Though nine people in ten questioned on a Manhattan street could not find them on a map, the Adirondacks comprise nearly a quarter of the state, an area bigger than Vermont or New Hampshire, bigger than Yellowstone, Grand Canyon, Yosemite, and Glacier National Parks combined. Five hours drive from the city, it is full of moose and coyote and bear and beaver, swamp and spruce and blackfly.

Though very few people live here—barely a hundred thousand through the winter, fewer than any twenty blocks of the Upper West Side—it is also a place filled with human history, an experiment in human possibility just as comprehensive as the one long underway in New York City. Barely a hundred years ago, these vast forests were all in private hands, and they were being cut with the same ferocity that Oregon or the Amazon is being cut today. But folks from the city had begun to venture here for their vacations—the Adirondacks were the first "adventure travel destination." Appalled by the destruction, and worried that silt rolling down the nude hillsides would plug the Hudson, they persuaded the legislature to draw a line around the park and begin acquiring land. New York now owns nearly half the property within the Adirondack Park, and under an amendment to the constitution that land is "forever wild"—not a branch ever to be cut. The remaining private property—my home for instance—exists under a fairly strict zoning code that has kept much of the park looking and seeming wild. Wilder all the time, in fact, for the forest has grown back in and with it have come most of the animals that belong here. My neighbors can remember back fifty years when the first bear returned to town; now it's the return of the moose that excites us. There aren't many yet—but it shouldn't take too long.

The Adirondacks are the largest recovered ecosystem on earth, one of the few places demonstrably healthier with each generation that passes. And in their health and vigor they remind me of the city as I imagined and loved it: a place of endless surprise. You could walk forever in the Adirondacks and never exhaust the subtly different landscapes: the beaver ponds and deer yards and bear trees, the bogs and fire scars and alpine meadows, the whitewater rivers and the cold ruffled lakes. And there is a human glory here too—the small towns hanging on amidst the wilderness, filled with people who have learned to adapt themselves to the natural world instead of, as in most places, the other way round.

The forces that undercut the city may undercut the park as well. There is too little money for many of the people who live here: the state's poorest counties are all in the Adirondacks, and privation breeds a quiet discontent, especially in people who live, via the satellite dish, in the mental world of uptown and not backcountry. Many of us are trying to solve those problems—to build decent schools and health care, and also to show that we might take our pleasure from the natural glory around us and not the material culture that leaks in on the airwaves.

There's something even harder than poverty to deal with, though, and that is the pool of money floating around the surrounding region. Money from those former yuppies that seeks now to take concrete form in second homes, vacation developments, in all the schemes that will cut short this Adirondack experiment and spread the blandness here. But for now the cold winters and the crazed insects of the spring keep some of that pressure at bay. For the moment this place remains impeccably *real,* as real as the Garment District on a busy afternoon or Hunts Point Market at five in the morning. There are no fireworks in the Adirondacks, but on a clear night the sky is still dark, the Milky Way a creamy ribbon.

———————

BILL MCKIBBEN, *a 1982 graduate of Harvard College, has written for a wide range of publications, including the* Atlantic Monthly, *the* New York Review of Books, *the* New York Times *magazine,* Esquire, Natural History, Audubon, Outside, *and* Rolling Stone. *As a staff writer for The New Yorker from 1982-1987, he wrote hundreds of articles for the magazine, primarily for "Talk of the Town," but also longer pieces and humorous fiction. He has been a free-lance writer since 1987, as a Lyndhurst Fellow from 1988-1991 and a Guggenheim Fellow from 1993-1994.*

His books are The End of Nature *(1989, now with fourteen foreign language editions);* The Age of Missing Information *(1992);* The Comforting Whirlwind: God, Job, and the Scale of Creation *(1994); and* Hope, Human and Wild *(1995). He is co-author, with Alex MacLean, of* Look at the Land *(1993) and editor of the 1992 book* Birch Browsings: A John Burroughs Reader.

After living in the Boston and New York areas, he now makes his home in the Adirondack Mountains of New York with his wife, writer Sue Halpern, and their daughter.

"Elsewhere in the Empire" was written for Leaving New York.

Edward Hoagland

The Courage of Turtles

Turtles are a kind of bird with the governor turned low. With the same attitude of removal, they cock a glance at what is going on, as if they need only to fly away. Until recently they were also a case of virtue rewarded, at least in the town where I grew up, because, being humble creatures, there were plenty of them. Even when we still had a few bobcats in the woods the local snapping turtles, growing up to forty pounds, were the largest carnivores. You would see them through the amber water, as big as greeny wash basins at the bottom of the pond, until they faded into the inscrutable mud as if they hadn't existed at all.

When I was ten I went to Dr. Green's Pond, a two-acre-pond across the road. When I was twelve I walked a mile or so to Taggart's Pond, which was lusher, had big water snakes and a waterfall; and shortly after that I was bicycling way up to the adventuresome vastness of Mud Pond, a lake-sized body of water in the reservoir system of a Connecticut city, possessed of cat-backed little islands and empty shacks and a forest of pines and hardwoods along the shore. Otters, foxes, and mink left their prints on the bank; there were pike and perch. As I got older, the estates and forgotten back lots in town were parceled out and sold for nice prices, yet, though the woods had shrunk, it seemed that fewer people walked in the woods. The new residents didn't know how to find them. Eventually, exploring, they did find them, and it required some ingenuity and doubling around on my part to go for eight miles without meeting someone. I was grown by now, I lived in New

York, and that's what I wanted to do on the occasional weekends when I came out.

Since Mud Pond contained drinking water I had felt confident nothing untoward would happen there. For a long while the developers stayed away, until the drought of the mid-1960s. This event, squeezing the edges in, convinced the local water company that the pond really wasn't a necessity as a catch basin, however; so they bulldozed a hole in the earthen dam, bulldozed the banks to fill in the bottom, and landscaped the flow of water that remained to wind like an English brook and provide a domestic view for the houses which were planned. Most of the painted turtles of Mud Pond, who had been inaccessible as they sunned on their rocks, wound up in boxes in boys' closets within a matter of days. Their footsteps in the dry leaves gave them away as they wandered forlornly. The snappers and the little musk turtles, neither of whom leave the water except once a year to lay their eggs, dug into the drying mud for another siege of hot weather, which they were accustomed to doing whenever the pond got low. But this time it was low for good; the mud baked over them and slowly entombed them. As for the ducks, I couldn't stroll in the woods and not feel guilty, because they were crouched beside every stagnant pothole, or were slinking between the bushes with their heads tucked into their shoulders so that I wouldn't see them. If they decided I had, they beat their way up through the screen of trees, striking their wings dangerously, and wheeled about with that headlong, magnificent velocity to locate another poor puddle.

I used to catch possums and black snakes as well as turtles, and I kept dogs and goats. Some summers I worked in a menagerie with the big personalities of the animal kingdom, like elephants and rhinoceroses. I was twenty before these enthusiasms began to wane, and it was then that I picked turtles as the particular animal I wanted to keep in touch with. I was allergic to fur, for one thing, and turtles need minimal care and not much in the way of quarters. They're personable beasts. They see the same colors we do and they seem to see just as well, as one discovers in trying to sneak up on them. In the laboratory they unravel the twists of a maze with the hot-blooded rapidity of a mammal. Though they can't run as fast as a rat, they improve on their errors just as quickly, pausing at each crossroads to look left and right. And they rock rhythmically in place, as we often do, although they are hatched from eggs, not the womb. (A common explanation psychologists give for our pleasure in rocking quietly is that it recapitulates our mother's heartbeat *in utero*.)

Snakes, by contrast, are dryly silent and priapic. They are smooth movers, legalistic, unblinking, and they afford the humor which the humorless do. But they make challenging captives; sometimes they don't eat for months on a point of order—if the light isn't right, for instance. Alligators are sticklers too. They're like war-horses, or German shepherds, and with their bar-shaped, vertical pupils adding emphasis, they have the *idée fixe* of eating, eating, even when they choose to refuse all food and stubbornly die. They delight in tossing a salamander up towards the sky and grabbing him in their long mouths as he comes down. They're so eager that they get the jitters, and they're too much of a proposition for a casual aquarium like mine. Frogs are depressingly defenseless: that moist, extensive back, with the bones almost sticking through. Hold a frog and you're holding its skeleton. Frogs' tasty legs are the staff of life to many animals—herons, raccoons, ribbon snakes—though they themselves are hard to feed. It's not an enviable role to be the staff of life, and after frogs you descend down the evolutionary ladder a big step to fish.

*　　*　　*

Turtles cough, burp, whistle, grunt and hiss, and produce social judgments. They put their heads together amicably enough, but then one drives the other back with the suddenness of two dogs who have been conversing in tones too low for an onlooker to hear. They pee in fear when they're first caught, but exercise both pluck and optimism in trying to escape, walking for hundreds of yards within the confines of their pen, carrying the weight of that cumbersome box on legs that are cruelly positioned for walking. They don't feel that the contest is unfair; they keep plugging, rolling like sailorly souls—a bobbing, infirm gait, a brave, sea-legged momentum—stopping occasionally to study the lay of the land. For me, anyway, they manage to contain the rest of the animal world. They can stretch out their necks like a giraffe, or loom underwater like an apocryphal hippo. They browse on lettuce thrown on the water like a cow moose which is partly submerged. They have a penguin's alertness, combined with a build like a brontosaurus when they rise up on tiptoe. Then they hunch and ponderously lunge like a grizzly going forward.

Baby turtles in a turtle bowl are a puzzle in geometrics. They're as decorative as pansy petals, but they are also self-directed building blocks, propping themselves on one another in different arrangements, before upending the tower. The timid individuals turn fearless, or vice versa. If one gets a bit arrogant he will push the others off the rock and afterwards climb down into the water and cling to the back of one of those he has bullied, tickling him with his hind feet until he bucks like a bronco. On the other hand, when this same milder-mannered fellow isn't exerting himself, he will stare right into the face of the sun for hours. What could be more lionlike? And he's at home in or out of the water and does lots of metaphysical tilting. He sinks and rises, with an infinity of levels to choose from; or, elongating himself, he climbs out on the land again to perambulate, sits boxed in his box, and finally slides back in the water, submerging into dreams.

I have five of these babies in a kidney-shaped bowl. The hatchling, who is a painted turtle, is not as large as the top joint of my thumb. He eats chicken gladly. Other foods he will attempt to eat but not with sufficient perseverance to succeed because he's so little. The yellow-bellied terrapin is probably a yearling, and he eats salad voraciously, but no meat, fish, or fowl. The Cumberland terrapin won't touch salad or chicken but eats fish and all of the meats except for bacon. The little snapper, with a black crenelated shell, feasts on any kind of meat, but rejects greens and fish. The fifth of the turtles is African. I acquired him only recently and don't know him well. A mottled brown, he unnerves the greener turtles, dragging their food off to his lairs. He doesn't seem to want to be green—he bites the algae off his shell, hanging meanwhile at daring, steep, head-first angles.

The snapper was a Ferdinand until I provided him with deeper water. Now he snaps at my pencil with his downturned and fearsome mouth, his swollen face like a napalm victim's. The Cumberland has an elliptical red mark on the side of his green-and-yellow head. He is benign by nature and ought to be as elegant as his scientific name (*Pseudemys scripta elegans*), except he has contracted a disease of the air bladder which has permanently inflated it; he floats high in the water at an undignified slant and can't go under. There may have been internal bleeding, too, because his carapace is stained along its ridge. Unfortunately, like flowers, baby turtles often die. Their mouths fill up with a white fungus and their lungs with pneumonia. Their organs clog up from the rust in the water, or diet troubles, and, like a dying man's, their eyes and heads become too prominent. Toward the end, the edge of the shell becomes flabby as felt and folds around them like a shroud.

While they live they're like puppies. Although they're vivacious, they would be a bore to be with all the time, so I also have an adult wood turtle about six inches long. Her top shell is the equal of any seashell for sculpturing, even a Cellini shell; it's like an old, dusty, richly engraved medallion dug out of a hillside. Her legs are salmon-orange bordered with black and protected by canted, heroic scales. Her plastron—the bottom shell—is splotched like a margay cat's coat, with black ocelli on a yellow background. It is convex to make room for the female organs inside, whereas a male's would be concave to help him fit tightly on top of her. Altogether, she exhibits every camouflage color on her limbs and shells. She has a turtleneck neck, a tail like an elephant's, wise old pachydermous hind legs, and the face of a turkey—except that when I carry her she gazes at the passing ground with a hawk's eyes and mouth. Her feet fit to the fingers of my hand, one to each one, and she rides looking down. She can walk on the floor in perfect silence, but usually she lets her plastron knock portentously, like a footstep, so that she resembles some grand, concise, slow-moving id. But if an earthworm is presented, she jerks swiftly ahead, poises above it, and strikes like a mongoose, consuming it with wild vigor. Yet she will climb on my lap to eat bread or boiled eggs.

If put into a creek, she swims like a cutter, nosing forward to intercept a strange turtle and smell him. She drifts with the current to go downstream, maneuvering behind a rock when she wants to take stock, or sinking to the nether levels, while bubbles float up. Getting out, choosing her path, she will proceed a distance and dig into a pile of humus, thrusting herself to the coolest layer at the bottom. The hole closes over her until it's as small as a mouse's hole. She's not as aquatic as a musk turtle, not quite as terrestrial as the box turtles in the same woods, but because of her versatility she's marvelous, she's everywhere. And though she breathes the way we breathe, with scarcely perceptible movements of her chest, sometimes instead she pumps her throat ruminatively, like a pipe smoker sucking and puffing. She waits and blinks, pumping her throat, turning her head, then steps off like a loping tiger in slow motion, hurdling the jungly lumber, the pea vine and twigs. She estimates angles so well that when she rides over the rocks, sliding down a drop-off with her rugged front legs extended, she has the grace of a rodeo mare.

But she's well off to be with me rather than at Mud Pond. The other turtles have fled—those that aren't baked into the bottom. Creeping up the brooks to sad, constricted marshes, burdened as they are with that box on their backs, they're walking into a setup where all their enemies move thirty times faster than they. It's like the nightmare most of us have whimpered through, where we are weighted down disastrously while trying to flee; fleeing our home ground, we try to run.

I've seen turtles in still worse straits. On Broadway, in New York, there is a penny arcade which used to sell baby terrapins that were scrawled with bon mots in enamel paint, such as KISS ME BABY. The manager turned out to be a wholesaler as well, and once I asked him whether he had any larger turtles to sell. He took me upstairs to a loft room devoted to the turtle business. There were desks for the paper work and a series of racks that held shallow tin bins atop one another, each with several hundred babies crawling around in it. He was a smudgy-complexioned, bespectacled, serious fellow and he did have a few adult terrapins, but I was going to school and wasn't actually planning to buy; I'd only wanted to see them. They were aquatic turtles, but here they went without water, presumably or weeks, lurching about in those dry bins like handicapped citizens, living on gumption. An easel where the artist worked stood in the middle of the floor. She had a palette and a clip attachment for fastening the babies in place. She wore a smock and a beret, and was homely, short, and eccentric-looking, with funny black hair, like some of the ladies who show their paintings in Washington Square in May. She had a cold, she was smoking, and her hand wasn't very steady, although she worked quickly enough. The smile that she produced for me would have looked giddy if she had been happier, or drunk. Of course the turtles' doom was sealed when she painted them, because their bodies inside would continue to grow but their shells would not. Gradually, invisibly, they would be crushed. Around us their bellies—two thousand belly shells—rubbed on the bins with a mournful, momentous hiss.

Somehow there were so many of them I didn't rescue one. Years later, however, I was walking on First Avenue when I noticed a basket of living turtles in front of a fish store. They were as dry as a heap of old bones in the sun; nevertheless, they were creeping over one another gimpily, doing their best to escape. I looked and was touched to discover that they appeared to be wood turtles, my favorites, so I bought one. In my apartment I looked closer and realized that in fact this was a diamondback terrapin, which was bad news. Diamondbacks are tidewater turtles from brackish estuaries, and I had no seawater to keep him in. He spent his days thumping interminably against the baseboards, pushing for an opening through the wall. He drank thirstily but would not eat and had none of the hearty, accepting qualities of wood turtles. He was morose, paler in color, sleeker and more Oriental in the carved ridges and rings that formed his shell. Though I felt sorry for him, finally I found his unrelenting presence exasperating. I carried him, struggling in a paper bag, across town to the Morton Street Pier on the Hudson River. It was August but gray and windy. He was very surprised when I tossed him in; for the first time in our association, I think, he was afraid. He looked afraid as he bobbed about on top of the water, looking up at me from ten feet below. Though we were both accustomed to his resistance and rigidity, seeing him still pitiful, I recognized that I must have done the wrong thing. At least the river was salty, but it was also bottomless; the waves were too rough for him, and the tide was coming in, bumping him against the pilings underneath the pier. Too late, I realized that he wouldn't be able to swim to a peaceful inlet in New Jersey, even if he could figure out which way to swim. But since, short of diving in after him, there was nothing I could do, I walked away.

EDWARD HOAGLAND *is one of this country's finest contemporary essayists and author of fifteen books, including the novel* Seven Rivers West. *A disciple of H. D. Thoreau, he discovered his talent for writing essays in 1968. Hoagland was born in New York City in 1932. For twenty years, he divided his time between a Manhattan apartment and a house without electricity in northeastern Vermont.*

Among his collections of essays are Walking the Dead Diamond River *and* Balancing Acts. *"The Courage of Turtles," which appeared originally in the* Village Voice—*purchased for a sum of thirty-five dollars—is the title essay of a collection published in 1970. Long out of print,* The Courage of Turtles *was reissued by Lyons and Burford in 1993. Hoagland's 1969 book,* Notes from the Century Before, *is a 1995 Sierra Club reissue.*

Terry Tempest Williams

Water Songs

Lee Milner and I stood in front of the diorama of the black-crowned night heron at the American Museum of Natural History in New York City. *Nycticorax nycticorax:* a long-legged bird common in freshwater marshes, swamps, and tidal flats, ranging from Canada to South America.

We each had our own stories. My tales were of night herons at the Bear River Migratory Bird Refuge in Utah—the way they fly with their heads sunken in line with their backs, their toes barely projecting beyond their tail, the way they roost in trees with their dark green feathered robes. Lee painted them at Pelham Bay Park on the northern edge of the Bronx, where, she says, "they fly about you like moths." Both of us could re-create their steady wingbeats with our hands as they move through crepuscular hours.

Two women, one from Utah and one from the Bronx, brought together by birds.

We were also colleagues at the American Museum. I was there as part of an exchange program from the Utah Museum of Natural History, on staff for six weeks. Lee was hired to manage the Alexander M. White Natural Science Center while the program director was on medical leave. The center is a special hands-on exhibit where children can learn about nature in New York City.

We worked together each day, teaching various school groups about the natural history in and around their neighborhoods. In between the toad, turtle, and salamander feedings, we found time to talk. Lee was passionate about her home. She would pull out maps of Pelham Bay Park and run her fingers over every slough, every clump of cattails and stretch of beach that was part of this ecosystem. She would gesture with her body the way the light shifts, exposing herons, bitterns, and owls. And she spoke with sadness about being misunderstood, how people outside the Bronx did not recognize the beauty.

I wasn't sure I did.

Lee and her father had just moved to Co-op City, and she described the view from their apartment as perfect for looking out over cattails. She promised to take me to Pelham Bay before I left.

The opportunity finally came. Our aquarium had been having bacteria problems that had killed some of the organisms. We decided we could use some more intertidal creatures: crabs, shrimps, and maybe some barnacles. We needed to go collecting. Pelham Bay was the place.

David Spencer, another instructor, agreed to come along. The plan was to meet Lee at Co-op City in the morning. David and I packed our pails, nets, and collecting gear before leaving the museum for the bus. Our directions were simple—one crosstown transfer, a few blocks up, and we were on the Fordham Road bus to Co-op City.

The idea of finding anything natural in the built environment passing my window seemed unnatural. All I could see was building after building, and beyond that, mere shells of buildings burnt out and vacant with empty lots mirroring the human deprivation.

"South Bronx," remarked David as he looked out his window.

Two elderly women sitting across from us, wrapped in oversized wool coats, their knees slightly apart, smiled at me. I looked down at my rubber boots with my old khakis tucked inside, my binoculars around my neck and the large net I was holding in the aisle—how odd I must look. I was about to explain, when their eyes returned to their hands folded neatly across their laps. I asked David, who was reading, if he felt the slightest bit silly or self-conscious.

"No," he said. "Nothing surprises New Yorkers." He returned to his book.

We arrived at Co-op City. Lee was there to meet us. I was not prepared for the isolating presence of these high-rise complexes that seemed to grow out of the wetlands. Any notion of community would have to be vertical.

From her apartment, Lee had a splendid view of the marshes. Through the haze, I recognized the Empire State Building and the twin towers of the World Trade Center. The juxtaposition of concrete and wetlands was unsettling, as they did nothing to inspire each other.

"The water songs of the red-winged blackbirds are what keep me here," Lee said as we walked toward Pelham Bay. "I listen to them each morning before I take the train into the city. These open lands hold my sanity."

"Do other tenants of Co-op City look at the marsh this way?" David asked.

"Most of them don't see the marsh at all," she replied.

I was trying hard not to let the pristine marshes I knew back home interfere with what was before us. The cattails were tattered and limp. Water stained with oil swirled around the stalks. It smelled of sewage. Our wetlands are becoming urban wastelands. This one, at least, had not completely been dredged, drained, or filled.

It was midwinter, with an overcast sky. The mood was sinister. But I trusted Lee, and the deeper we entered into Pelham Bay Park, the more hauntingly beautiful it became, in spite of the long shadows and thin silhouettes of men behind bushes.

"This is a good place for us to collect," she said, putting down her bucket at the estuary.

Within minutes, we were knee-deep in tide pools and sloughs. My work was hampered by the ensuing muck that leached into the water. I could not see, much less find, what one would naturally assume to be there. More oil slicks. Iridescent water. Yellow foam. I kept coming up with gnarled oysters with abnormal growths on their shells. I handed an oyster dripping with black ooze to David.

"Eat this," I said.

"Not until you lick off your fingers first," he replied, wiping the animal clean.

These wetlands did not sparkle and sing. They were moribund.

Lee didn't see them this way. She knew too much to be defensive, yet recognized her place as their defender, the beauty inherent in marshes as systems of regeneration. She walked toward us with a bucket of killifish, some hermit crabs, and one ghost shrimp.

"Did you see the night heron?" she asked.

I had not seen anything but my own fears fly by with a few gulls.

We followed her through a thicket of hardwoods to another clearing. She motioned us down in the grasses.

"See him?" she whispered.

On the edge of the rushes stood the black-crowned night heron. Perfectly still. His long white plumes, like the misplaced hairs of an old man, hung down from the back of his head, undulating in the breeze. We could see his red eye reflected in the slow, rippling water.

Lee Milner's gaze through her apartment window out over the cattails was not unlike the heron's. It will be this stalwartness in the face of terror that offers wetlands their only hope. When she motioned us down in the grasses to observe the black-crowned night heron still fishing at dusk, she was showing us the implacable focus of those who dwell there.

This is our first clue to residency.

Somehow, I felt more at home. Seeing the heron oriented me. I relaxed. We watched the mysterious bird until he finally outpatienced us. We left to collect a few more organisms before dark.

I made a slight detour. I wanted to walk on the beach during sunset. There was no one around. The beach was desolate, with the exception of a pavilion. It stood on the sand like a forgotten fortress. Graffiti looking more like Japanese characters than profanities streaked the walls. The windows, without glass, appeared as holes in a decaying edifice. In the middle of the promenade was a beautiful mosaic sundial. Someone had cared about this place.

In spite of the cold, I took off my boots and stockings and rolled up the cuffs of my pants. I needed to feel the sand and the surf beneath my feet. The setting sun looked like the tip of a burning cigarette through the fog. Up ahead, a black body lay stiff on the beach. It was a Labrador. Small waves rocked the dead dog back and forth. I turned away.

Lee and David were sitting on the pavilion stairs watching more night herons crisscross the sky. Darkness was settling in. Lee surmised we had wandered a good six miles or so inside the park. Even she did not think we should walk back to Co-op City after sunset. They had found a phone booth while I was out walking and had called a cab.

"So are we being picked up here?" I asked.

They looked at each other and shook their heads.

"We have a problem," David said. "No one will come get us."

"What do you mean?"

"The first company we dialed thought we were a prank call," said Lee. "Sure, you're out at Pelham Bay. Sure ya'll want a ride into the city. No cabby in hell's dumb enough to fall for that one . . . click."

"And the second company hung up on us," David said. "At least the third cab operation offered us an alternative. They said our only real option was to call for a registered car."

"Let's do it," I said.

"We would have except we've run out of change," Lee replied.

I handed her what I had in my pockets. She called a gypsy cab service.

Waiting for our hired car's headlights to appear inside this dark urban wilderness was the longest thirty minutes I can remember. We stood on the concrete steps of the pavilion like statues, no one saying a word. I thought to myself, We could be in Greece, we could be in a movie, we could be dead.

The registered car slowly pulled up and stopped. The driver pushed the passenger's door open with his foot. Because of all our gear, I sat in front. Our driver could barely focus on our faces, let alone speak. I noticed his arms ravaged with needle tracks, how his entire body shook.

Eight silent miles. Thirty dollars. I gave him a generous tip and later felt guilty, knowing where the money would go. David and I hugged Lee, thanked her, and took the specimens, buckets, screens, and net with us as we caught the bus back to Manhattan. The hour-long ride back to the city allowed me to settle into my fatigue. I dreamed of the pavilion, the stiff black dog, and the long-legged birds who live there.

David tapped me on the shoulder. I awoke startled. Disoriented.

"Next stop is ours," he said.

We got off the bus and walked over to Madison and Seventy-ninth Street to catch the crosstown bus back to the museum. We kept checking the fish to see if they were safe, surprised to see them surviving at all given the amount of sloshing that had occurred throughout the day.

As we stood on the corner waiting, a woman stopped. "Excuse me," she said. "I like your look. Do you mind me asking where you purchased your trousers and boots? And the binoculars are a fabulous accessory."

I looked at David, who was grinning.

"Utah," I said in a tired voice. "I bought them all in Utah."

"I see . . . " the woman replied. "I don't know that shop." She quickly disappeared into a gourmet deli.

Back at the museum, the killifish were transferred safely into the aquarium with the shrimp and crabs. Before we left, I placed the oysters in their own tank for observation. With our faces to the glass, we watched the aquariums for a few minutes to make certain all was in order. Life appeared fluid. We turned off the lights and left. In the hallway, we heard music. Cocktail chatter. It was a fund-raising gala in the African Hall. We quietly slipped out. No one saw us enter or leave.

Walking home on 77th Street, I became melancholy. I wasn't sure why. Usually, after a day in the field I am exhilarated. I kept thinking about Lee, who responds to Pelham Bay Park as a lover, who rejects this open space as a wicked edge for undesirables, a dumping ground for toxins or occasional bodies. Pelham Bay is her home, the landscape she naturally comprehends, a sanctuary she holds inside her unguarded heart. And suddenly, the water songs of the red-winged blackbirds returned to me, the songs that keep her attentive in a city that has little memory of wildness.

———

TERRY TEMPEST WILLIAMS *lives in Salt Lake City with her husband, Brooke, and is naturalist-in-residence at the Utah Museum of Natural History. She is the author of* Pieces of White Shell: A Journey to Navajoland *(1984),* Coyote's Canyon *(1989), and two children's books. Her book* Refuge: An Unnatural History of Family and Place *(1992) chronicles the rise of the Great Salt Lake and the mysterious frequency of cancer in her family. A collection of experiences and portraits,* An Unspoken Hunger: Stories from the Field, *was published in 1994.*

"Water Songs" is reprinted from An Unspoken Hunger.

Amy Clampitt

Times Square Water Music

By way of a leak
in the brickwork
beside a stairway
in the Times Square
subway, midway
between the IR
and the BM T, weeks
of sneaking seepage
had smuggled in,
that morning,
a centimeter
of standing water.

To ward off the herd
we tend to turn into,
turned loose on
the tiered terrain
of the Times Square
subway, somebody
had tried, with
a half-hearted
barricade or tether
of twine,
to cordon off
the stairway—
as though anyone
could tie up seepage
into a package—
down which the
water, a dripping

escapee, was surrep-
titiously proceeding
with the intent,
albeit inadvertent,
in time, at an
inferior level,
to make a lake.

Having gone round
the pond thus far
accumulated, bound
for the third, infra-
infernal hollow
of the underground,
where the N, RR,
and QB cars are
wont to travel,
in mid-descent I
stopped, abruptly way-
laid by a sound.

Alongside the iron-
runged nethermost
stairway, under
the banister,
a hurrying skein
of moisture had begun,
on its way down,
to unravel
into the trickle
of a musical
minuscule
waterfall.

Think of spleen-
wort, of moss
and maiden-
hair fernwork,
think of water
pipits, of ouzels
and wagtails
dipping into

the course of it
as the music
of it oozes
from the walls!

Think of it
undermining
the computer's
cheep, the time
clock's hiccup,
the tectonic
inchings of it
toward some
general crackup!
Think of it, think of
water running, running,
running till it
         falls!

Poet AMY CLAMPITT *moved to New York after spending her childhood in her birthplace, New Providence, Iowa, and her college years at Grinnell, where she received her undergraduate degree. She taught and lectured at several colleges and universities and was honored with a Guggenheim Fellowship, a fellowship of the Academy of American Poets, and the MacArthur Prize Fellowship.*

Her poetry first appeared in the New Yorker *in 1978. Among her notable poetry collections are* What the Light Was Like *and* Westward. *"Times Square Water Music," reprinted here, is from her first collection of poems,* The Kingfisher. *Amy Clampitt died in New York last year.*

James Wright

Greetings in New York City

A man walking alone, a stranger
In a strange forest,
Plucks his way carefully among brambles.
He ploughs the spider pits.

He is awake and lonely in the midday,
The jungle of the sun.

He steps out of the snaggle, naked.

A hundred yards away,
One more stranger steps out of the dank vines,
Into the clearing.

Nothing is alone any more.

Two alone, two hours, they poise there,
Afraid, gazing across.

Then,
The green masses behind one shoulder
Cluster their grapes together,
And they become night. And by night each stranger
Turns back into a tree and lies down,
A root, alone.

Sleepless by dawn,
One rises
And finds the other already awake,

Gazing.
Weary,
He lifts his hand and shades his eyes.

Startled,
He touches his chin.
The other stranger across the distance
Touches his chin.
He pauses, then leans down,
And lifts a stone.
The other stranger leans down
And lifts a stone.

All the long morning
They edge the clearing
With little patterns of stones.
Sometimes they balance
Three pebbles on boulders

Or patterns of stars.
Or they lay out new flowers
In circles
Or little gatherings of faces
That neither stranger
Had ever seen.

And then, when noon comes,
Each stranger
Has no room left in the light
Except for only his hands.
Here are mine. They are kind of skinny. May I have your
lovely trees?

———————

JAMES WRIGHT *(1927-1980) earned the Pulitzer Prize for
poetry for his 1971* Collected Poems. *He was the recipient of
two Guggenheim Fellowships.*

*Born in Martins Ferry, Ohio, he served in the United
States Army in Japan and returned to attend Kenyon
College, where he received his bachelor's degree in 1952. He
studied at the University of Vienna on a Fulbright*

scholarship and later pursued graduate study at the University of Washington, Seattle. His manuscript The Green Wall *was chosen for the Yale Series of Younger Poets in 1954 and published in 1957.*

In the 1950s and '60s James Wright taught in the Twin Cities, at the University of Minnesota and Macalester College. In 1966 he went to New York to accept a position at Hunter College. "Greetings in New York City" was published in This Journey *(1977).*

Acknowledgements

Grateful acknowledgement is made for the permission to include the following works:

"Heartbeat"; from *A Hunger* by Lucie Brock-Broido. Copyright © 1988 by Lucie Brock-Broido. Reprinted by permission of Alfred A. Knopf, Inc.

"Return of the Native," by Harold Brodkey. Reprinted by permission of Wylie, Aitken & Stone, Inc.

"A House on the Heights;" from *Selected Writings of Truman Capote,* by Truman Capote. Copyright © 1959 by the Curtis Publishing Co. Reprinted by permission of Random House, Inc.

"Times Square Water Music;" from *The Kingfisher* by Amy Clampitt. Copyright © 1983 by Amy Clampitt. Reprinted by permission of Alfred A. Knopf, Inc.

"Une Letter à New York;" from *The Look of Things* by Henri Cole. Copyright © 1995 by Henri Cole. Reprinted by permission of Alfred A. Knopf, Inc.

"Goodbye to All That;" from *Slouching Towards Bethlehem* by Joan Didion. Copyright © 1967, 1968 by Joan Didion. Reprinted by permission of Farrar, Straus & Giroux, Inc.

"Canary," by Rita Dove. Reprinted from *Grace Notes* by Rita Dove, with the permission of the author and W. W. Norton & Company, Inc. Copyright © 1989 by Rita Dove.

"Autumn in New York;" words and music by Vernon Duke. Copyright © 1934 Warner Bros. Inc. (renewed). All Rights Reserved. Used by Permission. Warner Bros. Publications Inc., Miami, FL 33014.

"Hard Times in New York Town" and "Talking New York." Words and music by Bob Dylan. Copyright © 1962 Duchess

Permission to quote letters comes from the Academy of American Poets and the estate of Elizabeth Kray Ussachevsky.

"3 A.M. in New York;" from *Ordinary Things* by Jean Valentine. Copyright © 1974 by Jean Valentine. Reprinted by permission of Farrar, Straus & Giroux, Inc.

"A Village Life;" from *Collected Poems 1948–1984* by Derek Walcott. Copyright © 1986 by Derek Walcott. Reprinted by permission of Farrar, Straus & Giroux, Inc.

"A Phonecall from Frank O'Hara," by Anne Waldman. Originally appeared in *Helping the Dreamer* by Anne Waldman, Coffee House Press, 1989. Reprinted by permission of the publisher. Copyright © 1989 by Anne Waldman.

"Water Songs," from *An Unspoken Hunger* by Terry Tempest Williams. Copyright © 1994 by Terry Tempest Williams. Reprinted by permission of Pantheon Books, a division of Random House, Inc.

"Greetings in New York City:" from *Above the River* by James Wright. Copyright © 1990 by Anne Wright. Reprinted by permission of Farrar, Straus & Giroux, Inc.

"Stalking the Billion-Footed Beast," by Tom Wolfe. Copyright © 1989 by *Harper's Magazine*. All rights reserved. Reproduced from the November issue by special permission.